W9-CCR-868

WITHDRAWN
UNIVERSITY OF PENNSYLVANIA
LIBRARIES

CASEWORK: *A Psychosocial Therapy*

CASEWORK

A

PSYCHOSOCIAL

THERAPY

by

FLORENCE HOLLIS

Columbia University School of Social Work

Preface by Charlotte Towle

Professor Emeritus
School of Social Service Administration
University of Chicago

Random House   New York

FIRST PRINTING

© Copyright, 1964, by Random House, Inc.

All rights reserved under International and Pan-American Copyright Conventions. Published in New York by Random House, Inc., and simultaneously in Toronto, Canada, by Random House of Canada, Limited.

Library of Congress Catalog Card Number: 64-11828
MANUFACTURED IN THE UNITED STATES OF AMERICA BY
The Book Press, Brattleboro, Vt.

Design by Tere LoPrete

Preface

Without benefit of an author's Preface, which traditionally has served to reveal the author, the readers of this book will see Florence Hollis as a full-fledged social worker in action as educator and as casework practitioner.* Having thoroughly integrated her professional experience, she functions freely in both roles. Master of her subject, she is also perceptive of the integrative task confronting the reader, as she shows not only in her steadfast concern to convey methods of thinking in the content of the rich knowledge she imparts, but also in her concern to clarify, to point out what is merely speculative, and to provide evidence to support assertions. Her understanding is evident in her rare ability to involve the reader in the feeling, thinking, and doing which she not only is portraying but in which she herself is engaged as she envisages casework practice.

To an exceptional degree Miss Hollis dares to teach the hows of practice, the specific technical means which workers have used, or conceivably might use, with specific individuals in specific situations. In so doing she upholds the principle of individualization through imaginative consideration of possible and probable variables. Although she does not need to fear the stigma of technicianship, she misses this pitfall by a wide margin. The whats and hows of casework which she leads the reader to consider are rooted in basic principles of practice, which are steadfastly oriented to the whys implicit in individualization of

---

* For the traditional purpose of the preface see *Famous Prefaces* (The Harvard Classics, Volume 39: Introductory Note, p. 3).

persons in relation to time, place, other persons, and social circumstances. This work therefore has a dimension far beyond that of a textbook.

The author's use of the direct influence implicit in instruction sustains rather than devitalizes reflective thinking. Thus Miss Hollis, in her role as educator, adapts technical measures which she and her associates have formulated for use in casework practice, on the assumption that one fosters rational behavior through providing the means to think rather than through "thinking for"—a weakness in many an author's approach to his readers, even as in many a caseworker's approach to his clients.

I welcome the author's abundant use of case citations. Technical means establish the validity of diagnostic thinking and treatment choices. With exceptions, in social work writing we have been more free in our use of case material to demonstrate what was done and why it was done than how it was done. Many factors doubtless have operated in our withdrawal from delineation of specific means. Among them one reason perhaps has been the unfortunate circumstance that, through removal from practice, some of us who write have not been sufficiently secure to risk facing or exposing our technical measures. There has also been a fear of technicianship, with its use of stereotypes rather than differential application of methods. The reflective consideration of possible "hows" should ease rather than heighten our fear.

This book will make an outstanding contribution to those who come to grips with what the author as educator teaches of psychosocial study, diagnosis, and treatment. Notably in two chapters on treatment, one on objectives, and one on procedures, Miss Hollis differentiates casework objectives and procedures from those in other kinds of therapy, but she does not divorce the two; in fact, casework help may bulwark other kinds of therapy. This is in contrast to the theory and practice of many social workers, who have disentangled therapy, casework, and relief-giving out of a concern to develop social work as a profession in its own right, distinct from psychiatry. Such a separation also has been justified, often in the light of reality pressures, as a necessary means of bringing the demands of practice within the scope of agency function and resources. The limitation in this has been the tendency to think categorically about the values of method, rather than about its appropriateness for the client.

The relationship among study, diagnosis, and treatment is demonstrated in the cases discussed in the chapter entitled "Three Variations in Treatment Emphasis" in which cases demonstrate the relationship between them. They are models of brief but comprehensive case summarization, with fine-point appraisal of movement in treatment, appropriate modification of diagnosis, and well-developed assessment of the factors operating in the treatment outcome. The author emphasizes that these cases are offered not as proof of theories or results but rather as demonstrations of the relationship among psychosocial study, diagnosis, and treatment. They were selected because the individuals involved were markedly similar, but their problems and social situations called for variation in treatment. They thus demonstrate the need for individualization within categories at a time when there has been a trend toward short cuts in diagnosis and in case analysis as a means to the formulation of principles of practice.

Certainly a profession does not come of age until it develops its own theory. The oversimplification at the root of shoddy practice is more likely to occur through the annexation of theory from other disciplines. Unassimilated, such borrowings may become cliches and easy generalizations which lend themselves to indiscriminate, patchy, or blanket use. Miss Hollis warns against oversimplification as "one of the worst traps into which a worker can fall." She herself clarifies without simplification by providing the wherewithal for coping with complexity. Her use of case materials has obvious value for teachers, supervisors, practitioners, and students. One must not overlook its value also for consultants in other disciplines—psychiatrists, psychoanalysts, psychologists and social scientists—from whom social caseworkers have derived formulations which, despite their value, have sometimes operated against differential thinking to raise the question: diagnosis and treatment of whom—this person or a type, this person or a disease entity, this specific social situation or a comparable one commonly encountered? Assumption of responsibility for engaging our consultants to think with us rather than for us may be facilitated not only through our grasp of case analysis but also through sharing our thinking with them.

This book is a timely contribution to the current interprofessional scene. Among the professions directly concerned with human welfare this is a period of synthesis. Cross-fertilization has been an integrative force in providing a common conceptual framework to serve as a means to communication and collaboration among the segments within social work and among disciplines formerly incompatible in their thinking. It has served to produce common principles of practice and some valid overlapping in practice. Inevitably, however, it has also brought invalid fusions which have fostered coalescence rather than integration. Within social work this synthesis has been expressed in the generic movement, a sound development when it has not surpassed the limits of what can be integrated, and also in an amalgamation rather than in a nice articulation of professional functions. In many multidisciplinary settings, the primary function of each profession in a clinical team has been subordinated or even defaced as social workers, psychologists, and psychiatrists have become psychotherapists operating with negligible difference from one another, and the psychiatrist has become more consultant, supervisor, and teacher than practitioner of his specialty. The pervasive influence of this abortive development on social work practice beyond clinic walls is progressively being corrected by a counter-movement instigated largely by social workers, which gives hope that in synthesizing we will not in the long run become synthetic. Miss Hollis's work heightens this hope, for it forthrightly establishes what social casework is and what it is not in all its helping measures.

Despite the headway made by the counter-movement, the coalescence of the several professions engaged in psychotherapy has fathered a new movement for the establishment of a "profession of psychotherapy," in which the basic education of the several disciplines involved would be merged to produce a unified profession.* An argument in favor of such a step is that

* One step in this direction has been taken in a conference on "An Ideal Training Program for Psychotherapists" held at Gould House, Ardsley-on-Hudson, New York, March 21–24, 1963, under the auspices of New York

the "dead wood" for psychotherapy in each profession's basic education could be sloughed off. This raises many questions, of which the most important are: Would there not be heavy losses to those served and those serving? Should not each profession retain responsibility for its therapy and therefore for its basic training? A well-reasoned answer to these questions as they bear upon social casework is to be found in Miss Hollis's conception of social casework as an organic whole, in which treatment is a blend of the diagnostically determined technical procedures. Therapy in the sense of consideration of "dynamic and genetic intrapsychic factors" cannot be set apart from other measures which may support the client or which are indicated in the light of changing responses and goals. Generic casework principles still persist. A social worker may need to use all that he knows of social casework in the conduct of psychosocial therapy.

Now that the cause of social work is fast becoming a world cause, the community's expectations of it, as well as social work's expectations of itself, have mounted. The push for growth has stimulated, on the one hand, a quest for the new and much experimentation in an endeavor to expand the ways and means of social work. On the other hand, it has marshaled unconscious and conscious concern to synthesize as a means to the preservation of integrity. Periods of synthesis, in that they bring about new integrations which determine future developments, call for judicious extensions and discards, as Miss Hollis is aware. She perceptively has chosen to deal with a segment of casework practice because such a choice permits concentration upon basic well-established methodology, rather than upon the exploration of new trends still in the early stages of experimentation and assimilation. In closing the introduction she states:

A clear understanding of fundamental principles is never more needed than when theory is being expanded and choices must be made between what is to be retained and what discarded of both the new and the old. It is therefore perhaps especially timely for caseworkers to formulate as clearly as possible the

University and with the support of the Aaron E. Norman Fund. Representatives of the fields of clinical psychology, social work, psychiatry and psychoanalysis attended. A continuing committee was formed to consider the issues opened at this conference.

nature of their basic frame of reference. Treatment will become more effective only when what is potentially sound and useful in the new is admitted to the main body of principles whose value has already been demonstrated.

In these times of pressure for marked change, these lines place the author among those social workers who might be described as evolutionists rather than as revolutionists, and whose behavior might be characterized as more adaptive than defensive. Throughout this book she tends to deal with a part with reference to the whole, in fact, to maintain the intactness of a valued whole. To this end she brings together what belongs together and excludes the discrepant, pending the establishment of its relevance. She contends against those dichotomies which have been erected as defenses against complexity or against that which is emotionally unacceptable. Her guides have much in common with those developed by other writers as social casework has shifted progressively from the simplicity of its early focus on problems to the complexity of person or persons in the matrix of agency and social situation. She goes beyond many authors in her fine-point orientation of diagnosis and treatment to personality dynamics in normal and pathological behavior, individual and group.

The author's propensity to conserve wholeness, in the process of integrating the new, or in reviving old discards which now have a new dimension through their growth or through the growth of social work in ability to use them, is shown in her union of the psychic and the social. In considering the implications of such a union for the relationship of psychiatry, social casework, and the social sciences, she contests social work's substitution of the social scientist for the psychoanalytic psychiatrist as a mentor. She asserts that "sociological data amplify the rich understanding of the internal dynamics of the personality developed by the Freudian school of thought; they do not replace it." In elaboration she decries the "either-or" trend represented by those who would explain human behavior primarily in interpersonal terms, omitting intrapsychic phenomena. She argues for the use of both. She shows acceptance of specific contributions of the sociologist, notably the role concept, with reservations, however, about precipitous annexation of theory, pending exploration. When one recalls that the early split between social work and the social scientists occurred largely around the issue of individualization versus categorization of people, one finds, now, that social casework is better able to generalize its experience. The author is not retreating, however, from the formulation and use of categories. She individualizes within categories and thus brings individualization and categorization together. She raises hope that we may now integrate the contribution of the social scientist and not repeat the past through erecting dichotomies.

Miss Hollis holds the past, present, and future of the client together in study, diagnosis, and treatment. Some social workers have simplified through centering on the present, trusting, first, that the discernible imprint of the past will serve as a reliable basis for inference, and second, that future difficulties may well be averted through meeting current needs and solving current problems. Miss Hollis, in contrast, while focusing on the present, draws on the past in understanding the client and, where indicated, helps him cope with the persistence of the past in the present. She is concerned to reckon with the client's future both through reflective consideration of his aspirations, goals and fears, and through helping him plan for the future whenever possible.

Miss Hollis brings the intellect and the emotions into a two-way relationship. The concept of man as a rational being dominated the caseworker's early thinking on this relationship; therefore intellect was expected not only to govern thinking and doing, but also to fashion it. The caseworker accordingly relied heavily on imparting information and on appealing to reason in effecting change in behavior. Psychological insight, however, brought a focus on the irrational self. It gave prominence to the point of view that feelings fashion thinking and prompt action. Therefore rational behavior was contingent on a change in feeling. The treatment sequence began with understanding and modifying feeling, after which change in thinking and doing would follow almost automatically. If it did not, it was because the client was resistant to change or for some reason inaccessible to help. Perception of the fact that what a man knows and what he thinks may be the source of his feeling again reversed the sequence. But progressively the "either-or" sequence has given way to one in which the two conceptions interplay. The saying, "As a man thinketh in his heart, so is he" has become a generic concept in social work; without reference to a school of thought, in fact, it is central in the philosophy of social work. But a philosophy and technical procedures which make it come alive in practice have not readily been attained.

This philosophy was beautifully expressed by Jessie Taft in a paper entitled, "Living and Feeling," written in 1933 and recently reissued.* It has been variously stated and restated in the literature throughout the years, notably encapsulated long ago by Gordon Hamilton in the comment, "Casework lies midway between therapy and education," and developed further by other writers on casework.** It has been reflected in accounts of desirable practice, but it is my impression that it has not pervasively influenced practice. There is still evidence that heavy reliance on modifying feeling without reference to the part played by distorted thinking out of ignorance or error persists. We have had valid fear of intellectualization, out of past lack of skill in imparting knowledge and in helping individuals think —in short, out of lack of facility in our use of educational method. It is probable also that our identification with the psychoanalytic therapist's methods has impeded acceptance of our re-educative role. An outstanding contribution of Miss Hollis's book is the place given to a rational approach in which knowledge is imparted and thinking anew is engaged through reflective discussion. Miss Hollis formulates this approach as a major technical procedure of central importance when it is combined with other procedures which make it something more than the worker's intellectualization.

Finally, the author's organization and evaluation of technical procedures conserves the wholeness of social casework. Con-

---

* Jessie Taft, *Therapist and Social Work Educator*. Edited by Virginia P. Robinson (Philadelphia: University of Pennsylvania Press, 1962).
** See Helen H. Perlman, *Social Casework: A Problem Solving Process* (Chicago: University of Chicago Press, 1957). See also Charlotte Towle, *Common Human Needs* (Washington, D.C.: Federal Security Agency, 1945; and New York: National Association of Social Workers, 1954), and *The Learner in Education for the Professions* (Chicago: University of Chicago Press, 1954).

tinuity, sequence, and integration of the parts emerges chapter by chapter and the wholeness is seen clearly in the summarization in the last chapter. The procedures are not arranged in a hierarchy of values; for example, insight therapy is not more valued than environmental modification. The author comments, "One technique is of no more value than another." The value lies in the blending of the procedures, in the matching and timing of them to the client's needs and abilities and in the skill with which any procedure is used. A decisive demand is that they support one another. The part played by the casework relationship and the worker's understanding of the unconscious in the conduct of all the procedures is well developed in two chapters and recaptured in the summarization in the final chapter, as well as in the presentation of case examples throughout the book.

Among the types of procedure by which change can be wrought in the client's social effectiveness, the place the author gives to direct influence and to reflective discussion of the person-situation configuration affirms a trend which I, among others, have welcomed. As one member of what has seemed to be a minority group in the recent past, I have held steadfastly to these procedures as being the very stuff of social casework. I have decried the evisceration implied in the past depreciation and even discard of these procedures. Miss Hollis has restored these discards not only in reviving these aspects of early practice, but in making them an integral part of psychologically oriented casework.

In relation to the reflective discussion of the person-situation configuration, my role as educator has convinced me that, just as what we have learned in casework has been used adaptively in education, so what we have learned as educators may be used adaptively to a greater extent than formerly in casework. It is to be hoped that the imprint of the social worker's own educational experience may lay the groundwork for this and become influential in begetting his professional identity. When one recalls that a primary aim of social casework is to help clients become more rational social beings, one firmly supports Miss Hollis's emphasis on this procedure, for she would have us relate to the client's rational self and thereby affirm this potential. It is only as we treat man as rational that he may become more so.

In this work Miss Hollis has not only delineated the relationship between the social and psychological components of casework therapy, but has also shown the line between psychoanalysis or psychoanalytic therapy on the one hand, and the practice of the social worker as caseworker or therapist on the other. In doing so, she has carried forward the work of others. We will be in a better position to appraise new directions in casework practice, and to define and clarify issues, as this work excites controversy. It is less important that we all think alike than that we know our likenesses and differences, so that we can speak intelligibly from group to group, within social work and within the inter-professional scene. In serving this purpose the book will meet an urgent need.

CHARLOTTE TOWLE

September, 1963
School of Social Service Administration
The University of Chicago

ACKNOWLEDGMENTS

The writing of acknowledgments for a book is a happy moment for its author. The work is done and the book is safely in the hands of the printer, finished but still protected for a brief interlude from the friendly but nonetheless critical scrutiny it must soon undergo.

This book was written with the generous help of many colleagues to whom I am deeply grateful. First of all the caseworkers who were willing for their work to be studied: protection of the anonymity of their clients who appear in the book prevents my mentioning them by name, but I do want here to express my gratitude to them and to the agencies which generously allowed me to read and use data from their records. The agencies which contributed to the development of the book include:

The Community Service Society, New York, New York
The Family Service of Greater Boston, Boston, Massachusetts
The Family Service Society, Hartford, Connecticut
The Jewish Board of Guardians, New York, New York
The Judge Baker Guidance Center, Boston, Massachusetts
The Massachusetts General Hospital, Boston, Massachusetts

These agencies are in no sense to be held responsible for the content of the book, but I trust that their staffs will feel that my use of their work has lead to formulations which ring true in the light of their own professional experience.

In the writing of Chapters IV through VII on the classification of treatment procedures, I have drawn upon work done under grant OM-513 of the National Institute of Mental Health. I am indeed grateful for this support, which is continuing and which will, I hope, make possible further developments in the use of the casework typology introduced in these chapters.

A number of colleagues have given many hours of their time to reading and criticizing the manuscript in its several drafts. Nothing is more important in the final stages of a book than for the author to be able to profit by the frank and discerning criticism of trusted colleagues. This preliminary putting of one's ideas to the test brings to light discrepancies between the intent and the actuality of communications, adds valuable ideas, and serves to protect the final readers from notions that cannot stand up to criticism or that are so poorly formulated that they do not deserve to see the light of day.

My first reader, the friend and colleague who has so generously shared her professional wisdom throughout the years, is Rosemary Reynolds. Others to whom I wish to express my appreciation are Lucille Austin, Esther Clemence, Jeanette Regensburg, Ruth Schwarz, Ann Shyne, Isabel Stamm, and Dr. George Wiedeman.

I should like to mention too that the beginnings of this book included early conversations with Florence Day and Annette Garrett. They both wanted the book to be written and contributed to that initial impetus which sets a study going. In addition, Annette Garrett helped in the location of suitable agencies from which to request material. It has been a great pleasure also to have Charlotte Towle consent to write the preface and to have her express her response to the book in such generous terms.

My thanks go also to the secretaries who in successive stages struggled with the manuscript and to the editors who finally weeded out the worst of my academese.

FLORENCE HOLLIS

New York City
October, 1963

CONTENTS

Preface by Charlotte Towle

Introduction: Purpose and Scope

PART ONE THE THEORETICAL FRAMEWORK

*Chapter I • Personality, Social Adjustment,
and the Casework Method* 9

    Casework, Psychiatry, and Social Science
    The Basic Values of Casework
    Personality and Social Functioning
    Causes of Interpersonal Adjustment Problems
    Treatment Through Reducing Environmental Press
    Treatment of Internal Factors
    Direct Work with the Individual
    Directive vs. Rational Therapies

*Chapter II • Some Examples of Casework
in Practice* 33

    Negative Complementarity in a Marriage
    A Superego Disturbance
    Understanding Early Life Experiences

*Chapter III • Classifications of Casework
Treatment* 50

    Early and Current Classifications
    Personality Changes and Methodology
    Diverse Approaches
    Personality Changes Without Clarification

Chapter IV · *A Classification Based on*
Dynamic Considerations   65
  A False Start
  Basic Considerations
  The Main Divisions of the Classification
  Environmental Treatment

PART TWO   TREATMENT: AN ANALYSIS
OF PROCEDURES

Chapter V · *The Sustaining Process, Direct*
Influence, and Ventilation   83
  The Sustaining Process
  Direct Influence
  Ventilation

Chapter VI · *Reflective Discussion of the*
Person-Situation Configuration   100
  The Situation: People, Conditions, Events
  Decisions and Consequences
  Inner Awareness, Responses, and Distortions
  Reactions to the Worker and to Treatment
  Environmental Work

Chapter VII · *Reflective Consideration of*
Dynamic and Developmental Factors   117

Chapter VIII · *Casework and the Unconscious*   131
  Unconscious or Preconscious?
  Levels of Consciousness in Casework Treatment
  Casework and Other Professions
    Practicing Psychotherapy

Chapter IX · *The Client-Worker Relationship*   149
  Realistic Attitudes and Responses
  Unrealistic Attitudes and Responses:
    Transference and Countertransference

Problems of Communication Between Client
and Worker
The Client-Worker Relationship in the
Dynamics of Treatment

PART THREE DIAGNOSIS AND
TREATMENT PLANNING

Chapter X · The Psychosocial Study   167

Chapter XI · Diagnosis   178

Assessment
Organizing the Facts
Diagnosis: Dynamic and Etiological
Categorization

*Chapter XII · The Choice of Treatment
Objectives*   204

Goals: Intermediate and Long Range
Goals and Motivation
Goals and Causation
Intervening Variables

*Chapter XIII · The Choice of Treatment
Procedures*   219

Environmental Change: By Client or Worker
Internal Change: The Range of Possibilities
Dynamic and Genetic Understanding
Anxiety and Guilt as Key Factors
Other Important Personality Factors
Significance of the Clinical Diagnosis
Treatment Procedures and the Problem

*Chapter XIV · Three Variations in
Treatment Emphasis*   246

A Character Disorder: Acting Out and
Self Devaluation

A Character Disorder: Guilt and
Impulsive Hostility
A Character Neurosis: Displacement and
Inhibition of Aggression

Chapter XV • Perspectives and Current Issues   265
Perspectives
Current Needs and Practical Problems

BIBLIOGRAPHY   277

INDEX   291

CASEWORK: *A Psychosocial Therapy*

Introduction:
Purpose
and
Scope

THE CONCERN OF THIS BOOK is the analysis of a particular segment of casework practice—the treatment of individuals experiencing problems in their interpersonal relationships. The book deals primarily with marital and parent-child adjustment problems of clients in family service agencies, child guidance clinics, psychiatric clinics and mental hygiene centers serving either children or adults. Its ultimate purpose is to contribute to the improvement of the quality of casework treatment offered such clients. The data upon which the book rests is drawn from the work of highly skilled caseworkers. We have endeavored to analyze the dynamics of the treatment procedures in such a way that the principles underlying them are sufficiently clear for the reader to understand the essentials of this type of treatment and thereby to enhance his own treatment skill.

Treatment of interpersonal adjustment problems does not constitute a separate form of casework, but when the problem is chiefly one of intrapsychic disturbance certain procedures of treatment necessarily receive greater emphasis while others would be stressed if we were discussing problems due primarily to reality pressures. Nevertheless, in analyzing this treatment approach, we are inevitably also discussing general casework principles. Throughout, the work in the cases considered is seen as lying within the general matrix of casework, and the principles involved are expressed in terms of their general applicability.

For the most part this study draws upon interviews with individuals rather than upon interviews with two or more people jointly. But the fact that this has been done does not represent any "position" concerning the value of the increased use of interviews with more than one person. Rather it in part reflects the practice at the time at which this material was collected and in part the intent to concentrate upon basic, well-established methodology rather than to explore newer trends which, though promising, are still in early stages of experimentation and assimilation.

There are currently many new emphases in the field of casework, as there are in the entire range of social work. For casework, at least, these are evolutionary rather than revolutionary in nature. There is undoubtedly value in the renewed concern for the total family, the bringing of fathers into treatment, the increased use of the home visit especially for diagnostic purposes, the experimentation with controlled and systematic use of the multiple-person interview. Of great importance also is the wider and more sophisticated use of the knowledge the social sciences are acquiring of ethnic, class, and regional factors in personality and social adjustment; of role behavior; of various aspects of group behavior, especially as seen in institutional life; and of social interaction, family structure, and other related matters.[1]

The task of evaluating these new emphases and enlarging the knowledge and understanding of the caseworker so that he can incorporate them into his own practice to the degree that they prove useful may seem formidable. It is made relatively easy, however, by the fact that these new trends represent additions to already well-established casework treatment methods rather than anything in essence diametrically opposed to them. Rather than to tear down an erroneous or inadequate frame of reference, the task is one of filling in parts of the framework that had perhaps been under-emphasized or even unexplored, although they were theoretically provided for in the overall scheme.

We shall therefore begin by attempting to clarify the nature of the interaction between inner psychological and outer social components in the individual's development and functioning. The theoretical framework of casework already embraces both these components, providing a meeting ground for psychodynamic theory and theories dealing with the impact upon man of his social environment.

A clear understanding of fundamental principles is never more needed than when theory is being expanded and choices must be made between what is to be retained and what discarded of both the new and the old. It is, therefore, perhaps especially timely for caseworkers to formulate as clearly as possible the nature of their basic frame of reference. Treatment will become more effective only when what is potentially sound and useful in the new is admitted to the main body of principles whose value has already been demonstrated.

NOTE

1. A good introduction to pertinent material from the social sciences can be found in Herman Stein and Richard Cloward, *Social Perspectives on Behavior*, The Free Press, Glencoe, Ill., 1958. Two articles by Herman Stein are also of interest: "Social Science in Social Work Practice and Education," *Social Casework*, 36 (April, 1955), 147–155, and "The Concept of the Social Environment in Social Work Practice," *Smith College Studies in Social Work*, 30 (June, 1960), 187–210.

Part One

THE
THEORETICAL
FRAMEWORK

I

Personality, Social Adjustment, and the Casework Method

CASEWORK HAS ALWAYS BEEN a psychosocial treatment method. It recognizes both internal psychological and external social causes of dysfunctioning, and endeavors to enable the individual to meet his needs more fully and to function more adequately in his social relationships. Throughout its history it has drawn continuously from other scientific fields as they uncovered data and developed theory that promised to throw light upon either the psychological or the social side of human problems.

] *Casework, Psychiatry, and Social Science*

Today casework finds its own characteristic psychosocial approach gaining recognition in two closely related fields—psychiatry and the social sciences. Psychiatrists have long been working in close collaboration with social workers in psychiatric clinics, child guidance clinics, and family service agencies, and the two professions have greatly influenced each other. Less extensively, individual psychiatrists and analysts have collaborated with

individual social scientists in bringing clinical practice and
personality theory into a closer relationship with academic psychology and sociology. As a result, psychiatry has gained additional impetus toward understanding the social component in
human ills, and the social sciences are increasingly interested in
the interaction between characteristics of the social structure
and the psychology of the individual as determinants of behavior.[1] This heightened understanding is now bringing the social
sciences and social work closer to each other, with the prospect
of further mutual influence and gain.

Central to casework is the notion of "the-person-in-his-situation"[2]
as a threefold configuration consisting of the person, the situation, and the interaction between them. The terms "internal
pressure" and "external pressure" are often used to describe
forces within the individual and forces within the environment
as they impinge upon or interact with each other. Translated
into sociological terminology, external pressure becomes *press*
and internal pressure, *stress*.

Casework recognizes this interaction as highly complex. It is
not by any means a billiard ball type of action and reaction
between man and his environment, as the conditionists would
have us believe, for the external press is immediately modified
by the way in which the individual perceives it. Depending upon
his nature, upon his need or internal stress, the individual will
react to his perception of the press in his own peculiar way.
Furthermore, as the term "situation" implies most often a human
situation—family, friends, employer, teacher, and so on—the
situation is as complicated as the "person" who confronts it.
When the person reacts to the external press, this reaction in turn
becomes a press upon some other human being, who then responds with his own set of perceptions and needs. Hence understanding of the person-in-his-situation requires varying degrees
of understanding of the psychology of all the people involved in
the gestalt. For the situation is never just one person but rather
a multiplicity of persons (to the sociologist a "role network")
having varying degrees of importance in the life of the client.

Social scientists have particularly illuminated one dimension
of both the person and the situation: that of the nature of beliefs,
values, and expectations held by different groups of people which

influence the beliefs, values, and expectations of individuals.[3] Freud long ago sketched some of the mechanisms by which such influence takes place, as for example identification and superego and ego-ideal formation. Sociological study of different ethnic groups and social classes has increased our knowledge of the varying content of these beliefs, values, and expectations. It has also emphasized the extent to which these forces continue to influence individual psychology long after the formative years in which the main tendencies of the personality take form.

These sociological data amplify the rich understanding of the internal dynamics of the personality developed by the Freudian school of thought; they do not replace it. Freud's discoveries concerning the libidinal and aggressive drives and their stages of maturation, the effect of infantile thought processes on the child's perception and understanding of the world, the influence of early relationships within the immediate family, and the profound effect of all of these as they continue, through their persistence in the unconscious, to influence later thought processes and emotions, remain basic to the understanding of the individual. Casework will drastically impoverish itself if it follows the lead of Horney and Sullivan in trying to explain human behavior primarily in interpersonal terms, omitting those key intrapsychic phenomena that from the start influence the child's perception of and reaction to his interpersonal experiences. But it can use their insights, just as it can use the insights of the sociologists as additions to the knowledge of the inner life of the child uncovered by Freud.

To say that casework is directed toward the better social functioning of the individual by no means distinguishes it from all other professions. Such a definition distinguishes casework from, say, general medicine or from engineering, but not from psychiatry, which also aims to bring about better social functioning. It has sometimes been said that casework is directed toward the social side of man's adjustment and psychiatry to his inner psychological adjustment, but this is a false distinction. Although certain branches of psychiatry explore regions of intrapsychic functioning which casework does not investigate, casework characteristically must deal with mental processes, and psychiatry with interpersonal material. Both are concerned with effecting improvement in social functioning, and both deal with intra-psychic functioning toward the end, in many instances, of bringing about personality change. The distinction between the two is mainly a matter of technical methods. The nature of the differences involved will be explored in detail in succeeding chapters.

] *The Basic Values of Casework*

Casework is characterized also by its direct concern for the well-being of the individual. It is not primarily an organ of social control, designed to bring the individual into conformity with society and thus rid it of the social hazard presented by the discontented, unsatisfied, rebellious individual. On the contrary, casework came into being as a response to the needs of human beings for protection against social and natural deprivations and catastrophes. Historically it represents a turning away from the laissez faire doctrines that followed the unhappy combination of Malthusian thinking with Darwin's emphasis on the development of strength through the survival of the fittest. From its inception it has stressed the value of the individual, and for the past thirty years, at least, has been quite outspoken about the right of each man to live in his own unique way, provided he does not infringe upon the rights of others.[4] This emphasis upon the innate worth of the individual is an extremely important, fundamental characteristic of casework. It is the ingredient that makes it possible to establish the relationship of trust that is so essential for effective treatment. From it grow the two essential characteristics of the caseworker's attitude toward his client: acceptance and belief in self-determination.

By acceptance we mean the maintaining of an attitude of warm good will toward the client, whether or not his way of behaving is socially acceptable and whether or not it is to the worker's personal liking. It is true that we cannot always live up to this ideal in actual practice, but the more we do so the more possibility there is that the goals of casework will be accomplished. Acceptance must not be confused with refraining from evaluating the appropriateness or usefulness of the client's ways of functioning. But such evaluation is of little use if it is accompanied by feelings of condemnation or hostility toward the client.

Self-determination is perhaps not too felicitous a term; it is too absolute in its implications. What we really mean by this concept is that self-direction, the right to make his own choices, is a highly valued attribute of the individual. The more he can make his own decisions and direct his own life the better, and the less the caseworker tries to take over these responsibilities the better. No one in this world can continually do exactly as he wants, but he can make his own decisions about how to find his way among the limitations and opportunities presented by external reality. In extreme situations, where there is danger of real harm to others or to the client himself, or where the client is incapable of carrying this responsibility, the caseworker must take over and make decisions for him. But he docs so only where the necessity for such action is clear.

ₓA belief in the value of self-determination does not mean, however, that the caseworker plays a passive role with his clients. He does of course sponsor changes in the client's functioning which he believes will enable him to meet his needs more effectively. The caseworker's belief in self-direction is not always shared by the client, but the means the worker chooses to bring about change must ever be consistent with this end. Thus the relationship is consistently an honest one, the worker showing respect for the wishes of the client and sometimes offering suggestions and advice, not, however, as directives but as opinions which the client is free to accept or reject. Whenever possible— and this is most of the time—the client is helped to think things through for himself, to correct his own misconceptions, and to accept the maximum responsibility of which he is capable for formulating his own ideas. This procedure requires of the worker development of techniques for drawing out the client's own reasoning capacities, rather than the use of didactic, or directive, methods. ₓ

] *Personality and Social Functioning*

In this book we will be considering casework procedures as they are used to bring about change in the individual's social functioning and particularly in his interpersonal relationships. As we noted in the introduction, this is not the whole of casework, but it is an extremely important part of the whole and is carried on by all caseworkers under whatever auspices they work. Although the data on which this book is based derive from family, medical and psychiatric settings, the principles presented hold for casework in any setting in which interpersonal relationships are a treatment concern.

THE SOCIAL ENVIRONMENT

Before we can comprehend the dynamics of this type of casework treatment, however, we must have a clear picture of what the caseworker understands by personality and its social functioning. Social functioning represents the interplay between the two major variables—the social environment and the individual—each of which, in its turn, is a composite of various forces. The environment offers opportunities and gratifications, frustrations and deprivations. It consists not only of concrete realities—such things as the availability of food, clothing, shelter, medical care, employment opportunities, physical safety, recreational opportunities, educational opportunities—but also of sociopsychological realities expressed through interpersonal relationships. For human beings need social relationships as much as they need food and shelter. We know that a baby can die not only because of lack of food but also because he is deprived of mothering.[5] An individual must rely on the environment to provide him with opportunities for social relationships of all sorts—parents, brothers and sisters, extended family relationships, marriage partners, friends, acquaintances. The quality of these relationships is to no small degree determined by forces independent of his own efforts and choices. While the qualities of "other people" exert especial force in childhood family relationships, in varying measure they exercise a potent influence upon adult relationships too.

Socially determined psychological realities also exert profound pressures, particularly in the areas of values and perceptions. Ethnic, class, regional, and role factors influence standards of behavior, aspirations, and perceptions of others and of self. At first these influences are transmitted primarily through the parents, later through other social relationships. The total environment, then, as experienced by any individual, is a complex set of interacting forces impinging upon him simultaneously from many different directions and interacting with an equally complex set of forces within his own personality.   ✕

THE INDIVIDUAL: THE CONTRIBUTION OF FREUDIAN THEORY

Most caseworkers have found in the work of Freud and his followers[6] a valuable frame of reference for the understanding of the individual.* Without attempting a detailed review of Freudian theory, I should like to comment on certain features of importance for understanding the nature of personality changes induced by casework and for distinguishing these from changes brought about by other treatment methods.[7]

First, it is assumed that the individual from birth onwards is characterized by certain sets of drives, libidinal and aggressive in nature. These vary in both absolute and relative strength in different individuals and constitute a continuing and unique demand upon the environment. Moreover, the personality from birth onwards includes a set of adaptive qualities, known in composite as the ego. These qualities also vary in strength and quality in different individuals. The personality proceeds in its development under two major influences: internal biologically determined stages of maturation in both the drives and the ego, and interaction between the individual and his environment. Under these combined influences the drives change their form of demand and expression during the familiar oral, anal, oedipal, and genital stages of growth; the ego moves from primary to secondary modes of thought, develops its superego formation, builds its mechanisms of defense, adapts its perceptions and judgments to reality, and strengthens its capacities for direction and control. The libidinal drive proceeds from its early narcissistic stage, forming first oral dependent relationships, then moving to adult object relationships. Sexual feelings develop and are gradually sorted out for their special function in the range of libidinal feelings: love, affection, and less intense positive responses. The

---

* A divergent point of view is held by the functional school of social work, which bases its work in part upon the writings of Otto Rank. Karen Horney and Harry Stack Sullivan have also contributed insights to current casework practice and are considered of paramount importance by some caseworkers.

aggressive drives differentiate into hostility and constructive aggression harnessed to the job of mastering the environment and the self.[8]

Because Freud elaborated more upon the needs and responses of the individual than upon the impact of the environment, it has become popular to regard Freudian theory as a theory of the instincts or a biological theory, and to accuse it of disregarding environmental influences. But the truth is that Freud strongly emphasized the influence of both intra- and extra-familial life experiences. Indeed, one of his major departures from predecessors such as Janet and Charcot, who regarded neurosis as a manifestation of constitutional weakness, was to see neurosis in terms of human relationships. The person with a hysterical paralysis, for example, is using this symptom to protect himself from something he fears in his relationships with other people. Neurosis springs not only from conflict between inner drives and the superego and ego but also from the interaction between the child and the parents. Freud's theory definitely rests upon social interaction as well as upon intrapsychic factors; it is therefore harmonious with the long standing psychosocial orientation of casework and can be part of a total frame of reference which includes whatever data the social sciences can provide to illuminate the nature of the environment and the social forces with which the individual interacts.

This dual orientation lends itself very well to the systematizing of casework findings. Since the caseworker's laboratory is the common everyday world, he has had ample opportunity to observe the interplay between inner and outer forces. He has repeatedly seen people change for better and for worse under the impact of both benign and traumatic environments. He has observed people of diverse classes, ethnic origins, and regions and is well aware that adult behavior varies not only from group to group according to group norms but also within each group in accordance with the individual personality differences and life experiences of its members. Because traditionally the caseworker has dealt with family units, he is particularly aware of the interplay between family members and of the profound influence of parents as well as other members of the family upon the develment of the child's personality.

On the other hand Freudian theory stoutly maintains that man is not the mere product of his environment, clay upon which social influences leave their imprint. It insists, and rightly, that the individual makes his own demands upon his environment. This assertion of the individual's role in shaping his interaction with his environment carries with it the corollary implication that even if it were possible to provide exactly the same environment for two different babies the resultant adult personalities would differ.

While the foregoing may seem highly theoretical, it has major practical implications. It shifts emphasis from manipulation of the environment and a conditioning type of approach to emphasis upon *interaction,* particularly upon the individual's part in that interaction. In cases of marital adjustment it guards the worker against seeing the partner to whom he is talking as merely the victim in the relationship. In parent-child disorders it leads to a balanced examination both of what the parent is doing to the child and of what the child is doing to and demanding of the parent. In general, it leads to the assumption that the individual himself can almost always do something about his problem and that the worker's task is to increase his capacity to do so. This by no means, however, precludes recognition of realistic environmental pressures where they exist, nor does it deny the responsibility of the caseworker to ameliorate such pressures.

INTERACTIONS BETWEEN INDIVIDUAL AND ENVIRONMENT

The individual does not react to his environment as it exists but rather as he sees it, and a host of internal factors influence his perceptions. Among these are the primitive thought processes which distort the world of early childhood. Wishes are embued with magical power. Hence when the child wishes that a parent or brother or sister should get hurt, he may feel that he has actually caused any mishap that subsequently occurs, and therefore fear retaliation. When someone close to him has died, he may regard this as an act of purposeful abandonment and resent it accordingly. He cannot always distinguish his own thoughts and feelings from the thoughts and feelings of others: when he is angry he believes others are angry at him. Contradictory ideas exist side by side in his mind and he has no need to reconcile them. When he is crossed, his anger is not tempered by the good things he has experienced from the same source that now frustrates him. He generalizes indiscriminately, often expecting all grown-up men to be like father, all women like mother. His misperceptions cause him to react in a way that actually affects the response of his environment to him. Hence he is already to a degree creating his own environment.

These early distortions would not be quite so serious a matter if childish things were always left behind, but unfortunately the adult to a greater or lesser extent continues these infantile thought processes. They become an important ingredient in certain ego defense mechanisms. In the mechanism known as *projection* the individual will confuse his own thoughts and feelings with those of others. In *transference* he will either generalize indiscriminately or actually confuse one person with another because of superficial similarities. In *isolation* he will separate parts of his experience so that matters that are actually interrelated do not affect each other.[9] He will often fail to correct misapprehensions about his environment although contrary evidence is readily at hand.

Indeed, the individual's whole perception of the world around him is a combination in varying degrees of what is actually there and what he expects to find. We often do not see what we do not look for, but we create for ourselves what we seek to find. The person who anticipates that someone else will be hostile will read into the other person's behavior belligerent meanings whether or not they actually exist, and by his own responses may very well give rise to hostility in the other person. In so doing, he has to a high degree created his own environment: another form of the self-fulfilling prophecy.

Such misperceptions are not entirely a matter of individual psychology. A child learns that a radiator is hot not only by direct experience but also by being told so by a person whose words he trusts; and if he trusts another person, he will believe a false statement as readily as a true one. Indeed, if it is "everybody" who holds something to be true, it becomes extremely difficult for even the good adult mind to have a contrary opinion. How many generations saw sails disappearing over the horizon and continued to believe the world was flat? Belief is often so strong that the believer is cut off from even the opportunity of testing it. Race stereotypes are a cardinal example: in many communities people of different races never have a chance to meet and correct their mistaken ideas about each other because their preconceptions cause them to avoid all social contact. The element of expectation that is part of one's perception of his environment is a joint product of actual experience, individual distortion growing out of faulty thought processes, ideas incorporated from the idiosyncrasies of close associates, and ideas learned by personal contact but actually the product of group opinion—class, ethnic, regional, occupational, religious, political, and so on. Certain ideas are commonly held in the Middle West but not in the East, in the North but not in the South, in cities but not in rural areas, in Russia but not in the United States, among white-collar workers but not among industrial workers, among women but not among men, in poverty-stricken city areas but not in suburbia, and so on.

Role expectation is a form of group opinion especially significant for social work.[10] Specific ways of behaving are commonly accepted as appropriate or necessary for the individual in certain areas of functioning—e.g., as parent, as husband or wife, as employer—and he is perceived in terms of the way his role performance conforms to the norms held by his group. For instance, a man's perception of whether or not his wife loves him depends upon quite different cues in different groups. In some cultures the wife's housekeeping tasks are deemed so important that the husband would see subordination of them to interest in a job as personal neglect and evidence of lack of love, and his perception would be reinforced by the opinions of his friends, before whom he would be disgraced. Similarly, a parent's view of his child depends very greatly upon the extent to which he behaves according to group-influenced expectations. In some groups a child who dares strike his parent is perceived as very bad; in others he is merely high spirited.

The client will also have certain expectations of how the caseworker will act, and these will vary according to his personal and social experience. If the worker is to convey the same impression of good will, objectivity, and competence to clients of varying life experience he will need to be aware of their preconceptions and of the different interpretations they will make of his actions. He will need to be more "friendly" with some, more "professional" with others. With the "hard-to-reach," months of generous "doing for" may be necessary to overcome the stereotype of the caseworker as an interfering, hostile do-gooder. But the different methods employed do not mean that the underlying attitude of the worker is different.

Inaccurate perception can extend toward the self as well as toward others. An important component in the way we regard ourselves is the way in which other people regard us. A child who is constantly told he is stupid often believes this himself, whether or not it is true. A boy who is labeled a delinquent because he truants from school may begin to classify himself as a delinquent and start to associate with boys who actually are delinquent or think of themselves as such. (Who can doubt that this is a factor in the development of delinquent patterns?) This particular mechanism has a circular effect. When an individual feels himself an outcast for any reason, he begins to distort his perception of how other people react to him. Even when their behavior toward him does not fit his stereotype of rejection, he reacts as if it did and uses this belief to reenforce his picture of himself—a vicious circle, indeed.

] Causes of Interpersonal Adjustment Problems

Clients come for casework treatment because there has been a breakdown in their social adjustment. This breakdown has three possible sources: (1) infantile needs and drives left over from childhood which cause the individual to make inappropriate demands upon his adult world; (2) a current life situation which exerts excessive pressure upon him; and (3) faulty ego and superego functioning. The degree to which each of these is present varies with different people.

Persisting infantile needs and drives may lead to exaggerated narcissistic needs, excessive dependence or hostility, fixations on early family figures, fear of separation (with resulting anxiety or timidity which makes the individual require excessive protection and prevents him from assuming adult responsibilities), and abnormalities in the expression of sexual and aggressive drives.

While it is sometimes possible for people to find social situations where such abnormal needs can be gratified, for the most part this does not occur. The individual is then left with a constant sense of frustration, and characteristically behaves in a way that creates antagonism in his social environment and cuts him off from gratifications he might otherwise receive.

Common among current life pressures are those of economic deprivation (often due to unemployment or marginal working conditions), poor housing and neighborhood conditions, substandard educational opportunities, illness, and loss of love by death or separation. To these must be added innumerable individual life experiences that arouse anger-provoking frustration or feelings of inadequacy or guilt. They may occur in family relationships, when the needs of one individual conflict in a major way with those of another. They may occur when employment and living conditions are realistically very frustrating and pressing, although they may in no sense be substandard. And they may occur when general social conditions, such as racial discrimination, create constant environmental pressure of major proportions.

Faulty ego functioning includes distorted perception of either the outside world or the self, poor judgment, insufficient ability to control impulses or to direct behavior, poor reality testing, and inappropriate uses of the ego defenses. Faulty superego functioning may be of several kinds. Sometimes the superego is so primitive that the individual has not incorporated much in the way of standards at all. He just doesn't care about "right and wrong." More frequently, he does care but his standards and self-requirements are either too high, or too low, or otherwise out of harmony with his environment.

Faulty ego and superego functioning add substantially to the environmental pressures felt by the individual. If he misperceives pressures, the stress actually experienced in response to his distorted version of reality may be more severe than would have been appropriate to the actual life pressures. Such faulty functioning may also lead him to behave in such a way that he deprives himself of satisfactions he might otherwise have, creates guilt-arousing situations, exposes himself unnecessarily to situations in which he is inadequate, and surrounds himself with people who confirm his childish distortions of the world, thus reenforcing his tendency to faulty functioning. It is in reducing the extent of this secondary elaboration that the caseworker can be particularly helpful. Freed from some of these selfcreated pressures, the individual may be able to find in his life sufficient satisfaction of his basic needs to maintain a fairly comfortable equilibrium even though many childish needs and reactions remain untouched.

] *Treatment Through Reducing Environmental Press*

When a major part of the cause of the client's discomfort is in the environment, it is sometimes possible for the caseworker to modify the pressure directly. The public assistance program, for example, provides money for food, clothing, and shelter in cases of financial need. Other life pressures can be overcome by such direct services as obtaining medical care during illness, placing the homeless or neglected child in an adoptive or foster home, locating better housing, opening up educational and recreational opportunities. Attitudes of other individuals who are creating difficulties for the client can sometimes be modified by casework contact; when such modification is required, environmental manipulation itself becomes psychological in nature. Some of the services mentioned—child placement is a prime example—can be extremely complicated in the treatment required. And environmental services never stand alone. They are always accompanied by work directly with the client in which his reactions become the focus of attention. The public assistance client may not understand or respond realistically to the eligibility process. The hospital patient may be unwilling to undergo the recommended medical procedures. The child may not be ready to use the educational or recreational services that have been opened up. Much preparation involving both the resource and the client may be required before environmental pressure can be relieved.

Often, instead of meeting the need directly, it is advisable to help the client bring about a change in the situation himself. The caseworker's effort is then directed toward telling the client about possible opportunities, helping him decide whether or not he wants to use them and, if so, how to go about using them. Whenever a client can effectively do his own manipulation of the environment, this is the preferable course.

Environmental changes brought about solely for the purpose of removing unusual pressures or deficiencies need not involve an effort to change the personality of the individual. He may function more comfortably as a result of such change, but his inner balance may remain the same.

] *Treatment of Internal Factors*

When the major causative factors in the client's problem lie either in too great a residue of infantile desires and needs or in faulty ego and superego functioning, it is necessary to emphasize treatment directed toward the person himself. Such treatment may attempt to bring about either lasting changes in the client's personality or way of functioning or temporary adjustments of behavior during a period of stress.

Environmental change can sometimes become the means through which changes in personality are brought about. With children especially, lasting personality change occurs rather readily in response to environmental change, and this is the predominant method of casework treatment used with children. We try either to bring about changes in the parents' attitudes and behavior or to find substitute parents who can provide the child with a better milieu than that of his natural home. Major personality changes in the child—particularly the young child— often result. Less profound changes are promoted by modifications in the school environment, or by the provision of recreational and other group experiences such as camping, bringing a "big brother" into the situation, and so on. Because the child's personality is still so fluid, environmental changes profoundly affect his view of the world, the extent to which infantile strivings remain a part of his adult personality, his identifications, his ability to bear frustration, and in general the quality of his ego functioning.

With adults, the chances of bringing about personality change through environmental means are considerably narrowed. A radical change in environment will sometimes bring about a genuine personality change, as for example when a particularly fortunate choice of marriage partner leads to a long period of satisfying living that seems to undo the effects of earlier misfortune and brings about a real reorientation to life, or when events of traumatic proportions cause lasting regression in adult personality patterns. Sometimes the constant repetition of small traumata can have a cumulative effect of similar proportions. It is rarely possible, however, to arrange favorable environmental experiences of proportions sufficient to bring about significant personality changes in the adult. Changes in behavior, yes, but changes built into the personality, hardly ever. For example, a woman may become less tense, less hostile, and more able to give love to her children when she is working outside the home and having others care for her children than when she devotes her own full time to their care. If the caseworker helps her to recognize this and to arrange her life so that she can take a job, there may be marked improvement in her functioning. It should be noted, however, that a change in personality is not involved. Rather, the client has wisely provided herself with a set of circumstances within which she can use her current adaptive patterns to better advantage. If for some reason she has to give up her work, her functioning in relation to her children and her husband will again deteriorate. In many instances, however, such a change in functioning alone is an entirely appropriate treatment aim. Indeed, looked at as a way of providing the client's children with a better emotional environment, it may be the means for bringing about substantial changes in *their* personalities.

] Direct Work with the Individual

Intrapsychic factors causing personal difficulties for adults are usually modified through work with the individual directed toward modification of the dysfunctioning aspect of the personality. (This approach is also used with children, but usually in combination with whatever environmental changes can be achieved.) Casework uses for this purpose memories and current reactions and behavior that are either immediately accessible to consciousness or else suppressed, unverbalized or uncomprehended, but not repressed or so remote from consciousness that only such means as free association, hypnosis, or therapy under drugs can bring them to the surface.*

To understand how work with this part of the personality can be effective, we must appreciate the extent to which the personality is really a balance of forces. On the one side we have the immature or unusual needs and drives, the view of the world distorted by early childhood experiences, and the infantile modes of thoughts. On the other side, we have the healthy or potentially healthy part of the personality. When the inner drives push the individual toward socially unwise or self-destructive behavior, the healthy ego says "No." When the irrational part of the ego distorts reality by projection or magical beliefs, or other unconscious or primitive thought processes cause distortions, the healthy ego corrects this and keeps the irrational tendencies in check. It is often nip and tuck as to which side will win, depending upon the relative strength the two sets of forces can bring to bear in any particular situation. "If she had said just one more thing, I would have thrown the hammer at her. . . ." That is, "If I had been just a little more angry, nothing my ego was telling me would have been enough to keep me in control. . . ." One of the interesting aspects of this balance of forces is that while the decision to act may hang upon a hair's weight of difference between them, the action which this slight difference triggers may be of major proportions and have extensive consequences. A series of such issues and actions can combine to make a pattern of considerable strength and significance. It is not alone the strength of a drive, such as a tremendously strong impulse or the degree of a tendency toward distortion, that determines whether an action is to be taken, for these may be opposed by an equally strong counterforce, in the form of capacity for reality testing and ability to control impulses. Insofar as the opposing strengths are almost equally balanced, a relatively small amount of improvement in ego functioning may be enough to enable the individual to make significant changes in his total social functioning. This is one of the answers to the oft-repeated question: "If the infantile demands and distortions are not modified, how can there be any real change?" The

---

* See Chapter VIII for a full discussion of this point.

demands and distortions may remain untouched, but the person may handle them differently if his ego is functioning better.

It is also important to remember that all formative influences do not occur in infancy, nor are they all unconscious. If unresolved oedipal rivalries have made a daughter see her mother as hostile, the daughter's feeling may be reenforced by experiencing actual hostility from her mother in the later years of growth, or it may be somewhat lessened by experiences of a contrary nature. In the latter instance, not only is the original tendency not reenforced but the ego is given a means by which to counteract the effect of the original distortion. In the former instance, when the mother's later behavior reenforces the daughter's belief that enmity must exist between them—a belief that may affect her attitude toward other women—several modes of attack are open.

In one approach, the client is encouraged to ventilate her feelings about the events she spontaneously remembers or can recall with the help of "eductive" interviewing techniques. For a person who has not previously been able to express her anger toward her mother this in itself may have a useful cathartic effect, reducing the amount of suppressed hostility pressing for displacement on current female figures in the client's life. If there has been guilt over the angry feelings, the worker's acceptance of these feelings as warranted may reduce the guilt and subsequent need to use defenses such as hostility, projection, or turning against the self. If the anger has been displaced on a female child or on other adult women, it may be possible to enable the client to recognize and to stop behavior which provokes counter-hostility and is thus causing her to experience constant repetitions of her original unhappy experience with a woman.

Another approach is to provide the client with an opportunity for a corrective relationship. By allowing a relationship to develop in which the client regards the worker as a mother figure, it may be possible to counteract the earlier bad mother-daughter experience by enabling the client to see that the characteristics of her own mother which caused her unhappiness are peculiar to her mother and are not general characteristics of all women. This experience may also tend to undo some of her attitudes about herself, about sex, marriage, child raising and so on which she acquired in her early relationship with her mother.

A further alternative is to enable the client to review her conscious and preconscious or near-conscious early memories of her experiences with her mother. By seeing their effects on her personality and current reactions to life she may free herself to a degree from these childhood and adolescent reenforcements of her oedipal distortions and, in turn, reduce the degree of distortion with which her adult ego must now deal. Along with this reduction of the force of her childhood experiences, she may be helped to recognize her tendency to carry over feelings from her childhood to her current relationships and may learn to improve these relationships by careful testing of her own reactions against the realities of other people's behavior.

Now, none of these procedures will have touched directly the infantile core of the client's trouble. She will still have in her unconscious whatever hostilities and distortion tendencies, whatever component of infantile oedipal rivalry was there before the treatment. But the effect of some of the later childhood experiences which reenforced the earlier ones will have been reduced, the ego will have been strengthened in its efforts to correct and control destructive behavior, and the tendency to create repetitive hostile life experiences will have been lessened. Such changes in the balance of forces within the individual may well bring about marked improvement in functioning and constitute an internalized change in adaptive patterns.

] *Directive vs. Rational Therapies*

Casework is a form of treatment that relies primarily on "rational" measures, and makes use of directive techniques like suggestion, advice, and persuasion only when diagnosis indicates that the client is unlikely to respond to measures that rely upon his own active thinking. This may be the case when he is so overwhelmed by pressing happenings in his life—sickness, death, desertion—that he is unable to make use of his usual reflective powers, or when he is in large measure inherently incapable of doing so, as with individuals suffering from severe character disorders or borderline psychosis, or recovering from a period of mental illness.

In truly directive therapies the therapist prefers to take a very active part in advising the client, relying primarily upon the weight of his "professional authority" and upon the positive transference to modify the client's, or patient's, responses. Casework differs markedly from such therapies. It never uses directive procedures in isolation from rational measures, and employs them only when the client is not ready or able to use rational procedures. Even with the very severely disturbed or inadequate person with whom methods of "direct influence" may need to play a relatively large part in treatment, they would never, in casework, constitute the sole ingredient. Students sometimes ask whether there is not an incompatibility between the employment of directive procedures to even this limited degree and the principle of self-determination. But they fail to see that self-determination is not an absolute value. Whereas it requires that every effort be made to increase the client's capacity for self-direction, it also recognizes that clients vary in this capacity and that a limited amount of directiveness in treatment is sometimes advisable.*

Some writers recognize only two ways of influencing behavior: one characterized by the bringing of unconscious factors under the control of the ego, the other by methods that rest essentially on the therapist's authority and the influence of the transference. The second type of treatment, which certain writers, such as Eissler,[11] refer to condescendingly as "magic," is considered to be mainly manipulative and to bring only unstable changes in functioning, because such changes are not truly built into the personality but remain a reflection of the continuing relationship with the therapist. There is no doubt that truly directive therapies do rely very heavily upon the techniques Eissler terms "magic."

The first method referred to is, of course, psychoanalysis. Psychoanalysis attempts to modify infantile drive derivatives and needs which have partly become unconscious, cause intrapsychic conflict in the individual, and interfere with the adaptive functioning of the ego and superego. By inducing a strongly regressive transference in the patient, it enables his adult ego to relive and reevaluate early life experiences so that infantile attachments

---

* See Chapter V, page 95, for further discussion of this point.

and fantasies can truly be relinquished and infantile misconceptions corrected. But as Greta Bibring[12] has so clearly pointed out, psychoanalysis, in addition to this process of enabling the ego to assume control over unconscious factors, also makes use of "techniques of influence" such as those described in Eissler's second category. There is no question but what psychoanalysis does bring about profound changes in personality. These changes often give promise of being permanent, though they are not necessarily so.

In casework we find a kind of treatment of which Eissler does not take note. It is clearly not psychoanalysis, but neither is it mainly manipulative. Like analysis it sometimes uses techniques of influence, and it does so to a greater degree than is true in analysis. It is, however, by no means primarily a directive therapy, relying on the worker's professional authority to persuade the client to change his behavior in a given direction. Rather it seeks to engage the client's ego—his capacity to think, to reflect, to understand—in a reevaluation of himself-in-his-situation. It engages the client as fully as possible in his own treatment, endeavoring not only to preserve but to enhance his reliance upon himself and the extent to which he is able to guide his actions by realistic understanding.

In addition to improvement in external functioning, such treatment often brings about such internalized modifications as improvement of the ego's perception and reality testing ability, shifts in the use of defenses, changes in the demands—or in the reaction to the demands—of the superego, lasting reductions in the strength of destructive character traits such as chronic latent hostility and dependence, relinquishing of parental ties, and maturation in the instinctual life. Such shifts are built into the personality and enable the individual to function better even when he is confronted by circumstances identical or essentially similar to those under which his functioning was previously impaired. Such changes can be expected to continue after treatment has ended.

In summary, then, when casework is employed to help the client achieve better social functioning, it becomes a form of psychosocial therapy. It relies mainly on rational procedures closely allied to psychoanalytic techniques, augmented by methods of direct influence when diagnosis indicates that these will be more effective. Focus is always upon the person-situation gestalt, which is seen as an interacting balance of forces between the needs of the person and the influence upon him of the environment. Individual functioning is the end result of a complicated interaction between complementary parts of the personality highly susceptible to outside influences. In psychosocial therapy influence is brought to bear on either the environment or the personality or both. When it is directed toward the personality, it can reduce the force of destructive trends in the individual by decreasing the force of earlier life experiences and by increasing the capacity of the ego and superego to handle current life experiences more realistically. ⌡

NOTES

1. For discussions of this, see Talcott Parsons, "Psychoanalysis and the Social Structure," in *Essays in Sociological Theory,* The Free Press, Glencoe, Ill., 1954; and Geza Roheim, *Psychoanalysis and Anthropology: Culture, Personality and the Unconscious,* International Universities Press, New York, 1950.

2. Gordon Hamilton and many other writers have stressed this point of view. See her *Theory and Practice of Social Work,* rev. ed., Columbia University Press, New York, 1951.

3. Florence Kluckhohn's work in this area has been of special interest to social workers. See Florence Kluckhohn, "Variations in the Basic Values of Family Systems," *Social Casework,* 39 (February–March, 1958), 63–72; and Florence Kluckhohn and John P. Spiegel, "Integration and Conflict in Family Behavior," Committee on the Family of the Group for the Advancement of Psychiatry, Report No. 27, August, 1954.

4. For a fuller discussion of casework values, see Herbert Bisno, *The Philosophy of Social Work*, Public Affairs Press, Washington, D.C., 1952. Also see the author's "Principles and Assumptions Underlying Casework Practice," *Social Work* (London), *12* (1955), 41–55.

5. For comprehensive review of the findings concerning the effects of maternal deprivation, see John Bowlby, *Maternal Care and Mental Health*, 2nd ed., World Health Organization: Monograph Series No. 2, Geneva, 1952; and Mary D. Ainsworth, "The Effects of Maternal Deprivation: A Review of Findings and Controversy in the Context of Research Strategy," in *Deprivation of Maternal Care: A Reassessment of Its Effects*, World Health Organization, Geneva, 1962.

6. For comments on this, see Annette Garrett, "Modern Casework: The Contributions of Ego Psychology," in *Ego Psychology and Dynamic Casework*, Howard J. Parad, ed., Family Service Association of America, New York, 1958, pp. 38–52, and Gordon Hamilton, "A Theory of Personality: Freud's Contribution to Social Work," in Parad, *ibid.*, pp. 11–37.

7. For a brief and modern presentation of the main outlines of Freudian theory, see Charles Brenner, *An Elementary Textbook of Psychoanalysis*, Doubleday Anchor Books, Garden City, N. Y., 1955.

8. Ways of thinking and feeling characteristic of the young child are vividly portrayed in the studies of Jean Piaget and Susan Isaacs. See especially Jean Piaget, *The Child's Conception of the World*, Harcourt, Brace & Co., New York, 1929; and Susan Isaacs, *Social Development In Young Children*, Harcourt, Brace & Co., New York, 1937.

9. For a full and clear discussion of these and other mechanisms of defense, see Anna Freud, *The Ego and the Mechanisms of Defense*, International Universities Press, New York, 1946. For a condensed discussion, see Lucille N. Austin, "Some Psychoanalytic Principles Underlying Casework with Children," in *Child Therapy—A Casework Symposium*, Family Service Association of America, New York, 1948, pp. 10–15.

10. A brief presentation of the use of role concepts in casework is given by Henry Maas in his chapter "Social Casework," in *Concepts and Methods of Social Work*, Walter A. Friedlander,

ed., Prentice-Hall, Englewood Cliffs, N. J., 1958, pp. 48–65. Other useful references on role concepts include:

Edgar F. Borgatta, "Role and Reference Group Theory in Social Science Theory and Social Work Research," in *Proceedings of an Institute Held by the Research Section of the National Association of Social Workers,* L. Kogan, ed., National Association of Social Workers, New York, 1960.

Neal Gross, Ward S. Mason, and Alexander McEachern, *Explorations in Role Analysis: Studies of the School Superintendency Role,* John Wiley & Sons, New York, 1958.

L. J. Neiman and J. W. Hughes, "The Problem of the Concept of Role—A Re-survey of the Literature," *Social Forces, 30* (1951), 141–149, also in Herman Stein and Richard Cloward, *Social Perspectives on Behavior,* The Free Press, Glencoe, Ill., 1958.

Victoria Olds, "Role Theory and Casework: A Review of the Literature," *Social Casework, 43* (January, 1962), 3–8.

Helen Perlman, "The Role Concept and Social Casework: Some Explorations. II. What is Social Diagnosis," *Social Service Review, 36* (March, 1962), 17–31.

Beatrice Werble, "The Implications of Role Theory for Casework Research," *Social Science Theory and Social Work Research,* L. Kogan, ed., National Association of Social Workers, New York, 1960.

11. Kurt R. Eissler, "The Chicago Institute of Psychoanalysis and the Sixth Period of Development of Psychoanalytic Technique," *Journal of General Psychology, 42* (1950), 118ff.

12. Grete L. Bibring discusses "manipulation" as a technique of both casework and psychoanalysis in "Psychiatry and Social Work," *Journal of Social Casework, 28* (June, 1947), 203–211, and in "Psychiatric Principles in Casework," *Journal of Social Casework, 30* (June, 1949), 230–235.

II

Some Examples of Casework in Practice

BEFORE WE PROCEED with further discussion of theory, some case illustrations may be of value in demonstrating the use in actual practice of the concepts presented in the introductory chapter. The case of Mr. and Mrs. Ryman,* for example, is of particular interest because the problems in social functioning encountered by this couple reflect all three types of causation described in Chapter I, and the dynamics of the treatment processes by which they were enabled to achieve better functioning demonstrate clearly many of the points made there.

] *Negative Complementarity in a Marriage*

Mrs. Ryman, the wife of a successful young executive, was on the point of leaving her "impossible" husband when she came to the agency. There were violent quarrels in which he swore at her abusively. He was jealous of their children, particularly of the older child, Alice, a nine-year-old born while he was overseas; towards her he was critical and hostile, favoring the second daughter, two years younger. Mrs. Ryman felt that she received

---

* All case material in this book is disguised and fictitious names are used throughout.

no love from her husband. She objected to sexual relations with him and wanted either to separate from him or to continue in a purely practical living arrangement which would provide financial support for herself and the children. She desired no companionship with her husband and wanted to exclude him from the upbringing of the children, since she considered this a woman's job and also thought his influence on the children was harmful. In this view she was reenforced by her mother's attitude that it was hopeless to try to improve her relationship with her husband.

The current situational pressures in this case are obvious. Mrs. Ryman was receiving very little love from her husband; instead, he was verbally abusive to her. He was also handling the children badly, creating problems with which she was left to deal. Her mother's attitude pushed her further in the direction of quarreling with her husband, rather than of trying to improve their relationship.

What infantile needs did Mrs. Ryman bring to her situation from her childhood? When she was two or three years old, her father left her mother, eventually divorcing her. For a number of years he was in and out of the house, remaining an extremely attractive figure to Mrs. Ryman, but also a deserting one. She was his favorite child. When she was seven her mother remarried, but this marriage also ended in separation when Mrs. Ryman was thirteen or fourteen. She remembers her stepfather as violently hostile. Her mother hated men and inculcated this hatred in her daughter.

As a result of her early life, Mrs. Ryman carried over into adulthood a number of childish needs and reactions which caused her to make unusual demands on her adult world. She was partially frigid, fearful of sex, guilty on the few occasions when she allowed herself to enjoy it, and prudish in her refusal to participate in anything but the most conservative form of sex relationship, wanting for herself a husband who had little or no sex interest himself. She was overly devoted to her mother and so dependent upon her approval that she allowed her to continue to guide her adult life. Lacking other love gratification, she became overly possessive of her children, excluding her husband from participation in their upbringing. She also brought into adulthood excessive hostility to men, displaced from her feelings toward her two fathers and reenforced by her mother's attitude which had been instilled in her.

There was also faulty ego functioning in her evaluation of her husband, whom she could not see as the fundamentally loving person he was. Because of her earlier experiences Mrs. Ryman anticipated hostility and desertion on his part, and was unable to believe that he really loved her and wanted to find ways of improving their relationship. In the early years of their marriage, Mr. Ryman was devoted to his wife, hoping to be able to "awaken" her. But when he returned from overseas service, he found her so preoccupied with the children that she had little interest in him, and was resistive to sex relations. A number of times he lost his temper with her and with the older child, and from that point on she became increasingly cold, withdrawn, and hostile despite all his warm efforts to make amends.

Because of her distorted attitude toward men, Mrs. Ryman now saw her husband as the bad father her mother had pictured and she had experienced in childhood. Indeed, her husband's absence during the war must have encouraged displacement of the feelings she had had toward her deserting father. It was impossible for her to understand or sympathize with her husband's needs. Instead, she deprived and belittled him in a way that brought to the fore immaturities in his own personality—a strong need for mothering and a degree of insecurity about his masculinity. Thus, because of her own personality impairment, Mrs. Ryman had created for herself a hostile, attacking husband out of a fundamentally loving one and had deprived herself of the love she could have had because of her own inability to receive it.

Looking at the problem from Mr. Ryman's side, what do we see? He was somewhat over-attached to his mother, although not in a truly neurotic way, with correspondingly excessive needs for mothering from his wife, and with some adolescent-like insecurities about his masculinity. Late in treatment, he recalled his hurt and anger when an older sister who had been very much of a mother to him had turned her affections to a younger brother born when he was seven. At the beginning of his marriage, nevertheless, he appeared to be a fairly mature young man, with a normal capacity for love and free of marked neurotic traits.

Upon his return from military service, however, he met what was essentially a traumatic situation. We tend to think of a trauma as a sudden dramatic event, but in actuality the repeated shock of lesser events can have an effect comparable in its proportions to a single major blow. Although Mr. Ryman came gradually to realize his wife's consistently unyielding hostility, this realization was, in effect, a trauma for him. For a long time he denied the severity of her reaction, alternately trying in every way he knew to recapture their earlier relationship and responding with fury when his efforts were frustrated.

As he became lonelier and more frustrated and angry, regression set in; his need for the sort of love he had had from his mother and sister increased. He responded with the jealousy he had felt for his brother, displacing his anger from his brother to his older child, who seemed to have stolen his place. His adolescent-like doubts about his own virility were also rearoused now that the realities of his life seemed to indicate that he was unable to awaken response in his wife. Earlier guilt feelings about sex, not quite outgrown, reasserted themselves, and he began to feel that some of his less conventional sex desires might be wrong and were contributing to his troubles. In his need to defend himself against these anxieties, he became at times short-tempered, unreasonable, and sharply attacking. He saw his wife as hostile and destructive, and lost to a large degree his former ability to understand her needs.

Three sets of forces, then, had combined to create their present dilemma for the Rymans: infantile needs and weaknesses in functioning deriving from childhood, current life deprivations and pressures, and nonadaptive ego functioning which united with the childish remnants to create additional environmental hazards.

Mr. and Mrs. Ryman began treatment simultaneously, each coming for weekly interviews. At the beginning they had different workers; later, Mrs. Ryman at her own request transferred to her husband's caseworker. At first Mr. Ryman needed to talk in detail about his wife's cold and hostile behavior, but he immediately followed this up by talking about his own angry reactions and his guilt about his inability to control himself. The caseworker was able to reduce some of his tension by showing sympathetic understanding of the frustrations by which he was confronted and of his unhappiness about them. This laid the groundwork for his later ability to work on the shortcomings in his own responses. She did not give false reassurance about his inability to control his anger, but instead agreed without condemnation that it was a problem for him and worked against his own expressed desires for his family.

In this atmosphere Mr. Ryman became increasingly able to describe the details of interaction between himself, his wife, and his children. As he recounted incidents involving the children, he became more aware of the effect of his angry spells on them, both in confusing and frightening them and in alienating them from him. He also began to see that much of his anger toward Alice was really intended for his wife, and that he was using the child to hurt Mrs. Ryman. This realization made it more possible for him to control his outbursts against Alice. But his wife, unfortunately, did not show any appreciation of his efforts to change, nor did she respond any more generously to his need for love.

As Mr. Ryman's description of his wife's treatment of him increased in freedom and vehemence, he suddenly saw that he felt she was taking away his masculinity and was trying to destroy him. It was apparent to the worker that this in turn aroused his doubts about himself and that he defended himself against his self-doubts by a show of masculine aggression punctuated with crude and abusive language. The worker rightly saw that Mrs. Ryman's attack was not a product of Mr. Ryman's manipulation but a realistic pressure growing out of Mrs. Ryman's distorted reactions to men. Since it was not yet possible to bring about a change in Mrs. Ryman, efforts were made in two directions to strengthen Mr. Ryman's ability to withstand his wife's continuing hostility. One approach rested in its dynamics upon the relationship between the client and therapist. Wherever possible the worker conveyed to Mr. Ryman her own view of him as an adequate male; she expressed directly her opinion that his sexual desires were normal, as they were. The worker's continued acceptance of the healthiness of Mr. Ryman's desires and the naturalness of his anger made it possible for him to begin to regain his self-confidence and opened the way for his trying to understand his wife. He was increasingly able to see that his wife had great anxiety about sex. He went over the early life experiences that had brought about the sex inhibitions which she could not control.

The more he saw the problem in her, the less anxious he became about himself. He was freed to understand and appreciate her unhappiness and to see more fully the way in which his angry behavior had increased her fears. As he became more able to place the blame for their sexual problem on his wife where, in this case, it really belonged, Mr. Ryman was in large measure relieved of his own reawakened doubts about himself and his sexual needs and competence. Thus a large part of his need to become hostile towards his wife was also removed.

The balance of forces within his personality was now shifted sufficiently to enable him gradually to acquire control of his own reactions. When he did become angry he was repeatedly able to trace his anger to its current source in the frustrating sexual situation and keep it where it belonged—as he said, "in the bedroom"—instead of allowing it to spill over to do harm in other areas of his family life where it did not belong; he could also keep himself from acts of retaliation which worsened rather than improved his situation. Thus the area of social disturbance was greatly narrowed.

Toward the end of treatment, as Mrs. Ryman also began to change, Mr. Ryman showed sympathetic understanding of her problems and tried to help her to become less fearful in their sexual relationship. He also examined more fully his jealousy of his children and came to see its similarity to his childhood reactions to his mother; this in turn gave him greater motivation for controlling his responses and keeping them from doing harm to the children.

The treatment of Mr. Ryman scarcely touched the childish components in his adult personality; it was concerned almost exclusively with strengthening the healthy part of his ego in order to enable it to deal better with frustrations. His perception of himself as a healthy male was shored up, and he was enabled to see the realities of his situation more clearly, thereby ridding himself of harmful distortions. He was also helped to understand the interaction between himself and his family and the effects his own responses were having on them. Perceiving and comprehending the situation more clearly, he was better able to judge the direction he wanted his affairs to take and to control his own responses in a way more likely to bring his goal about.

The initial period of work with Mrs. Ryman was not fruitful. Her repetitious and extensive expressions of anger at her husband brought her little relief. She was completely unwilling to examine her own reactions to their relationship or accept even a modicum of responsibility for their troubles. She was aware of the effect on their marriage of her lack of participation in their sex life, and more superficially that the cause of her fears lay in her own childhood, in the absence of her father and in her mother's insistence that she see all men as bad. But instead of trying to free herself from these influences, she used them as an excuse and demanded that her husband adjust to her inhibitions.

The next step in treatment, which occurred after Mrs. Ryman began to be seen by the same worker as her husband, became one of helping Mrs. Ryman recognize that despite her husband's use of treatment to improve his behavior toward her, she still wanted to hold on to her grudges and refused to change her side of the relationship. The worker did not express criticism of Mrs. Ryman for this nor did she urge her to change, but limited herself to pointing out that there would be no purpose in setting up interviews if Mrs. Ryman really was satisfied to continue the status quo.

Gradually Mrs. Ryman acknowledged that she was fighting a battle from her past; she accepted the worker's comment that in so doing she was making trouble for herself as well as for her husband and volunteered that she played favorites with the children, preferring Alice, the child toward whom her husband was hostile. As Mrs. Ryman began to consider her mistakes, the worker kept herself oriented to Mrs. Ryman's own well-being, so that the client would see the need for change not as a dutiful adaptation to her husband but as a way of better achieving her own deepest wishes for herself and her children.

As Mrs. Ryman began to recognize instances in which she had distorted her husband's actions, assuming hostility when none existed, she was able to see that she had not been trying to understand him. She began to correct her distortions and to look more realistically at Mr. Ryman, as well as at her own tendency to blame him at times when she herself was at fault.

The beginnings of a better relationship with her husband, brought feelings of disloyalty to her mother to the fore. As she recognized these feelings her adult judgment gradually took hold and another obstacle to better adjustment lost some of its power. For the first time she began to talk about the positive elements in her marriage. She saw that she had been shutting her husband out of the lives of her children and began to handle herself differently in that triangular relationship. At this point in her adjustment her discussion of their sexual difficulties took on a different quality; she conceded that the problem was really hers and that she ought to try to get over it. For the first time she could truly understand her husband's feelings of rejection. Her attitude toward his sexual advances now changed, even though she was not yet comfortable in her own sexual responses.

Whether continued casework treatment would have brought about further improvement, we do not know, for at this point the couple had to leave the country because of Mr. Ryman's business, and treatment was discontinued. The total relationship between Mr. and Mrs. Ryman was markedly improved, however; the outright battles were a thing of the past, the children were no longer pawns in the marital struggle, and an atmosphere of true warmth had begun to emerge in the family.

In analyzing the case of Mrs. Ryman, we see again that treatment enabled the client's ego to take control over a larger part of her personality. First submerged feelings and wishes were brought clearly within the ego's perception. Then the realities and consequences of behavior to which the individual was previously blind emerged. As with Mr. Ryman, the direct influence of the worker, in the nature of a corrective experience in the treatment relationship, was of great importance. The therapist conveyed her own belief that Mrs. Ryman had a right to grow up and enjoy her marriage and that men were not by nature hostile and disloyal but rather capable of providing comfort and happiness to a woman.

] *A Superego Disturbance*

Casework treatment is "thematic." It does not attempt to deal thoroughly with all aspects of the client's adjustment or personality; rather, it studies the current adjustment and life history of the individual to ascertain where his functioning is inadequate and causes discomfort and what particular facets of his personality which need strengthening might be susceptible to change by casework methods. Certain social themes and certain psychological themes appear repetitively in interviews, their choice being determined partly by client interest and partly by conscious focusing on the part of the worker.

Work with Miss Emerson, for instance, viewed from the psychological side, concentrated on superego inadequacies. Viewed socially, it focused on her relationships with her friends and on her effort to find close relationships that would be both deeply satisfying and in harmony with the demands of her social environment.

In discussing changes in the superego, we must distinguish sharply between structure and content. A child learns very early in life that there is such a thing as right and wrong and acquires the desire to do "right" things and avoid doing "wrong" things in order both to please his parents and to avoid punishment. If this basic structure is absent or seriously defective in the adult, it is unlikely that casework methods can do much in the superego area. Fortunately, the basic structure is usually present, but the content—the pattern of what is believed right and what is believed wrong—is unrealistic. Sometimes it is consistently too high in the standard it requires, sometimes too low. At other times it is inconsistent, with contrary patterns or with lacunae, as Adelaide Johnson[1] has called them, curious blank spots where otherwise mature individuals seem to lack socially acceptable standards. It is this area of *content* that is amenable to casework influence.

Miss Emerson, a young woman in her early twenties, came to the agency to seek help in freeing herself from a group of young people with whom she had been associating. They were using marijuana and engaging in petty stealing. Miss Emerson had been in revolt against conventional behavior for many years, but her friends' activities had begun to dissatisfy and frighten her. She was in severe conflict both about what she thought she ought to do and what she wanted to do.

Miss Emerson's early life history embodied three factors often associated with later superego disturbance. In the first place, her mother used overly severe physical punishment as a form of discipline, setting up a rebellion against the very standards she was trying to inculcate. In the second place, she constantly warned against certain forms of forbidden behavior, as though she anticipated that her daughter would be unable to refrain from indulging in them. As Adelaide Johnson and others have pointed out, a child's ability to discipline his own impulses is greatly aided by a belief on the part of his parents that he will be good most of the time. The parent who constantly warns the child against misbehavior, as Miss Emerson's mother did, is actually dangling a temptation before him. In the third place, Mrs. Emerson's own superego was defective. She was extremely impulsive and inconsistent in behavior. As the child learns more rapidly from what the parent does than from what he says, Miss Emerson was thus influenced by her mother's unsound example.

Miss Emerson's father appears to have had a much more stable superego than her mother, but he was a weaker person and so was unable to make his influence felt as strongly as that of his wife. Nevertheless, he did contribute a positive element to Miss Emerson's development, which she became more able to use as she responded to treatment.

Work with Miss Emerson combined a corrective relationship experience with discussions of current realities designed to strengthen the ego in its perception, judgment, and ability to control. In turn changes in the content of the superego were brought about. Because of the nature of the transference, Miss Emerson identified with the worker and accepted some of her values. In addition, her own increasingly realistic ego began to build up values of a more socially useful type, which gradually became part of her ideal for herself.

To begin with, the worker showed interest in Miss Emerson, understanding of her plight, and appreciation of her conflict about it; but she carefully refrained from falling into the trap of immediately aligning herself with Miss Emerson's impulsive move toward a more conventional life. To have plunged immediately into approving and implementing her initial impulse would have been to overlook Miss Emerson's ambivalence, to mobilize her resistance to change and to provide her with an opportunity once again to act out the old mother-daughter drama, with the worker cast in the role of the strict, punitive, and distrustful mother. Even if ways could have been found to avoid this latter pitfall, had the worker moved too quickly in getting Miss Emerson away from her anti-social companions she would have run the risk of sacrificing the long-range goal of enabling her to build a new set of life objectives which would become a lasting part of her personality.

Early interviews, therefore, were used to encourage Miss Emerson to look at her proposed move from all angles, to face the loss of friendships that would be involved and to air her fears of not being able to find new ones. The worker made it clear that she was ready to help work out plans for such a move if and when Miss Emerson really decided to make it, but did not try to rush the decision. She assumed throughout, as was diagnostically indicated, that Miss Emerson was capable of deciding for herself what was wise and unwise activity and that she both desired and was capable of finding for herself a way of life in which she could be at peace with the world as well as with herself.

As Miss Emerson became more certain of her resolve, the worker showed her agreement with it and tacitly implied Miss Emerson would be able to carry it through. When the decision was finally made, she gave help in the form of suggestions about practical steps to take. When Miss Emerson moved to a new location she showed pleasure, but gentle pleasure geared to the client's own satisfaction in her accomplishments.

During the inevitable period of loneliness before Miss Emerson could find new friendships, the worker's friendly interest in her everyday life became an emotional crutch to tide her over until real life experiences could again meet her needs. She and the worker discussed her new acquaintances, including Miss Emerson's ways of reacting to them and her distorted evaluation of their attitudes toward her. They went into details of how she handled herself on her job. The worker shared her own interests in movies and jazz, so that Miss Emerson saw her as a person who thought it was good to have fun and who knew something about the ropes of a young person's world. As her growing interest in dating and eventual marriage aroused her interest in homemaking skills, the worker brought her recipes and even helped her in sewing a dress. As the worker gradually gained her trust and admiration, Miss Emerson began to identify with her and incorporate some of her values.

While there was a minimum of active direction on the worker's part, as the relationship between her and Miss Emerson grew stronger she was able to be more direct in expressing opinions when these were called for, thus providing Miss Emerson with guides for behavior which she had not had earlier in her life. As Miss Emerson herself put it toward the end of treatment, "When you are told you are a bum all your life, you begin to believe it"; and she particularly stressed the value of the worker's "believing" in her. At the same time she said she was glad the caseworker had not "indulged" her, referring to the fact that the worker had gradually cut through her self-deceptions and rationalizations, enabling her ego to make its decisions on the basis of facts rather than of self-coddling distortions.

Here again, as in the case of the Rymans, the early formative experiences in the client's life were touched on but by no means thoroughly explored. The main dynamics of treatment lay in strengthening the more accessible parts of the personality in ways that would enable them to counterbalance the early traumata.

While the effect of the client-worker relationship was by no means the only dynamic in treatment, it played a larger part in this case than it did in the work with the Rymans. There has been a tendency to belittle so-called transference cures. Some of our distrust of such cures is well based. When nothing more is done than to use suggestion as a way of directly removing symptomatic behavior, it is extremely likely that a new form of symptom will arise, and not infrequently a more harmful symptom than the one originally chosen by the client. If, however, the transference is used to remove or lessen the effect of factors causative to the maladjustment, we have an entirely different situation.

This principle may be seen in the work with Miss Emerson. Had the worker used her influence directly to induce her client to move to a different neighborhood, to give up certain friends, and to make certain other friendships, this would have been "symptomatic" treatment. The improvement would then very likely have been only temporary, because the forces originally at work would have pushed the client in the direction of repetitive behavior and she would have chosen acquaintances similar to the friends she had just relinquished. Instead, the worker-client relationship was used to counteract the self-image and values derived from earlier life experiences which were basic to later social adjustment.

Two additional factors would seem to influence the endurance of transference improvement. One, of course, is the length of time the transference itself remains alive. If the treatment has ended by mutual consent and with the positive transference elements in ascendancy, if dependence has been lessened before the close of treatment to a point where the client has confidence in his ability to maintain his improvement alone, and if the negative feelings inevitable in separation have been foreseen and worked through before ending, the effects of the transference may continue for indefinite periods of time.

A second important factor is the extent to which improved life conditions achieved through the behavior changes originating in transference reenforce the effect of transference itself. If the experience of living confirms the wisdom of ways of behavior promoted by the therapist through the medium of transference, the client may gradually be led to integrate the new ways into his ego structure, independently of their original transference source. This element was important in the Emerson case.

] *Understanding Early Life Experiences*

Not infrequently the caseworker does find it necessary to use early life material to develop a client's understanding of current reactions. This was true in the case of Mr. Fuller, who was having difficulty in two areas—his work and his relationship with his son. These became the social themes around which treatment revolved; but it soon became apparent that they were in large part a reflection of problems that had their roots in neurotic personality characteristics. Mr. Fuller's feelings toward his father and the subsequent displacement of these feelings in his current work and family relationships thus became the psychological themes of treatment, with the emphasis more upon self-understanding than was true in Miss Emerson's case.

Mr. Fuller had been complaining to the therapist at length about his employer's immoderate demands, spoke of his wife's impatience with his investing too much of himself in his job, and gave innumerable instances of his boss's stupidity and unreason-

ableness and of arguments in which Mr. Fuller was repeatedly
able to come out on top. When the worker asked why he worked
so hard for a man he disliked, Mr. Fuller said he thought the
cause lay in the ideas about work that his father had inculcated
in him. He described his father as a perfectionist demanding
high performance of his son, who had worked for him during his
adolescence. He told of his consequent fear of criticism, and his
efforts to avoid it by requiring more than adequate performance
of himself on a job. At the same time, he expressed great anger
at his boss for his unjustified criticisms. As a result of this discussion, Mr. Fuller began to think more objectively about his
father's standards and ideals and to realize that he as an adult
could set more realistic rules for himself.

Despite this new awareness, his troubles with his employer
and his complaints continued unchanged. The worker indicated
that she accepted the fact that this was a difficult reality situation and that his boss was unreasonable, but she added that there
were certain factors about his response to the situation that
needed further exploration and study. Why should Mr. Fuller
tire himself out working overtime with no extra pay to do a better
job for a boss he didn't like? Mr. Fuller was quick to see the
illogic of his own behavior and was astonished at his own foolish-
ness, when in reality he could easily make his boss hire additional
help. Spurred on by this, he admitted his feelings of inadequacy
and his need to show that he was really much better than the
boss, that he was, in fact, a superman.

This admission led to further discussion of his father's attitudes, and for the first time real ambivalence began to come
through. Mr. Fuller would swing from describing his father's
great strength and intelligence to belittling him as a vocational
failure and a man who only thought he ruled his family but was
actually under his wife's domination. He told of his father's disparaging treatment of him, of his domineering over him and his
refusal to try ideas Mr. Fuller had about improving the family
business. Finally he burst out that "he adored the old man in
many ways yet sometimes he hated him with every fiber in his
body." Subsequently, Mr. Fuller saw the repetitive nature of his
relationship with his employer as a displacement from his father.
His belligerent behavior with his boss was in part a living out

of suppressed and repressed anger at his father and in part an attempt to prove to himself that he was an ideal, loving son by carrying out his father's mandate to be a perfect, or superperfect, workman. He became able to handle his work life more realistically, and in time changed to a more remunerative and less demanding job.

Several processes were at work in bringing about this change. First came the step of convincing Mr. Fuller that his current behavior was irrational. Sometimes such a realization in itself is enough to enable a person to modify his reactions; but in cases where such modification does not occur, motivation has nevertheless been created for the client to pursue the matter further. A second factor was Mr. Fuller's recognition of the displacement from father to employer. Often a client is well aware of hostile feelings toward parents and blind only to the fact of displacement; but in more complicated situations, as with Mr. Fuller, the feelings are themselves half-concealed. A third factor, then, became the bringing to light of the strength of Mr. Fuller's anger at his father, together with the most important fourth factor, the worker's acceptance of that anger and the consequent reduction in Mr. Fuller's guilt about it.

Viewed in the framework of Freudian theory, this case is one of classical oedipal reactions. Mr. Fuller had recalled events in his adolescence which reflected and reenforced unresolved infantile rivalries with his father. Other material in the record substantiates this. At no point, however, did the therapist get into these underlying, unconscious reactions. The strength of the total oedipal component in Mr. Fuller's problem was, however, reduced in several ways: the reenforcement of the original experiences occurring in adolescence was greatly lessened; the constant confirmation of the original distortion in the reactions he evoked in "father persons" was removed; and some of the feeling itself was drained off as in his conscious mind the father became a less powerful figure, thus decreasing the guilt and the need for destructive, defensive behavior.

Very little, if any, of the material that came through in this instance had been unconscious; rather it was preconscious in nature. Occasionally, a very limited amount of unconscious data does come through in casework and this is well illustrated in the theme of Mr. Fuller's complicated relationship with his son. Mr. Fuller was very eager for his son to be an aggressive, masculine little boy, for, he said, he himself had been weak and delicate as a child. Yet there were situations in which he was extremely overprotective of the boy, as, for example, his insistence that Edward hold on to his hand when they were together on city streets. Once in discussing this, Mr. Fuller suddenly called Edward "Lester." By following up this slip, the worker learned that Lester was a younger brother who, at the age of six, had run into the street in the path of an automobile and been killed. The accident occurred just a few months after Mr. Fuller's father's death, when Mr. Fuller, then eighteen, had been delegated, as the oldest son, to take over his father's responsibilities in the family. As he told about the details of his brother's death, he described himself as so shocked that he fainted when he had to identify his brother's body in the morgue; but at the same time he had not cried and had been surprisingly unfeeling about his mother's grief. As he spoke, however, he suddenly began to cry violently and had considerable difficulty in regaining control. Mr. Fuller very easily made the connection to his present over-protectiveness with Edward.

Although the facts of this event had never been forgotten, the affect had in large measure been repressed. Its release probably reduced the extent to which the occurrence controlled Mr. Fuller's behavior. Awareness of the transference from brother to son also provided him with a means of combating it. It seems likely that despite his denials he did have irrational unconscious feelings of guilt about the accident, and the worker may have reduced these to a slight degree by her own acceptance of the fact that he was not at fault. Had this overprotectiveness continued, it might have been advisable to relieve his possible guilt feelings by bringing them to light.

Note that in both these instances of exploration of childhood material a principle of economy was followed. The caseworker pursued a theme only as far as seemed necessary to bring improvement in the social adaptation of the client. In the first instance, emphasis was upon modifying the hostilities and consequent fears which Mr. Fuller carried over from his childhood experiences with his father to adult life, where their inappropriateness created problems in his work. His adult ego was helped to become aware of these early feelings and to recognize their continued existence and destructive expression in his current life. In the second instance, recovery of the feelings about his brother's death and recognition of the effect his concern about his brother had on his relationship with his son enabled him to overcome the inconsistencies in his handling of the child. The balance between the adaptive forces of his ego and the drive toward behavior motivated by unresolved earlier life problems was tipped in favor of the adult ego. The reduction in the force of these childhood remnants was sufficient to enable the adaptive forces to achieve improved functioning both in his work life and in his relationship with his son.

NOTE

1. Adelaide M. Johnson, "Sanctions for Superego Lacunae of Adolescents," *Searchlight on Delinquency*, International Universities Press, New York, 1949, pp. 225–244.

III

Classifications

of

Casework Treatment

LOGIC WOULD DICTATE that we move into detailed discussion of the casework process by way of chapters on social study, diagnosis, treatment planning, and treatment procedures. But in order to understand what information we should seek in social study and what type of diagnosis will be useful in treatment planning, we first need further understanding of the nature of treatment itself as it has evolved in casework.

Every treatment step is a goal-directed procedure, and brings into action various dynamics to bring about its intended effect. Suppose our client is a widow who is afraid of an operation partly because she is too sick to work out plans for the care of her children during her absence from home, partly because she is going to a strange doctor and is uncertain about the outcome of the operation, and partly because unconsciously she fears punishment for her hostile attitudes toward her mother, who had a similar illness and became a permanent cripple following an operation which the client erroneously assumes was similar to the one she is about to undergo. Many different dynamics can be employed to reduce this woman's anxiety.

One alternative is the environmental one of providing for the care of the children during her absence. This can have a double effect: it will relieve her of that part of her anxiety which is caused by realistic concern for the welfare of her children; and it will demonstrate to her that others care for her welfare and are ready to come to her assistance when she is weak and unable to manage her own affairs. We know that in serious illness regression may lead to a state of intense dependence. It is extremely important at such a time for the patient to feel that someone with strength will take care of him. The way in which plans for the children are made will also be of importance. If relatives or friends toward whom the patient has warm feelings can care for them, so much the better. If agency care must be sought, the degree of relief from anxiety felt by the patient will vary with the amount of confidence she has in the good will and competence of the caseworker who makes this arrangement. Every effort should therefore be made to establish a strong, positive relationship with the patient.

A second possible mode of help consists of direct reassurance by the worker about her anxieties. He can encourage her to express her fears about the operation; he can show understanding of her anxiety, indicating that it is a natural reaction, not a sign of childishness on her part. Not infrequently, he may also be able to reassure her that the doctors are interested in her, are skillful, and so on. The patient's response to this approach will depend very largely upon the extent of her confidence in the worker.

A third way of reducing the anxiety would be to help the patient understand more fully the facts about the operation itself. Arrangement could be made for her to talk in detail with the doctor. Subsequently, she might again go over the facts with the caseworker, clarifying her understanding of what the doctor had told her.

A fourth alternative, to be undertaken only if it is both necessary and feasible, would be to help her gain understanding of the relationship between her feelings about her mother and her mother's illness and her current reactions to her own illness.

These procedures all have a common aim—to reduce anxiety—but the dynamics involved in each are different. In one instance one of the stimuli for the anxiety is removed by environmental measures; in another, reassurance is given by means of the client's confidence in the worker; in the third, the patient uses her rea-

soning powers to help her understand her situation more realistically; and in the fourth, she applies these reasoning powers
toward an understanding of early developmental factors which
affect her current reactions.

] *Early and Current Classifications*

There is as yet no entirely satisfactory classification of casework treatment methods. Mary Richmond made only the very
simple distinction between "direct" and "indirect" treatment. By
the former she meant those processes that take place directly
between the client and the worker—the "influence of mind upon
mind"—and by the latter, changes which the worker brings about
in the client's human and physical environment.[1] Porter Lee
made essentially the same distinction in his reference to "executive" and "leadership" forms of treatment, as did Gordon Hamilton in her early writings.[2] In 1947 Grete Bibring,[3] a psychoanalyst
who had worked closely with caseworkers for a number of years
in Boston, mentioned five groups of technical procedures used
by all types of therapists, including caseworkers. These were
suggestion, emotional relief, immediate influence (or manipulation), clarification, and interpretation. It was her impression that
interpretation was used sparingly in casework, and chiefly in
dealing with preconscious rather than unconscious material, but
she did not altogether rule out interpretation of unconscious
material. Her major distinction was between interpretation,
which she characterized as having as its goal insight development
(the principal objective of psychoanalysis), and the other techniques, for which insight development was not a goal.

Bibring's classification represented a distinct elaboration of the
earlier direct treatment method and reflected the influence of
psychoanalysis in enriching the caseworker's understanding of
the ways in which psychological forces can be used in treatment.
Suggestion, emotional relief, and manipulation, though not recognized in these terms, were undoubtedly a part of early casework
methodology, as was also a technique not mentioned by Bibring
—that of helping the client to reason his way through to a favorable solution of his problems. Clarification in the sense of helping
the client to separate objective reality from his own distortions of

the external world was, like insight development, the result of
our incorporation of analytic concepts and played little part in
casework until the 1930's and 1940's.

Also in 1947 the present writer suggested another classification
of treatment methods.[4] These were environmental modification
(corresponding to the earlier indirect method) and psychological
support, clarification, and insight development (representing subdivisions of direct treatment). This classification and Bibring's
were similar in that both attempted to group techniques according to the psychological dynamics by which they operated.
Bibring's suggestion, emotional relief, and manipulation corre-
sponded to different aspects of the Hollis psychological support;
insight development was the same in the two classifications. But
Hollis used clarification in a broader sense than did Bibring,
covering by that term the general encouragement of a reasoning
approach to problems as well as the separation of objective reality from distortions of external events—actually two different
processes, which experience indicates are better understood as
distinct categories.

In 1948 Lucille Austin suggested a somewhat different type of
classification,[5] directed primarily not toward separating clusters
of techniques by their dynamics but by their use in the pursuit
of a predominant treatment goal. "Social therapy" she described
as consisting primarily of "the use of techniques designed to
influence positively various factors in the environment and of the
effective use of social resources." In pursuit of this aim, psychological support and a rational approach to reality problems would
complement the Richmond indirect treatment techniques. When,
on the other hand, the aim was primarily that of modifying the
client's behavior, Austin suggested the term "psychotherapy" to
describe the treatment techniques, and proposed three subdivisions of this method. At the two extremes she placed supportive
therapy and insight therapy, and designated an intermediate
form "experiential" therapy.

Supportive therapy, as the name indicates, relies heavily on
the techniques of psychological support, but may often include
Richmond's indirect methods and a rational approach to reality
problems. The aim of this form of treatment is the prevention of
further breakdown in clients whose egos are weak and who may

be particularly vulnerable to further breakdown under pressure. Insight therapy aims at achieving a change in the ego by developing the patient's insight into his difficulties and increasing the ability of the ego to deal with them through the emotional experience in the transference situation. The cluster of techniques used in this type of treatment would include interpretation and clarification in the Bibring sense, in addition to selected use of all the other direct and indirect procedures. Experiential therapy is a blending of supportive and insight therapy, with the central focus on the development and use of the relationship as a corrective emotional experience; sometimes the techniques emphasized in supportive therapy are stressed and sometimes those more characteristic of insight therapy.

Austin recognized that although her supportive treatment was designed primarily to maintain present strengths, psychological improvement often occurred. "As anxiety diminishes the ego gains strength to handle immediate situations, and the experience of more adequate functioning becomes itself a growth process." Likewise in the experiential form of treatment, for although Austin at one point maintains that "in this group change represents primarily better adaptations within the existing personality structure," she goes on to say that "in certain cases maturation already under way is carried through to completion." She further maintains that the objectives of experiential treatment "are mainly loosening restrictive ties to figures in the past, redirecting emotional energies, and promoting growth through increased satisfactions in living."[6]

In 1953 a committee of the Family Service Association of America published a report[7] based in part on the reading of a series of cases in family service agencies. In this report a new classification of casework treatment was proposed. Type A, or "supportive casework," was designated as "treatment aimed at maintaining adaptive patterns," and Type B as "treatment aimed at modification of adaptive patterns." The first type of treatment was described as resting upon the use of such techniques as "manipulation of the environment, reassurance, persuasion, direct advice and guidance, suggestion, logical discussion, exercise of professional authority and immediate influence."[8] The second was characterized mainly by its use of the technique of clarification.[9]

The distinguishing feature of this classification is its use of the type of change anticipated in the client as the major basis for the classification. Austin had moved somewhat in this direction, but saw the outcome in much more flexible terms than did the F.S.A.A. report. We must consider the question of whether this is indeed a sound basis for classification. Is it true that only through the use of clarification do we aim to bring about modification of adaptive patterns? Or, on the contrary, is this also sometimes an aim of supportive techniques?

] *Personality Changes and Methodology*

To begin with, we need to consider what is meant by a change in adaptive patterns. The report distinguishes between a change in adaptive patterns and an improvement in social functioning without modification of habitual patterns of behavior. A change in adaptive patterns is one that is internalized, built into the personality. The implication is that it is not an improvement in functioning that can be accounted for by improved circumstances, the passing of a crisis, or the influence of the worker during the period of treatment; rather, it constitutes a change in the client's way of functioning that will enable him to respond differently even when his external situation has not changed and when the worker is not part of his current life. He will have learned to act differently and will respond more appropriately than he did before treatment to the same or similar life events.

Improvement in functioning without a change in adaptive patterns, then, might be said to occur in situations such as the following. A man has been quarreling with his wife because of anxiety about his business. In discussions with the worker, he comes to understand the cause of his irritability, transfers to another position in which he is under less pressure, and subsequently is more even-tempered at home. A widow is depressed because of the loss of her husband and is, therefore, unable to care adequately for her children. She is helped during this period of grief, and as it subsides, is able to function normally again in relation to the children. A structural iron worker loses a leg in an accident and is told he will no longer be able to continue in his line of work. He loses interest in life, does not try to obtain a prosthesis, and retreats to dependent, whining, childlike behavior, to the despair of his formerly dependent wife. After a good deal of skillful work, including some development of understanding of his current responses, he regains his former stability and finds a new work adjustment. In none of these cases, however, have new adaptive patterns been established.

Such improvements in functioning certainly do occur in response to supportive treatment methods. The question at issue is whether more can occur, whether internalized changes can be achieved without the development of self-understanding by means of clarification, that is, without procedures which involve the client's gaining awareness of habitual patterns of behavior and sorting out subjective and objective factors in his life experience.

In actuality, it is not hard to find cases in which modifications in adaptive patterns do appear to have taken place in response to the Type A, or supportive, treatment methods. We have already discussed at some length in Chapter II the work with Miss Emerson, in which only such supportive techniques were used. Nevertheless, the treatment had the aim of helping Miss Emerson to develop a socially realistic superego and the ability to function well and with satisfaction in her work and her human relationships. We have reason to believe that the new adaptive patterns had become so incorporated into her personality that these gains would hold as a permanent part of her functioning.

Another client, Mr. Graham, wavered between compulsive and impulsive behavior when he came to the agency. He was in trouble because of debts, excessive drinking, and instability in his relationships with women. The worker became the good, kind, but gently firm parent, and used "logical discussion" to guide the client away from the impulsive patterns through which he made so much trouble for himself and others. The client's dependency led him to want to please and imitate the worker. New adaptive patterns were reenforced by the experience of greater satisfactions when ego controls over impulsive behavior were strengthened. Again, there is reason to believe that an improvement in adaptive patterns had been achieved.

Mr. Ingersol, a married man of thirty-five, was repeatedly in trouble because of impulsive behavior at work and with his wife. Periodic drinking complicated the problem. The aim of treatment was to help him control his impulsiveness and his drinking, although at first he would not even admit that the latter was a problem. Through transference the worker came to represent the good father whom Mr. Ingersol very much admired and wanted to please. Logical discussion, advice, approval, and encouragement were all used in the effort to enable him to improve the quality and strength of his ego controls. At several points clarification was also used, but it was by no means the predominant technique. Considerable improvement in adaptive patterns seems to have occurred in this case. It is hard to predict, however, whether or not it will be maintained when the contact ends, as it is difficult to tell to what extent Mr. Ingersol has actually incorporated the new patterns. This was, however, the definite aim of treatment in this case even though clarification was used in only a minor way.

Mrs. Knight, an exceedingly immature young woman still in her teens, was married to a man old enough to be her father. At first he thoroughly enjoyed her childish dependence, but soon he became irritated by her inability to manage his home and be an adequate mother to the two children of his former marriage. Mrs. Knight sought help "in growing up" from the caseworker. The approach was one of guidance and support, with reliance on elements in the relationship, on considerable logical discussion, on extensive use of a visiting homemaker and of a nurse whose role was that of educating the client in matters concerning her own and the children's health. With the ego strengthened by increased knowledge and skill, the psychosocial maturation that had been arrested when Mrs. Knight was overwhelmed by demands so far beyond her ability to meet began again to take place, with marked improvement in her functioning as a wife and mother. There is every reason to believe that the improvement in adaptive patterns will be lasting.

Mrs. Landers, the mother of five children, was driven by a strong need to succeed which showed itself in the form of perfectionistic demands upon the children and excessive self-criticism when difficulties arose in her own relationship with them. The worker became the "good mother" and on the basis of this relationship was able to help Mrs. Landers to handle the children more realistically and to reduce the severity of the demands of her superego upon the children and upon herself. Mrs. Landers became able to set up more lenient goals for her family and to see at a number of points that she was overreacting in holding herself so completely responsible for their behavior. Once again, a nurse was used for discussion of health problems; better housing plans were worked out; camp opportunities were provided for the children. Mrs. Landers was learning new ways of handling her children, and had incorporated less demanding standards for herself and her family.

Miss Masters, a woman of twenty-nine, suffered from a character disorder which expressed itself chiefly in her social relationships. Although she thought she wanted to marry, she dated only men whom for one reason or another she could not marry. She had become a strict adherent of an ascetic philosophy which cut her off from many normal social pleasures. Exaggerated residual childish fantasies of omnipotence led her to undertake unrealistic educational plans. She complicated her social relationships by overreacting to slights, trying to solve by avoidance difficulties which she created for herself, and seeking to gain satisfaction by creating competition among her friends. Because it was feared that Miss Masters might be too disturbed to use clarification, it was decided to work through a supportive relationship and logical discussion of her way of handling her social situation. This method brought marked improvement in a number of areas, though not in all. Although there was very little modification of Miss Masters' fear of relationships with men, she became more realistic in her educational plans, less sensitive to slights, and more able to handle troubles with her friends in a straightforward way instead of by avoidance; she managed, moreover, to free herself from the more excessive features of her philosophical beliefs. In other words, there was great improvement in the quality of her ego functioning, and some modification of her destructive use of defenses.

In these six cases we believe modification of adaptive patterns has occurred; but are we justified in considering that these are changes in adaptive patterns and that they are directly the aim and result of treatment, rather than simply a by-product of general release of tension and a generalized sort of improvement called "greater integrative capacity"[10] of the ego? If by this latter term we mean a generally greater forcefulness and preciseness of ego functioning that comes with more self-confidence and freedom from tension and anxiety (comparable to the better functioning of the body when it is free from fatigue and tension), it seems apparent that something much more specific in ego and also superego modification has taken place.

] *Diverse Approaches*

Change in adaptive patterns can occur in a number of ways. There is first the basic personality change, often called "structural change" in psychoanalytic terminology, which occurs when some of the decisive formative experiences of life are reached with treatment and undergo reevaluation. This process involves bringing to consciousness and understanding material which was previously unconscious or repressed, such as memories, thoughts, or fantasies representing infantile destructive and sexual impulses and wishes, and reactions and distortions growing out of very early life experiences. Clearly, we do not attempt to achieve this type of change in casework.

We have earlier pointed out, however, that irrational and inappropriate responses are also often based on *preconscious* influences, on events that at most have been *suppressed* rather than repressed, and hence can be brought to the surface of the mind by the type of interviewing techniques used in casework. The ego defenses in particular often operate on a preconscious level, and a person not infrequently can become aware of and will modify defense patterns when he sees their irrationality or their harmfulness. This is a second way in which change in adaptive patterns can be brought about, the way that characterizes the Family Service Association's Type B treatment—that is, treatment through clarification.

A third way of bringing about changes in ego adaptive patterns is the use of later life experiences, for personality is formed not only by early experiences that have been repressed and suppressed but also by later life events, the memories of which have been neither repressed nor suppressed. Freud, in his *Outline of Psychoanalysis*, expressed the opinion that the superego, in addition to representing early parental influence, also "takes over contributions from later successors and substitutes of the parents, such as teachers, admired people in public life, or high social ideals."[11] By its very nature, its contact with external reality, the ego uses later life experiences to enable it to control harmful impulses and to combat irrational and inappropriate responses motivated by the unconscious part of the mind.* Current reality itself can therefore be used as a corrective in modifying ego patterns if a person is helped to examine and reevaluate the nature of significant people and situations in his life and the results of his ways of functioning. This type of logical discussion may also lead to a lasting modification of an individual's adaptive patterns.

A fourth method of effecting change depends primarily upon the use of the client's relationship to the worker. When the client responds to the worker as to a good parent, it is frequently possible to induce him to take on new attitudes. When he experiences greater ease and effectiveness in his life by virtue of these "borrowed" patterns, he may incorporate them as new adaptive patterns that will continue to serve him after the termination of treatment.

] *Personality Changes Without Clarification*

In the cases under consideration the last two kinds of change occurred in response to Type A, or supportive, treatment techniques. Mr. Ingersol, for instance, denied for a long time that his drinking was a problem and that his own behavior contributed to his quarrels with his wife. After treatment had advanced to a point where Mr. Ingersol trusted the caseworker, it was possible again and again to get him to go over the details of what happened between himself and his wife when he had been drinking excessively, to recall exactly how many drinks he had had and exactly what he did and said during the course of an evening.

---

* A pertinent illustration of this process is professional training itself. It has long been recognized in social work that during the training period the worker internalizes certain values of the profession and may need to modify his ego ideal in the process of developing into a fully qualified social worker. The sociologist refers to this as "acculturation to the profession." Social workers sometimes call it "the development of the professional self."

He gradually came to see that after a certain number of drinks he said things which he would not otherwise have said and that his behavior on such occasions precipitated certain responses from his wife which would not otherwise have been elicited. When he became able to admit to himself that his drinking really did cause trouble, he began to make a real effort to control it and actually succeeded in reducing it to a marked extent. A pattern of greater ego control was established, not by bringing suppressed material to consciousness or by seeking causative understanding of his drinking beyond current provocations, but by the effect of close examination of present realities.

Another factor at work in Mr. Ingersol's progress was the client-worker relationship itself. Mr. Ingersol was a dependent person who had greatly admired his father. He developed similar feelings toward his caseworker, whom he wanted to please as he had wanted to please his father. The worker used this dynamic also, giving Mr. Ingersol credit and appreciation when he showed understanding of the effects of his behavior patterns and when he tried to modify them. His efforts to change were further fortified by the satisfaction he secured during periods of better relationship with his wife.

An essentially similar process was used with Miss Masters. She often fancied that she had been slighted, and she handled difficulties that arose in her social relationships by avoiding discussing them with the people involved, instead of trying to straighten them out. Again and again the worker went over the details of what happened with her friends, had her repeat exactly what they said and did, and helped her to reexamine these current realities in the light of whether she really had been slighted or whether there might not be some other explanation of events. The workers also reviewed with Miss Masters the possibility of other ways to straighten out these difficulties, helping her to see that she was making the situation worse by avoiding direct discussion with her friends. Current realities rather than hidden influences were discussed, and causative understanding was not pursued. With this help, however, Miss Masters' ability to evaluate reality happenings improved, and she modified her pattern of avoidance.

What about the possibility of change in *superego* patterns

through Type A techniques? We have already discussed at length the changes in superego patterns brought about in Miss Emerson. Superego modification of a different sort occurred with Mrs. Landers, the mother who made perfectionistic demands of herself and her five children and was over-severe in her self-criticism. A relaxation of the demands of conscience set in as the worker, in the role of the good mother, helped the client to feel that she would still be a good mother if she set up more lenient goals for the children. By making use of concrete instances she showed her that she blamed herself unnecessarily, in overreacting to the ordinary ups and downs of her children's behavior.

In none of these cases were the techniques needed for clarification or for acquiring causative understanding of behavior used. There would seem to be clear evidence from these six cases that Type A and Type B forms of treatment cannot always be distinguished by differences in *aim*. We have, of course, selected for this discussion only cases in which the work was designed to bring about changes in adaptive patterns, but this by no means implies that Type A techniques are *always* used with this objective in mind. Often the client's problem does not indicate the need for such a change, or else, though modification might be desirable, the client lacks either the wish or the ability to use casework help in this way.

Type A or supportive treatment actually offers a range of treatment objectives. In some instances it aims to restore previous adaptive patterns; in others it seeks to prevent regression to patterns of less social effectiveness; in still others it endeavors to bring about better functioning only during treatment or in response to a situational change, but does not expect that it will be possible for the client to incorporate this better way of functioning as a new adaptive pattern. Not infrequently, however, as in the cases cited, it can and does bring changes in adaptive patterns. Hence, objectives cannot be considered as the distinguishing feature between the two treatment methods.[12]

The main difference between them lies in the means and dynamics they employ. Type B endeavors to improve functioning by increasing the ego's awareness of previously unrecognized aspects of its own functioning. To accomplish this end, it uses the technique of clarification of relationships between current social functioning and obscure, unverbalized, suppressed, or un-comprehended aspects of mental life, and promotes dynamic and historical understanding of these interrelationships. Type A, on the other hand, excludes clarification and relies entirely on environmental manipulation, reassurance, guidance, the direct influence of the worker, logical discussion, and similar techniques.

NOTES

1. Mary E. Richmond, *What is Social Casework?* *An Introductory Description*, Russell Sage Foundation, New York, 1922, p. 102.

2. Gordon Hamilton, "Basic Concepts in Social Casework," *The Family*, 18 (July, 1937), 147–156. Other references of interest are:

Virginia P. Robinson, "An Analysis of Processes in the Records of Family Case Working Agencies," *The Family*, 2 (July, 1921), 101–106; and *Social Casework, Generic and Specific: An Outline. A Report of the Milford Conference*, American Association of Social Workers, New York, 1929.

3. Grete L. Bibring, "Psychiatry and Social Work," *Journal of Social Casework*, 28 (June, 1947), 203–211.

4. Florence Hollis, *Casework in Marital Disharmony*, doctoral dissertation, Bryn Mawr College, 1947, microfilmed, University Microfilms, Ann Arbor, 1951. Also available in "The Techniques of Casework," *Journal of Social Casework*, 30 (June, 1949), 235–244.

5. Lucille N. Austin, "Trends in Differential Treatment in Social Casework," *Journal of Social Casework*, 29 (June, 1948), 203–211.

6. In a later article, "Qualifications for Psychotherapists, Social Caseworkers" (*American Journal of Orthopsychiatry*, 26 [1956], 47–57), Austin suggests giving up the term "insight therapy" as an inaccurate designation, since insight is a quality or experience that may result from different procedures.

7. *Scope and Methods of the Family Service Agency*, Report of the Committee on Methods and Scope, Family Service Association of America, New York, 1953.

8. *Ibid.*, p. 19.

9. See also *Method and Process in Social Casework, Report of a Staff Committee, Community Service Society of New York*, Family Service Association of America, New York, 1958, for a highly useful elaboration and refinement of this point of view. The "modifying treatment method" is here related to "modification of selected ego mechanisms of defense," rather than to adaptive patterns as a whole, as in the Family Service Association committee's classification.

10. *Scope and Methods of the Family Service Agency*, p. 18.

11. Sigmund Freud, *An Outline of Psychoanalysis*, authorized translation by James Strachey, W. W. Norton Co., New York, 1949, p. 17.

12. Sidney Berkowitz was the first writer to raise questions about this formulation. See his "Some Specific Techniques of Psychosocial Diagnosis and Treatment in Family Casework," *Social Casework, 36* (November, 1955), 399–406.

IV

A Classification
Based on
Dynamic Considerations

THE PREVIOUS CHAPTER SUGGESTS that the formulation of a logical and useful classification of casework treatment is no simple matter, especially if this formulation is to be rich enough in its dimensions to make conceptually worthwhile distinctions and yet not so elaborate as to be impractical.

But why, in any case, do we want a treatment classification? What purpose will it serve? Will it merely enable us to describe casework in an orderly way in writing and teaching? This is one important use of classification; the very need for such clarity constitutes a strong impetus toward classification. Agencies also feel a need for a systematic way of grouping cases for reports of accountability, work distribution, evaluation, and the like. More fundamental, however, is the necessity of classification for the study of casework itself. In order to use casework effectively we must ask ourselves for what sort of personality or problem is this or that treatment method or technique appropriate? What is the result of using this or that technique under such and such circumstances? What alternative means are available to the end we have in mind? Under what circumstances is one means more likely to serve the purpose than another?

Before we can answer these questions, the numerous variables involved must be separated. At the very least we will need to find some way of identifying and classifying not only treatment procedures but also types of personality, types of problems, types of outcome, as well as ways of establishing relationships between these variables. Currently available treatment classifications for the most part try to combine in composite form several of these different dimensions, as for example the effort, which we discussed at some length in the previous chapter, to combine in composite categories the type of change sought in the client and the treatment method. Only by examining aim and method as two separate matters can we test the relationship of one to the other and examine the conditions under which specific techniques can lead to specific results.

] *A False Start*

A first objective, then, is to develop a classification of treatment techniques or procedures independent both of the type of ultimate modification we are seeking to bring about and of the type of client for whose particular problem it might be of value. Several years ago, in an abortive effort to do this, I proposed a substitute definition for Type A and Type B of the 1953 Family Service Association report.[1] The true difference between Type A and Type B, it was suggested, lay in the kinds of material each used, A dealing entirely with fully conscious material and B with suppressed preconscious content and other preconscious material of equally anxiety-arousing potential. The B, or clarification, technique would, therefore, be used only with clients capable of bearing the anxiety aroused by such treatment and comparatively immune to the hazards of immobilization, development of more severe symptomatology, excessive regression, or acting out. Such clients would be people suffering from only a mild degree of neurosis, and would not include psychotics, severe neurotics, or, because of insufficient motivation, clients with character disorders.

Subsequently a small study was undertaken to see whether this distinction was a valid one and also to examine further the relationship of treatment procedures to diagnosis. Twenty-five cases drawn from six agencies representing family service agencies, child guidance clinics, and psychiatric clinics in four different communities were explored. Limited as this study was, it was nevertheless extremely fruitful in pointing up the problems involved in classification and in providing material for experimentation with a series of classifications, each successively introducing modifications designed to meet the shortcomings of its predecessor.

Each agency was asked to submit examples both of supportive treatment and of treatment in which the technique of clarification was used, including an example of a case representing the greatest depth in treatment carried on in the agency. It was at first disconcerting to discover that workers differed enormously in their interpretation of this request. Cases of a type considered clarification by one worker would actually involve less use of the technique of clarification than cases classified as supportive by another worker. Troublesome as this confusion was, it led to a very useful observation: namely, that there was no sharp dividing line between supportive and clarification cases. In actual practice there appeared to be a continuum, beginning with cases in which no clarification whatsoever was used, going on to those in which snatches of it were used only from time to time, proceeding to others where it played a considerable part in treatment, and finally arriving at cases in which clarification could be considered the predominant treatment method. Furthermore, it also became clear that in most cases treatment moved through phases in which the balance between supportive work and clarification was constantly changing. This discovery pointed in the direction of seeking a classification that would permit us to study the blending of different techniques as they are used over a period of time within a particular case, rather than one that classified a case in terms of an arbitrary degree of clarification.*

When the twenty-five cases were examined to test my own

---

* It is interesting that as far back as 1949, Annette Garrett, in reaction to the classifications then being devised, made essentially the same point in conversation with the author. She objected strongly to setting off insight development as a special method and maintained that in varying degrees insight development took place in a large range of cases.

hypothesis that supportive techniques did not deal with suppressed preconscious material, it became apparent that my suggestion for distinguishing between the A and B categories was one of those nice logical pieces of theory that are attractive for their simplicity but have little relationship to things as they are. To my chagrin it became clear that in a number of cases suppressed and other submerged material with anxiety-arousing potential came through in response to supportive techniques and played an important part in treatment in cases where clarification was purposely avoided. A closer inspection of supportive treatment then led me to realize that this category is far more complicated than has generally been supposed and embraces a variety of widely different techniques. Reassurance and advice-giving, to name only two of these, are utterly different techniques, suitable under different circumstances and leading to quite different results, despite the fact that they are sometimes appropriately used with the same individual. Clarification too, when looked at closely, can be subdivided into several processes. Our present classifications, then, would seem to be too "global." Each category embraces a number of different techniques, thus obscuring differentiations which may be of crucial significance. Finer distinctions must be made if we are to understand the nature of casework procedures, their potentialities and effects.

] *Basic Considerations*

With these observations in mind, a series of cases drawn from the original twenty-five was used as the raw material for a new classification. The material was selected because of the clarity of dictation and because it represented a variety of treatment methods when viewed globally. The material was gone over line by line in an effort to characterize each recorded happening in each interview. Various groupings of techniques were tried in an effort to arrive at meaningful and essential distinctions between different processes. The tackling of each new case became a testing of the system worked out on previous cases and frequently involved modifications in the system to accommodate the new material. The classification that resulted from this process has been experimented with and studied in a number of recent and continuing research projects.* Although many details have yet to be worked out, the main outlines of the classification seem well enough established to be shared with colleagues at this time.

The most difficult decisions to be made in evolving a treatment classification are those of level and logic. A classification can be too global for the uses for which it is intended; or it can be too fine for practical purposes. One can, for instance, note types of words chosen for communication, the use of declarative sentences versus questions, and so on. There are no doubt purposes for which this type of analysis is important. It would almost certainly, however, involve the use of electrically recorded interviews, because such information cannot be remembered consistently in recording interviews from memory. One guide to the level of classification, then, is the type of material upon which it is to be used. If a system is to be of value in ordinary casework practice, it must be suitable for use on interviews recorded from memory. While it has been demonstrated that caseworkers and clients are willing to have electrical recordings made of interviews and that the interview process is relatively unaffected by such recording, it is also well known that the processing of such interviews, running as they do to twenty-five or more pages per interview, is extremely expensive and possible only for carefully selected and generously financed research undertakings. A useful level of classification, then, lies between these extremes.

Furthermore, the rationale of the classification must be related

---

* I have been fortunate in being able to enlist the interest of two groups of students—one at the Smith College for Social Work,[2] the other at the New York School of Social Work (now the Columbia University School of Social Work)[3]—in applying the new system to the classification of techniques in two series of interviews. Their findings have become the basis for subsequent revisions of the typology and in general have indicated that the main outlines of the classification are applicable and potentially useful. Also of great value has been the work of Francis J. Turner, a doctoral student at the New York School of Social Work, who has experimented with the classification as a research instrument in his recent dissertation, "Social Work Treatment and Value Differences: An Exploration of Value Differences and Specific Use of Casework Techniques with Clients from Three Ethnic Groups Receiving Treatment in Family Agencies."[4] The latter study was supported in part by a grant from the National Institute of Mental Health, which is currently making possible further work to undertake examination of the usefulness of the classification for research purposes.

to the uses to which it will be put. This requires that the logic of the classification be related to the logic of the questions to be answered. We have already indicated some of the possible uses of a classification of this kind. It must help us to examine the dynamics of treatment, to answer such questions as: In what way does a given procedure affect a client? What is the relationship of type of client personality to choice of treatment method? What is the relationship between problem and treatment steps? What factors in the client's response in a particular interview indicate the advisability of using a particular procedure? What procedures in early interviews are most likely to encourage the client to remain in treatment? And so on.

For such purposes it has seemed best to base the classification on a set of hypotheses about the *dynamics of treatment,* that is, the *means* by which the treatment step or procedure is in general expected to produce its effect.

That is, the *type* of final change desired, and the *outcome* of treatment, are not the basis for the classification. As was pointed out in an earlier chapter in illustration of the different ways in which anxiety can be reduced, a given result can be achieved by a variety of procedures, ranging from direct reassurance to full understanding of the intrapsychic cause of the anxiety. However, under different circumstances and with different individuals one approach will be more effective than another. This question of which *means* is most useful under different conditions is central to any study seeking to understand and improve casework methodology and is therefore a particularly useful central dimension for a classification of casework procedures. The term "dynamics of treatment" is used to indicate that the classification revolves around the nature of the "change component" which the procedure is generally designed to bring into action.

The proposed classification also distinguishes sharply between the means employed and its actual effect. For example, the caseworker's expression of interest in and appreciation of a client's situation or feelings is generally thought to promote the client's perception of the worker as someone who is interested in him and capable of understanding him and his feeling that here is someone who will help or take care of him. By this means, it is

hoped, his anxiety will be lessened and, consequently, his functioning will be improved. A paranoid person, however, may interpret this same response on the caseworker's part as a kind of
magic mind reading, an effort to bring him under some obscure
influence, and the technique will not have the effect it is generally expected to have. Nevertheless, in the typology proposed,
the worker's technique would be classified as a "sustaining procedure," the term used for this type of potentially reassuring
technique. Such a separation of the means employed from the
outcome puts us in a position to examine the actual effect of a
treatment step, to study the circumstances under which it does
not have the desired effect, and thereafter to use it more appropriately; or, if we find it rarely has the effect we theoretically
thought it should have, we are in a position to correct our theory.

A classification of the sort proposed is not static: it can be
modified as research and study constantly correct and expand
our theories and can also lend itself well to expansion as new
techniques are developed. At the same time, if required, it can
be held static throughout a study or series of studies in which it
is used.

] *The Main Divisions of the Classification*

With these preliminaries, we may proceed to a brief description of the classification that has been evolving from the studies
described above. This classification is still tentative and is presented at this point in part as a stimulus to the reader's thinking
and criticism and in part as a logical structure for an organized
presentation of casework theory.

Detailed discussion of the specific technical procedures included under the main divisions of the classification will be found
in later chapters. The major dimensions of the classification will
be presented in this chapter, together with specific illustrations
used only to clarify the meaning of the main categories; we will
thus be able to discuss certain general theoretical questions before going extensively into details of techniques.

For the moment, I should like to set aside the question of
treatment through the environment—Richmond's indirect treatment—and deal only with direct treatment, those procedures that

take place between the worker and the client himself. Several clients within a given family, of course, may be receiving casework treatment at the same time through individual interviews. We are not at this point trying to adapt this classification to the work that is currently being done through "joint" or "family" interviews.[5]

In direct treatment, casework can be said to use six major groups of techniques. The first two of these derive their force or influence from the relationship that exists between client and worker, sometimes in actual fact, but more often in the way in which the client regards the worker and the degree of influence which he accords the worker or permits him to have in his life. The fourth, fifth, and sixth groups rest primarily upon various kinds of reflective consideration promoted within the client. The third, drawing its strength from catharsis or ventilation, lies midway between.

The first group of techniques may be called *sustaining procedures*. They include such activities on the worker's part as demonstration of interest, desire to help, understanding, expressions of confidence in the client's abilities or competence, and reassurance concerning matters about which the client has anxiety and guilt.

Sustaining techniques are used in varying degrees in all cases. Particularly in the early interviews, no matter what else is done, the worker usually tries, by giving the client a sympathetic hearing and by other sustaining techniques, to lessen his anxiety and give him the feeling that he is in a place where help will be forthcoming. Subsequently, cases vary a great deal in the extent to which sustaining techniques are needed, with marked fluctuations from time to time in the same case.

The second group may be called *procedures of direct influence*. These include a range of techniques among which suggestion and advice are most frequently used. They involve in one form or another the expression of the worker's opinion about the kind of action a client should take.

Procedures of direct influence are less universally used than sustaining techniques, although particularly in their more subtle forms they constitute a substantial part of casework treatment. One usually finds that where these procedures are being extensively used, they are either accompanied or preceded by considerable emphasis upon sustaining work. Their effectiveness depends to a high degree upon the existence of a strong positive relationship between client and worker, which in turn is promoted by sustaining procedures.

The third group of techniques may be called *catharsis or ventilation*. It employs procedures of encouraging the client to pour out in the interview pent-up feelings and emotionally charged memories. Often there is relief from tension just in the outpouring itself. Quite frequently the relief obtained by verbalization is supported by sustaining procedures which augment the reduction of the accompanying anxiety or guilt. At other times the content of the ventilating process is picked up for the purpose of promoting reflective consideration of it.

When we turn to techniques that rely upon the client's actively thinking about various aspects of his problem, it becomes more difficult to know where to draw the line between one kind of content and another. After experimentation with a number of groupings of these techniques, the one suggested here was chosen because it seemed capable of illuminating many of the processes that unfold in treatment practice.

The fourth grouping, designated by the lengthy descriptive name *reflective consideration of the current person-situation configuration*, is a broad category which has within itself several important subdivisions; later we shall explore the reason for distinguishing this kind of reflective consideration from the fifth and sixth groups which follow.

The first subdivision of this fourth category is directed outward. It includes procedures that require the client to reflect upon his situation—economic, social, physical, educational, etc.—or upon the nature of the people with whom he is associated, usually relatives or significant friends.

The second subdivision has to do with the client's thinking about the actual or probable effects of his actions on others or on himself. Its procedures include reflective discussion of the client's behavior, of alternative courses open to him concerning situational plans, of his use of available resources, or of his relation to people with whom he is associated.

The third subdivision is directed inward. It consists of a variety of procedures used to lead the client to discuss reflectively feelings, attitudes, or beliefs involved in the current or recent situation which have previously been withheld, unverbalized, or not recognized as significant; steps to encourage the client to think in a general way about the nature of current or recent activities or reactions that are inappropriate or unusual or pose problems; and steps to encourage him to examine or reflect upon factors in his situation or in the behavior of others or upon the realities of his own behavior when subjectively conditioned distortions about them have appeared.

The fourth and final subdivision of this category is concerned with the worker or agency as one facet of the client's situation. It consists of two kinds of procedures: activities used to encourage the client to discuss reflectively his reactions to the worker or to the agency or to treatment in general; and activities which may explain or clarify the nature of treatment or of the agency or of the worker's attitude toward the client.

It is impossible to imagine a case in which most of these procedures of reflective or logical discussion would not sometimes be used. The type of problem brought by the client is one of the important determinants of where the emphasis will be. The more realistic and external the problem, the greater the likelihood that interviews will emphasize procedures from the first two subdivisions; the greater the subjective involvement in the problem, the more likely it is that they will draw upon the third subdivision. The fourth is present in varying degrees of intensity in all cases. These procedures are combined to varying degrees with sustaining techniques and may be accompanied to a substantial degree by procedures of influence. They are techniques which are also always a part of the treatment process when other types of reflective considerations are in action.

The fifth main treatment category is another grouping that relies upon reflective discussion. It consists of procedures for encouraging the client to think about the *dynamics of his response patterns or tendencies.* The client is helped to reflect upon some of the internal reasons for his responses and actions. He is encouraged to look at the dynamics of his behavior by studying the relationship between one aspect of his behavior and another. He goes beyond thinking about a specific distortion of reality or inappropriate reaction toward consideration of the operations of the intrapsychic component itself. This type of reflective discussion includes thinking about the dynamics of his reactions to the worker, especially transference reactions.

The sixth treatment category, also a type of reflective discussion, includes procedures for encouraging the client to think about the *development of his response patterns or tendencies*—again, a subjective area. Here, the client is helped to deal with genetic* matters which are important because, although they occurred in the past, they have been internalized to such a degree that they are now part of his responses to current situations. As in the earlier category, treatment revolves around consideration of the relationship of one facet of behavior, one reaction to experience, to another; this time, however, in historical terms.

Obviously, the processes described in the fifth and sixth categories would never accomplish their aim without the aid of other techniques. Sustaining procedures lay the groundwork for the development of understanding and accompany it in varying degrees. When there is a strong emphasis on reflecting upon dynamic or genetic aspects of behavior, there is relatively little use of procedures of direct influence but they are by no means necessarily absent from the treatment blend. On the other hand, the mutual play between dynamic and genetic components and the current situation-response is constant. And whereas the degree to which reflection concerning dynamic and genetic content enters into any case can vary from not at all to its becoming a main theme throughout treatment, under no circumstances would this type of activity completely replace discussion of the current situation-response. Indeed, its only function is to clear the way to the client's understanding of his current life—his present situation, his response to it, and their interaction.[6]

] *Environmental Treatment*

We must now return to the knotty problem we had set aside for last—that of indirect, or environmental, treatment. One can,

---

* The word "genetic" is used here in the general sense of developmental or historical and is not meant to carry the implication, as it does in psychoanalysis, of reaching the infantile components in development.

consistently with the logic we have been following, regard environmental treatment in terms of the means by which it can be expected to affect the client. Such means may include environmental measures to provide for the better meeting of tangible basic needs or for the opening up of opportunities that go beyond basic needs but are of potential value to the client. Or they may consist of intervention to remove environmental pressures or obstacles or to change the attitudes of other people toward a client. Environmental measures can also be used to provide encouragement and to reduce anxiety. Or a person in the environment can be asked to carry an advisory or explanatory function.

When one's chief interest is in analyzing the dynamics of work with the client, a classification along these lines is useful. It is not of much value, however, in studying the way in which environmental work is actually carried out. Students who have used the classification in this form have complained—and I have agreed —that the environmental category was being slighted and not developed with the richness it deserved. As we began to look at client interviews in the terms suggested by this whole classification, it became apparent that one can also classify the content of interviews with people in the client's environment in some of the same terms one would use for classifying the content of client interviews. William Reid, then a doctoral student at the New York School of Social Work who is particularly interested in this problem, suggested that the distinction between environmental work and direct work with clients is really one that concerns the person toward whom the procedures are directed, rather than differences in the procedures themselves. This insight opened up an interesting line of thought, for it pointed the way toward a type of analysis of procedures used in the environment comparable to those used directly with the client.

In the course of our work, we use a great deal of rational or reflective discussion of both situations and persons with teachers, employers, landlords, and so on, the difference in approach from direct treatment being that our client, or our client and his family, have now become the "situation" concerning which we are working with the teacher, employer, or landlord. The principles involved, if not identical, certainly are remarkably similar to those involved in direct treatment. One can also see direct influence playing a part in environmental treatment, and not infrequently sustaining techniques as well; indeed, our environmental work might be more fruitful if we were more sustaining and less manipulative in our work with people of importance in our client's lives. It is unlikely that procedures of dynamic or genetic reflection would be used in environmental work, and certain subdivisions of reflective discussion of the situation-response area might not appear. Nevertheless, we can on the whole distinguish four categories of indirect treatment paralleling the first four used in direct work (sustaining and direct influence procedures, catharsis or ventilation, and reflective discussion of the current situation and responses). A fifth category must be added, however, to cover the direct provision of services such as financial assistance and the mobilizing of other resources on the client's behalf.

Not since Mary Richmond's time have we given the same quality of attention to indirect as to direct work. This neglect has tended to downgrade environmental treatment in the worker's mind, as though it were something one learned to do with one's left hand, something unworthy of serious analysis. We have furthermore tended to think of direct work as psychological and indirect as non-psychological, or "social." This is an absolutely false assumption. Environmental work also takes place with people and through psychological means. We cannot physically make a landlord, teacher, or anyone else do something for the benefit of our client. We have to talk with him about it, and in the process we must use psychological procedures of one sort or another. Broadening our view of casework in this way may help us to narrow the distance that seems so often to separate direct from indirect work.

In summary, then, this chapter offers a tentative classification of casework treatment methods. Starting out with the Richmond suggestion of separating casework into direct work with the client and indirect work with the environment on his behalf, it goes on to pick up the component parts of more recent classifications, arriving at a new arrangement in a pattern which uses as its logical foundation the major dynamics employed by modern casework in its effort to promote improvement in the client's functioning. Accordingly, six categories of direct treatment and five of indirect, or environmental, treatment are proposed. The six categories of direct treatment are (1) sustaining procedures, (2) procedures of direct influence, (3) catharsis or ventilation, (4) reflective discussion of the nature of the current situation, client responses to it, and their interaction, (5) reflective discussion of the dynamics of response patterns or tendencies, and (6) reflective discussion of the genetic development of response patterns or tendencies. The five categories of indirect or environmental treatment parallel the first four used in direct work, with a fifth subdivision consisting of the procedures involved in providing environmental service (such as financial assistance or visiting homemakers) through the resources of the agency itself or through the mobilization of other resources in the community.

According to this system, the treatment of any case as a whole is seen as an ever-changing blend of some or all of these treatment procedures. The nature of the blend will vary with the needs of the case and with the nature of the client's personality, his problem, and a number of other variables. ⅄

NOTES

1. Unpublished paper given at the 1956 Biennial Meeting of the Family Service Association of America.

2. Teresa P. Domanski, Marion M. Johns, and Margaret A. G. Manly, "An Investigation of a Scheme for the Classification of Casework Treatment Activities," unpublished master's thesis, Smith College School for Social Work, Northampton, Mass., 1960.

3. Jacqueline Betz, Phyllis Hartmann, Arlene Jaroslaw, Sheila Levine, Dena Schein, Gordon Smith, and Barbara Zeiss, "A Study of the Usefulness and Reliability of the Hollis Treatment Classification Scheme: A Continuation of Previous Research in This

Area," unpublished master's thesis, New York School of Social Work, Columbia University, New York, 1961.

4. Francis J. Turner, *Social Work Treatment and Value Differences*, unpublished doctoral dissertation, New York School of Social Work, Columbia University, New York, 1963.

5. For informative discussions of "joint interviewing," see: Sanford N. Sherman, "Joint Interviews in Casework Practice," *Social Work, 4* (April, 1959), 20–28; Frances H. Scherz, "Multiple-Client Interviewing: Treatment Implications," *Social Casework, 43* (March, 1962), 120–125; and Miriam Jolesch, "Casework Treatment of Young Married Couples," *Social Casework, 43* (May, 1962), 245–251.

6. Students considering experimenting with the usefulness of this classification as a research instrument will be interested to know that for the last four categories it is of value to use a parallel classification of the client's activities. This matches almost point by point the worker's activities: for example, the client "discusses reflectively" this or that. It is important, however, to be as discriminating as possible as to whether the client is actively thinking about something or, on the contrary, merely describing it. Content involving description without reflection can be grouped with ventilation. Purely exploratory comments of the worker can also be combined with this category.

Part Two

TREATMENT: AN ANALYSIS OF PROCEDURES

V

The
Sustaining Process,
Direct Influence,
and Ventilation

HAVING DISCUSSED THE SKELETAL OUTLINE of a new classification of casework treatment, we shall try in this and the following chapter to put flesh on its bare bones.

] *The Sustaining Process*

Sustaining procedures are perhaps the most basic and essential of all casework activities, for without them it would be extremely difficult even to explore the nature of the client's difficulties. It is well known that when a person must seek help from someone else, he undergoes discomfort and anxiety. Even when the assistance a client asks for is concrete and due him by right, he is uncertain whether the agency will recognize his eligibility. He finds himself in the humiliating position of having to ask even for recognition of his rights, dependent on the fairness of the worker in helping him establish these rights, and thrust into a situation in which he must answer questions about his financial, personal, and work life to the satisfaction of the interviewer. We know that the client will give more complete and less distorted information if his initial tension is relieved and he feels safe enough to discuss his situation frankly. The greater the degree of initial anxiety, the more important sustaining techniques become.

In problems that involve interpersonal adjustment, the anxiety typically continues, although with variations in level, throughout the whole period of treatment. Often the anxiety is itself one of the main problems in the individual's adjustment. Sometimes it is a general sense of incompetence or of inability to carry on life's activities adequately; sometimes it is acute concern about some external situation by which the client is confronted, such as an operation or a new and challenging job or a set of examinations; sometimes it is fear of inner impulses, aggressive or sexual; and very frequently it is fear of the superego or conscience, expressing itself as a sense of guilt.

In general it can be said that the greater the client's anxiety either initially or during the course of treatment, the more need there will be for the use of sustaining techniques. Chief among these is interested, sympathetic listening, which conveys to the client the worker's concern for his well-being. This skill comes naturally to most caseworkers, for it is an interest in people and their affairs that has brought them into social work in the first place. Nevertheless, workers do vary in their receptiveness and in their ways of showing it. It can be indicated by a subtle set of techniques, often not adequately recorded, for the necessary attitude is often expressed more in the worker's bodily behavior than in his words. Facial expression, tone of voice, choice of words, even his way of sitting as he listens, convey the worker's interest. The client is not seeking avid curiosity or over-solicitude on the worker's part, but neither does he want cold detachment.[1] An attitude of interest is essential throughout treatment. Special pains must be taken to communicate it to the client whenever his anxiety is high unless, as we will see later, there is some special therapeutic reason for allowing tension to remain unrelieved.

A sustaining procedure that goes beyond the basic attitude of interest and concern is that of conveying acceptance to the client. Despite the fact that the concept of acceptance has been emphasized in casework for many years,[2] it is still often misunderstood. It has to do with the worker's attitude—and hence communications—when the client is feeling guilty or for some reason unworthy of the worker's liking or respect. It is sometimes mistakenly assumed that the worker must be without an opinion about the rightness or wrongness, the advisability or inadvisability, of the client's activities. This would be impossible even if it were desirable—unless the worker were either an imbecile or a psychopath! It is true that the therapeutic attitude requires broad understanding of the validity of different values for people of different ethnic, religious, and class backgrounds. Furthermore individuals within all groups vary markedly from each other. The worker must see clearly that there are good reasons for such variations and that within broad limits many value questions are matters of individual preference; he must recognize where his own values are individual, too, and not necessarily better than those of the people with whom he is working. While all this is true and basic to the concept of acceptance, it by no means covers all of it. Acceptance means that whether the worker approves or disapproves of what the client has told about himself, he continues to convey a positive, understanding attitude toward the client. It is actually possible for the worker to communicate this attitude even when at the same time he expresses his agreement with the client that he was wrong in his action. Acceptance is not an expression of opinion about an act but an expression of continued good will toward the perpetrator of the act.[3]

A further step in the sustaining process consists of actual reassurance about the client's feelings of guilt and anxiety. For instance, a mother who has great difficulty in recognizing feelings of hostility may in the course of treatment become aware of considerable anger toward her child. The worker may seek to reassure her by commenting that the feeling is natural and that she has had ample provocation. This technique must be used with delicacy and discrimination. Yielding to the temptation to overuse reassurance in an attempt to build up a relationship or because the worker himself cannot endure the client's anxiety may merely leave the client with the feeling that the worker does not fully comprehend the reasons for his guilt or anxiety, or that the worker himself is deficient in moral discrimination and therefore not a person whose judgment matters. Moreover, when the client is ready to explore the reasons for his actions, the worker must be particularly careful not to give reassurance except when the client's anxiety is so great that he cannot proceed without it. If he is made completely comfortable, he may feel no need to seek reasons for troublesome behavior.

In the illustration just presented, for example, it was important to reassure the mother at first because she had unusually high guilt and could acknowledge her feelings only with great reluctance. But after a period of increased ability to talk about her angry feelings toward her child, the worker no longer needed to be reassuring; instead, she agreed that the feelings were unusually strong, and shifting to techniques for developing understanding, suggested seeking out some of the causes for this excessive irritation.

The worker must be even more careful in using techniques of reassurance when anxiety takes the form of fear of the external world or of internal drives which the client feels he may be unable to control. In the first place such reassurance must be justified by reality, or the client will almost always sense falseness and at best get only temporary comfort. It certainly does no good to tell the patient he need not fear an exploratory operation which he already knows may reveal the presence of cancer. It would be more helpful to provide him with opportunities for expressing his anxiety and at least gaining relief through the process of catharsis or ventilation. If the client is panicky about the operation, the worker's calm consideration of its possible outcomes will in itself be a reassuring process. Often the client is overreacting, either anticipating certain discovery of cancer when this possibility is not realistically justified, or ignoring the possibility of medical help for the condition even though it might be found to be malignant. Here logical discussion combined with reassurance may clarify the realities of the patient's condition by bringing to his attention the possible positive outcome of the operation and the fact that cure may be possible even if cancer is found. If the worker already has the confidence of the client, he may provide further reassurance of the sustaining type by expressing his confidence in the doctors, thus increasing the client's trust in them and correspondingly lessening his anxiety.

It is important to recognize that anxiety can be lessened by many different techniques. For example, the achievement of even a small area of self-understanding may remove the cause of guilt feelings or modify a distortion that has been causing anxiety. In sustaining work, however, the relief comes not from understanding but because the worker in whom the client has placed confidence has said in effect that it is not necessary to be so worried. The dynamic is not one of reasoning but of faith dependent upon the client's confidence in the worker's knowledge and good will.

A similar process takes place when the worker expresses confidence in a client's abilities, recognizes his achievement, shows pleasure in his successes, and so on. Encouragement is especially important in work with children, and is also effective with adults who either customarily lack self-confidence, are faced with especially difficult tasks, or are going through a period of anxiety in which their normal self-confidence is weakened. The worker must take special care, however, to discriminate between honest appreciation and false praise or flattery. The very fact that people are insecure often makes them extremely sensitive to hollow insincerity, and their confidence in the worker will evaporate if they once suspect his encouraging comments are merely a technique meant to inject courage into their personalities.

Above all, when expressing confidence in the client's ability to handle some task or situation, the worker must not only be realistic in his estimation of the client's capacity but must also be sensitive to the client's own conception of his abilities. Too-ready reassurance, even when realistically justified, causes the client to bottle up his anxiety, which may then reappear in full force at the very moment he most needs whatever self-confidence he possesses. If the lack of self-confidence is very great, initial ventilation may be called for, followed by whatever help the client is able to assimilate from rational consideration of the situation of which he is so fearful.

One other caution concerning procedures of encouragement. They inevitably arouse in the client a feeling that he should live up to the worker's expectations. Particularly if there is a possibility that the client will fail, it is important to deal in advance with the anxiety that this may create by making it clear that the worker will not be upset by failure, will continue his interest and confidence in the client, and will help him to deal with his disappointment and to find another solution. In other words, the other sustaining techniques of acceptance and reassurance must often go hand in hand with encouragement.[4]

At times the client's need for sustainment is so great that it can only be met by actual "gifts of love." We are most familiar with the use of such techniques with children who, it has long been recognized, need concrete evidence of the worker's good will. Small gifts have always been part of the worker's way of building up a positive relationship with children, especially young children. It is also customary for the worker to express his liking or fondness for them directly and, with small children, to convey it physically, by holding a child on his lap, putting his arm protectively around an upset youngster, and the like.

A comparable process is sometimes needed with adults. In recent years the literature on the "hard to reach" has emphasized the importance of winning the client's confidence partly by doing concrete things for his benefit,[5] such as working out difficult situations with a landlord or with the department of welfare, arranging for camp for the children, taking the children to busy clinics when the mother cannot do this herself, or even providing money for various household needs. While these services are given in their own right because of actual need, they often go beyond services that would be given routinely and are definitely understood as such by the client.

Sometimes "the gift" is a visit to the client in his home in a period of stress when the contact has usually been in the office; sometimes it is the arranging of an extra interview or even merely the giving of extra time in a regular interview. Whenever the worker's action is designed in part to impress upon the client his concern for and desire to help him, it represents this form of sustaining work. This approach is particularly called for when the client is distrustful of the worker or is in a state of anxiety where he needs the care of a "good mother." Again let it be said that it would not be the only procedure employed, but it might either accompany or be a necessary prelude to other techniques. In work with adults, such concrete demonstrations are not universally needed and in any case must be used with great discrimination based on sound diagnostic thinking; they should not grow out of the worker's enjoyment of the client's gratitude or out of his need to encourage a dependent relationship.

] *Direct Influence*

When we turn to our second set of procedures, those designated procedures of direct influence, we are considering the various ways in which the worker tries to promote a specific kind of behavior on the client's part, such as dealing more advantageously with an employer, consulting a doctor, going through with a medical recommendation, handling the children in a certain way, and so on.[6]

For many years this type of activity has been suspect in casework. In the days of innocence, when workers were universally thought to be wiser and better informed than clients, advice was one of the "visitor's" chief stocks in trade. Through bitter experience caseworkers gradually learned that the wife who took the worker's advice and separated from her alcoholic husband more often than not took him back again, despite her fear of the visitor's disapproval; that the mother who let herself be guided by child-rearing theories somehow managed to demonstrate that they did not work with her Johnnie; and that the housewife who let herself be taught how to make up a set of budget envelopes did not simultaneously learn how to keep her fingers out of the wrong envelope when the installment man came to the door. Out of such experiences came considerable healthy reluctance about telling the client how to run his life. To a certain extent the official position of casework on this matter has probably been more extreme than actual practice. Workers have probably intuitively recognized that there continues to be some need for guidance of at least some clients and have developed subtle ways of exercising such influence.

Now, however, it is recognized that to use the client's trust in the worker as a vehicle for influencing his behavior is sometimes a very useful form of treatment, but three main safeguards must be observed. First, the worker must be reasonably sure that he knows enough about what is best for the client. Especially on important decisions, the worker rarely knows enough to justify influencing him. Application of this test will go far in cutting down the temptation to give advice. For instance, in a decision to break up a marriage, a third person cannot sufficiently appreciate the subjective feelings and needs involved to weigh them adequately along with the objective realities that seem, perhaps all too obviously, to point toward the wisdom of separation. The worker is better advised to try to help the client through inducing reflective discussion to arrive at his own realization of both subjective and objective factors in his situation and to enable him to come to a wise decision for himself. Only then may there be reason for the worker's reenforcing the client's decision by expressing his agreement, but even this amount of influence must be sparingly used.

A second safeguard is to be quite sure that the need for advice rests in the client and not in the worker. This is a matter of self-examination for the worker. It is so tempting to tell people what to do; one feels so good to be called upon for professional advice! All the negative connotations of the word "authority" can be removed simply by putting "professional" in front of it and thereby transforming "authoritativeness" into "strength the client can lean on." That there is such a thing as professional authority is not to be denied, and under certain circumstances it can be put to very good use. However, the need to see oneself as an authority is not sufficient reason for invoking that role.

Our third safeguard is to induce the client, whenever possible, to think things through for himself. Clients often seduce the worker into thinking advice is necessary when it is not. Some people like to be told what to do because passivity or dependence interfere with their ability to think things out for themselves and later, if things go wrong, they can always blame someone else. Anxious people, people with little self-confidence, childish people who want very much to please others often ask for more direction than they really need. In casework we have found that the more people can do things for themselves, the more *self-directive* they can be, the more likely they are to continue functioning successfully after the end of treatment. Therefore, techniques of influence should be subordinated to the various types of procedures for developing understanding.

With these forewarnings, I hasten to add that there are many situations in which techniques of influence are appropriate. This is particularly true in matters of child rearing, where the worker, because of his expert knowledge, is able to give the client good advice. Often the client is not yet ready to think things through for himself, or strong cultural differences in his expectations of the worker may lead him to interpret the worker's refusal to give him direction as a sign of disinterest or incompetence. While the worker does not need to comply with such expectations throughout the whole of treatment, it is often important to do so at the beginning.

The very anxious client is also sometimes in need of direction, and it may be appropriate for the worker to provide it in the initial contact or throughout a period of crisis, gradually supplanting it, as the client's self-confidence grows, by methods that rest on understanding. Infantile personalities, too, are often not capable of complete self-direction and need at least a measure of guidance from the worker,[7] as may also people whose sense of reality is weak, such as ambulatory schizophrenics or borderline psychotics.[8] As long as the worker is philosophically committed to the value of self-direction, reasonably conscious of his own reactions to the client's need for dependence, and alert to every possibility of encouraging his client to think for himself, he will make wise use of procedures of influence.

As one works with these procedures, one discovers that they actually constitute a range of processes that form a continuum of degrees of directiveness. In the middle of the continuum one may place the giving of advice: definitely stating an opinion or taking a stand concerning actions the worker thinks the client should take. He may point out to a child's mother that Mary knows her way to school, is careful about crossing streets, and will have more chance to play with other children if her mother does not accompany her. Or he may comment to a man who is hesitating to ask for a seemingly deserved raise that several other men in his office have been given a raise and that the only way to find out if he can get one is to ask for it.

A less forceful way of presenting these same ideas might be for the worker to make a suggestion. He might comment to Mary's mother that it is only two blocks to the school and perhaps Mary is now able to walk this distance alone. Or he might wonder whether the second client has thought about asking the boss for a raise. The solution is raised in the client's mind in a way that conveys the worker's inclination toward it, but leaves the client with the alternative of rejecting the idea without feeling that he is going contrary to the worker's definite opinion.

A still milder form of influence is that of simply underlining, giving emphasis to, a course of action the client himself is already contemplating. A mother thinks it might be a good idea to let six-year-old Mary walk to school alone; the worker agrees it would be worth trying. Or the client says he is thinking of asking the boss for a raise, and the worker nods approvingly. Even if the client eventually decides against the step, there is very little likelihood that he will feel he has gone against the worker's opinion, for it was his own idea in the first place. If he does go ahead with it and it works, he takes the credit for himself; if it fails, the edge is taken off the failure, since the worker also made the mistake of thinking it would work.

At the other end of the continuum comes what may be called "advocating," the putting of a certain urgency behind the advice that is offered. The worker tells the mother that it is *essential* for her to take Mary to school, even though the child is frightened. Such pressure is often necessary in treatment of a true school phobia where the mother's own need to keep the child close to her is contributing to the difficulty, and the child herself cannot be properly treated unless she is put under considerable pressure to attend school despite her fears. Treatment of the child cannot wait upon a slow change in the mother's attitude, which might take months to bring about, for in the interim school problems will have been added to the initial phobia to such a degree that a permanent learning problem may ensue.[9]

Or the worker might tell the client he thinks it would be *very unwise* for him to ask for a raise when he is on such bad terms with his boss, that such an action might very well result in his being fired. When there is a possibility of severe consequences of an impulsive, ill-considered action, or when sufficient time is not available before action is threatened to help the client think such a matter through rationally, the technique of advocating may be worth trying. Sometimes it saves the client from unfortunate consequences. But if it does not work and the client suffers the predicted result, the worker must by all means avoid anything that can be construed as an "I told you so" attitude. Properly handled, with the client able to express his disappointment and to feel that the worker, too, regrets his disappointment, the failure may open the way to reflective consideration of what was involved and possibly ward off its repetition.

Most extreme of all the directive techniques is actual intervention in the client's life by such measures as removing a child from a home where he is subjected to cruelty or to a high degree of neglect, or taking a psychotic client to the receiving ward of a hospital. Such interventions must rest on two conditions: first, the worker must be fully convinced that the step is factually justified and not motivated by some overreaction on his own part; second, he must have thorough knowledge of the community resources involved in the action he has initiated and of the extent to which they will support it, for if it falls through he may well have lost his own contact with his client and made the situation worse. In the first illustration given, the worker must know the conditions under which a court would uphold his action in custody proceedings; in the second he must have sound clinical knowledge of the probable nature of the client's illness and of the procedures of the hospital to which he is to be taken. In both instances the action must be carried out with great skill. Firmness and kindness are needed. The probability of the client's acceding to the action with a minimum of resistance and disturbance is enhanced if in the first instance the worker is devoid of punitive motivation and in the second has his own anxiety sufficiently under control so that the client does not sense it. In both instances it is important for the worker to feel sufficiently confident of his ability to carry through the action that the client senses this strength and therefore rejects the temptation to test it.

Certain general rules can be laid down for the use of direct influence in casework. The first is that it should be used only in conjunction with procedures for developing understanding. In general, wherever understanding can be developed, this is preferable, with the worker's influence used only to support the client's own conclusions rather than to initiate them. The second is that preference should be given to the most gentle form of influence that can be successfully employed. Only the beginner or the clumsy worker makes major use of advice. The skillful practitioner finds ways of stirring his clients to thoughtfulness, for the most part simply by making a suggestion, or better still, merely reenforcing the client's own ideas. Only in exceptional cases does he employ much advice, and advocating is rarer still. Intervention, except in direct work with children, is limited to protective work, where it is necessary to safeguard the welfare either of the client or of other people who may be harmed by him.[10]

Among the types of clients who typically seek a great deal of advice are compulsive people.[11] Because they are usually very ambivalent, having a hard time making up their own minds, they consequently find an initial relief in being told what to do. Moreover, they are also usually dependent and have very strong superegos, so that they are very anxious to please people whom they regard as authorities. Asking for advice, in other words, is one way of showing that one is indeed a very good little boy or girl.

Because of the anxiety involved and the fact that the asked-for guidance becomes a gift (in the sustaining sense) that helps to build up a positive relationship, it sometimes is wise, especially in the early stages, to accede to the compulsive client's request. It is particularly important, however, to use the milder degrees of influence wherever possible. Direct advice should be given tentatively, the worker offering it as something the client might like to try or as something that is often found helpful. As the negativism of compulsive people sometimes leads them to ask for direction for the unconscious purpose of proving it will not work, this kind of qualifying comment will temper their need to show the advice is poor. If, on the other hand, they are truly trying to please the worker by following the advice, the tentative way in which it is offered will provide them with an anxiety-relieving excuse if they should fail.

It is obvious that a close relationship exists between sustaining techniques and direct influence, the latter techniques, except for intervention, being effective only in proportion to the client's trust in the worker. The client will come to the worker with certain preconceptions growing out of past experience with, or knowledge of, other social workers. Also, certain expectations are inherent in the worker's position—"ascribed," that is, to anyone functioning in this particular role. Immediately upon contact, the worker should begin to "achieve" the repute of a person to be trusted by virtue of his own ways of acting with the client. The client's trust in the worker will be made up mainly of two components—respect for the worker's competence and belief in his good will.[12] The latter is built up largely through sustaining processes, and is at least from the client's point of view the more important.

Both direct influence and sustainment draw upon the client's dependence on the worker, a fact which must be kept in mind both in using these techniques and subsequently in helping the client regain or strengthen his ability to be self-reliant. How can we justify the use of dependence in treatment while at the same time emphasizing the importance of the client's self-determination? Some years ago I suggested that "self-determination"[13] was an unfortunate choice of words, implying as it does an over-simplified notion of autonomy and self-sufficiency. "Self-direction" is perhaps a more accurate term, denoting not absolute independence but rather the capacity to guide oneself through the maze of interactions that make up the pattern of life. This is the capacity that the worker seeks to enable the client to increase. It is generally recognized that self-determination is a relative, not an absolute value. If the client is endangering others or himself, it must be superseded by another, namely, the worker's responsibility to prevent suffering; hence, the necessity for protective work. Most workers are ready to acknowledge this limitation to the client's right of self-direction but some flounder in another dilemma. What justification is there, they ask, for influencing the client at all? How can *you* have goals for treatment? Aren't goals the client's right of self-direction but some flounder in another

My answer is that, except for procedures of intervention, we do not influence the client without his assent. We may have our goals for him, but he makes them his own only to the extent that he is willing to accord us a place of influence in his life; some-times accepting our goals implicitly, sometimes explicitly, but insofar as possible with clear awareness of what they are. Any-one who deals with people inevitably influences them in one way or another, and whether he is conscious of it or not, he has a goal for his work. If one of the worker's primary values is the maximizing of the client's capacity for self-direction, he will relate his methods to that end. Again and again his choice of means will lead him toward the development of understanding. But he will also see that some clients are not ready to select their goals unaided, and that almost all clients require a degree of temporary dependence as a necessary bridge across which the processes of treatment move. The worker will acknowledge and grant this need, but he must be ever careful that the bridge of dependence he provides is no stronger than necessary for the work to be accomplished.

] *Ventilation*

Unlike sustaining procedures and techniques of direct influence, which are a composite of various procedures, catharsis—or ventilation, as it is sometimes called—is simply the process of encouraging the free expression of feeling by the client, or of providing an atmosphere that makes such free expression possible. This process needs to be distinguished from a straight exploration of the nature of the client's problem, which does not necessarily involve the expression of much emotion. But when the exploration deals with matters of high emotional import and involves much expression of feeling, the client often experiences considerable relief just from having talked freely about something that has been bottled up within him, even though the worker has not done more than listen. At such times catharsis, or ventilation, is occurring. It may also happen, however, that matters spoken of by the client during an emotional outpouring may have great diagnostic import. At such times, exploration on the worker's part, description and explanation on the client's, and catharsis are closely related. Sometimes it is hard to tell whether or not emotional release is occurring. The client may be so restrained or controlled in his manner that it is not till a later point in the contact that the therapist realizes that the client had deep feeling about the matter he was discussing and experienced great relief in talking about it.

Very often closely interwoven with the release of feeling in an interview other procedures will be used which draw upon the content initially brought into the interview by the ventilating process. Frequently, he will employ sustaining procedures, espe-

cially calling into play expressions of understanding and acceptance or even comments to relieve anxiety and guilt. At other
times he will use material discussed in the process of ventilation
to involve the client in reflective consideration about himself
and his situation.

Although a certain amount of emotional release is of value in
all cases, there are some circumstances under which it should
be held in check. Occasionally so much anxiety or other emotion
is ventilated that it actually seems to be feeding on itself. Talking
does not bring the client relief and a reduction of feeling but
engrosses him more deeply in it. Under these circumstances, the
expression of emotion is not helpful and the worker should
not encourage it to continue but rather turn the client's attention either to less emotionally laden content or to the question
of what can be done to modify the situation or the feelings
about which the client has been talking. The worker may even
have to say quite directly that it does not seem to help to go over
these matters and that it might be better to try not to dwell on
them so constantly. Occasionally, especially with the psychotic
or near-psychotic, ventilation may lead to the production of
increasingly bizarre material or become an incentive to irrational
action. Such a circumstance certainly needs to be foreseen and
warded off.

Occasionally the worker may realize that the client is deriving
marked gratification from talking freely about himself and seems
to be making no effort to use the interviews to move toward any
improvement in himself or his situation. This sometimes represents a passive type of self-pity, an effort to enlist the worker's
sympathy; at other times the client's complaints seem to be only
an excuse for not doing anything for himself and a way of putting
all the blame for his troubles on others. Occasionally, the talking
provides him with sexual or masochistic satisfaction. Gratification
of any of these types is of no value in helping the client to better
his plight and should not be continued once it becomes clear that
this is the prevailing mood. Sometimes, too, clients who seek
gratification in these ways are people who cannot be helped by
casework. Care should be taken, however, to move away from
this type of communication in a constructive rather than a destructive way. Often the reason for discouraging it can be explained directly to the client, thus leading him into a discussion

of this aspect of his resistance. But to do so successfully, the worker must be free of the hostile countertransference reactions that are so easily aroused by clients who make use of ventilation primarily for self-gratification.

NOTES

1. For an interesting discussion of this, see Clare Britton, "Casework Techniques in Child Care Services," *Social Casework, 36* (January, 1955), 3–13.

2. The importance of this concept was emphasized in many articles during the thirties. See especially Annette Garrett, *Interviewing: Its Principles and Methods*, Family Service Association of America, New York, 1942, pp. 22–24; Gordon Hamilton, "Basic Concepts in Social Casework," *The Family, 18* (July, 1937), 147–156; Fern Lowry, "Objectives in Social Case Work," *The Family, 18* (December, 1937), 263–268; Charlotte Towle, "Factors in Treatment," *Proceedings of the National Conference of Social Work, 1936*, University of Chicago Press, Chicago, 1936, pp. 179–191; and Marian Wyman, "What Is Basic in Case Work Practice?" in *Proceedings of the National Conference of Social Work, 1938*, University of Chicago Press, Chicago, 1939, pp. 179–191.

3. See Alice W. Rue, "The Casework Approach to Protective Work," *The Family, 18* (December, 1937), 277–282.

4. See Grace Nicholls, "Treatment of a Disturbed Mother-Child Relationship: A Case Presentation," in *Ego Psychology and Dynamic Casework*, Howard J. Parad, ed., Family Service Association of America, New York, 1958, pp. 117–125; and L. P. Laing, "The Use of Reassurance in Psychotherapy," *Smith College Studies in Social Work, 22* (February, 1952), 75–90.

5. For discussion of work with "the hard to reach," see especially Alice Overton, "Serving Families Who Don't Want Help,"

Social Casework, 34 (July, 1953), 304–309; Walter Haas, "Reaching Out—A Dynamic Concept in Casework," *Social Work, 4* (July, 1959), 41–45; and *Casework Notebook,* Family Centered Project, Greater St. Paul, Community Chests and Councils, Inc., St. Paul, Minn., 1957.

6. For an interesting study of one of these procedures, see Ruth T. Koehler, "The Use of Advice in Casework," *Smith College Studies in Social Work, 23* (February, 1953), 151–165.

7. For illustration, see Frances H. Scherz, "Treatment of Acting-out Character Disorders in a Marital Problem," *Casework Papers, 1956,* Family Service Association of America, New York, 1956.

8. See Margaret M. Heyman, "Some Methods in Direct Casework Treatment of the Schizophrenic," *Journal of Psychiatric Social Work, 19* (Summer, 1949), 18–24.

9. As suggested by Emmanuel Klein in "The Reluctance to Go to School," *Psychoanalytic Study of the Child, 1* (1945), 263–279.

10. Some general considerations involved in the use of authority of all degrees are well presented in Elliot Studt's "An Outline for Study of Social Authority Factors in Casework," *Social Casework, 35* (June, 1954), 231–238.

11. This is discussed by Sid Hirsohn in his "Casework with the Compulsive Mother," *Social Casework, 32* (June, 1951), 254–261.

12. This question has been studied by Norman Polansky and his associates. See Norman Polansky, and Jacob Kounin, "Clients' Reactions to Initial Interviews: A Field Study," *Human Relations, 9* (1956), 237–264; and Jacob Kounin, Norman Polansky, and others, "Experimental Studies of Clients' Reactions to Initial Interviews," *Human Relations,* 9 (1956), 265–293.

13. Florence Hollis, "Principles and Assumptions Underlying Casework Practice," *Social Work* (London), *12* (1955), 41–45.

Suggested Additional Reading

Lola G. Selby, "Supportive Treatment: The Development of a Concept and a Helping Method," *Social Service Review, 30* (1956), 400–414.

Fritz Schmidl, "A Study of Techniques Used in Supportive Treatment," *Social Casework, 32* (December, 1951), 413–419.

VI

Reflective Discussion
of the
Person-Situation
Configuration

CASEWORK PLACES GREAT EMPHASIS on drawing the client into reflective consideration of his situation and of his own functioning within it. In Chapter IV we suggested the usefulness of three major divisions in work of this kind: consideration of the nature of the current situation, one's responses to it, and the interaction of situation and responses; consideration of the dynamics of response patterns or tendencies; and consideration of the genetic or developmental factors in these patterns. The first category, the subject of this chapter, is a form of treatment universally used in casework. The worker always tries to help the client arrive at some measure of increased understanding, no matter how much reflective discussion may need to be buttressed by sustaining, directive, or ventilating work.[1] Because of the tendency in recent years to emphasize either supportive casework or work leading to clarification or insight development, the type of reflective discussion that leads to an understanding which is neither clarification nor insight has been lost sight of and never given the thorough study or accreditation it deserves. And yet this technique comprises a rich store of useful procedures that are perhaps more characteristic of casework than any others.

] *The Situation: People, Conditions, Events*

As indicated earlier, one can think in terms of four subdivisions of this category: consideration of the client's current situation, his own reactions, his inner responses, and, lastly, the treatment of relationship. The first of these has to do with the client's thinking reflectively about his situation. Here we are dealing partly with perception and partly with a question of knowledge. So often people see only a distorted or one-sided picture of the reality before them, either because they see or hear what they anticipate or because their feelings lead them actually to ignore or blot out important aspects of a situation. The father who is convinced that his son is stupid, like his own older brother, may remember or stress only those subjects or activities in which his son has failed, but may without noticing it reveal areas in which the son's learning has been unimpeded. The worker's first approach should be to call the father's attention to events that show the other side of the boy's capacities. In this sort of situation workers often err by rushing into a discussion of the distortion itself instead of seeing whether, when the client's attention is called to the reality picture, he is able by this procedure alone to modify his earlier misconceptions. It is only by testing the client's capacity to do this that one can measure the force of his need to distort.

There is a rule of parsimony in treatment as well as in science. If a person is able, with a little help, to perceive more realistically, it is not necessary to pursue the whys and wherefores of his previous failure to do so. If, on the other hand, the distortion does not yield to a look at the facts, the diagnostic information and material which this preliminary effort has provided can later be used to draw the client's attention to the discrepancy between reality and his view of it. For instance, he might say, "Have you noticed, Mr. Dawson, that even when Frank came home with a B+ in history you found it hard to believe he was doing better? . . . I wonder what makes it so hard for you to have confidence in him." Or, "It's hard for you to believe Frank really got that

B+, isn't it?" A perceptive client will often accept the cue and go on himself to talk about the things that complicate his feelings toward the child. Another will need more prompting from the worker, and when this occurs, treatment may move on from this first type of understanding to an effort to arrive at dynamic or genetic understanding.

A person's lack of understanding may be due not so much to distortion of or blindness to the facts as to actual lack of knowledge about normal reactions. Parents, unaware of the universal turmoil experienced by adolescents, become worried and angry in response to the unbearable behavior of their teen-age children. Often, an explanation by the worker of how common such behavior is in children of this age and of some of the reasons for it can do much to reduce parental worry and counterhostility. With more understanding, more tolerance and patience become possible.

Lack of imagination about another person's feelings or behavior or failure to identify with the feelings of another also may generate hostility between people. The husband intent on his own successful legal career fails to see that his college-trained wife is frustrated by household tasks and does not do them well because they do not seem to call on any of the knowledge she acquired in her college major in philosophy. Nor does it occur to him that since she really is inept at physical work, she needs some household help in caring for their three very young children, despite the fact that he has bought her expensive modern equipment. One man in such a situation had actually concluded that his wife was stupid because he did not realize the extent to which her feelings of frustration and anger were hindering her from learning new household skills. He was not incapable of understanding his wife's reactions when he was helped to do so—that is, to perceive her more accurately and fully—but without help, he was becoming constantly more irritated and more scornful of her capacities—the very thing that drove her to distraction.

The very process of understanding another person more fully sets in motion a change in behavior. As we saw earlier, we do not respond to the actual situation, but rather to our perception of it. Thus, when a distorted perception is corrected, the response often corrects itself.

The process of understanding the external world takes place not only in relation to people but also in respect to life events. Clients sometimes need help in understanding a budget, a business or work situation, medical recommendations, or the implications of their own or someone else's physical condition.[2] The more fully they can comprehend these things, the more appropriately will they handle them. Reflective consideration is a more tedious process than the giving of advice, but it increases the client's competence in a way that advisory processes do not.

Several choices of technique are open to the worker in helping the client reflect upon his understanding of people and situations. Some workers like to explain things to their clients in a more or less didactic way; others are more skillful in leading people to think things through for themselves. With a mother who does not understand the irritability of her three-year-old after the birth of a new baby, some workers immediately explain the universality of sibling jealousy. A better procedure is to ask the mother if she has herself thought of any explanation of the older child's peevishness. If she has not, there is still the possibility of inquiring whether she thinks the arrival of the new baby might be making Jane feel left out. The more one can get clients to think for themselves, the more conviction they will have about the answers they find. Furthermore, their dependency on the worker will not be so greatly increased, and at the same time they will be helped to develop an ego skill which they can apply to other situations.

] *Decisions and Consequences*

The second type of reflection concerning the person-situation gestalt involves decisions and activities of the client and their effects in interaction with his environment. Over and over again the worker strives to help the client think about the effect of his own actions on others, or about their consequences for himself.[3] An action may be a matter of practical decision, such as the advantages and disadvantages of moving into a housing project, the advisability of changing from one job to another, or the wisdom of training for a particular vocation. Or it may be a decision about a medical problem, such as whether or not to undergo recommended surgery. Often it involves a complicated interpersonal decision, such as whether or not to separate from husband or wife, to adopt a child, or to place a child for adoption. In any of these instances, the client tries imaginatively to foresee the consequences of a plan for himself and for the other people whose lives are involved in his decision. The worker contributes to the reflective discussion by bringing the client's attention to aspects of the situation which he may have overlooked, so that they can be adequately included in his considerations and decisions.

At other times it is not a direct decision but rather an understanding of the effects of the client's own behavior on someone else that is involved in the consideration. A mother may not realize that when she hits her fourteen-year-old son in front of his pals, she is compelling him to defy her in order to maintain the respect of his friends. A husband may not see that when he nags his wife about her figure, he is only making her more hungry for forbidden sweets.[4] A child may not realize that when he is a poor sport in losing games, his friends go to play with someone else.

Here as elsewhere, the best procedure for the worker is not to "explain" the relationship between behavior and consequences but rather to lead the client to see the sequence himself. What happened just before Johnny left you to play with Bud? Do you feel your wife eats less when you needle her about her weight? What did Mike do when you hit him in front of the other fellows? Many times the client will draw his own correct conclusions once the two aspects of his behavior are brought to his attention. If he needs more help, the worker may go on with, "Do you suppose that . . ." or "Have you noticed that . . ." or "Often boys of this age. . . ." When a full explanation is really needed, the worker should give it but not until an effort has been made to see whether the client can arrive at conclusions on his own, so that he will at least gain experience in thinking in terms of consequences in general as well as some understanding of the particular matter under discussion.

] *Inner Awareness, Responses, and Distortions*

The third subdivision of this type of treatment, which parallels the procedure of helping the client look outward with greater perceptive accuracy, has to do with increasing the client's *inner* awareness. This process is sometimes regarded as very complicated, particularly if it involves awareness of so-called hidden feelings or reactions. There are many degrees of "hiddenness." The client may be perfectly aware of his reactions but afraid to speak of them because he is ashamed of them or fears ridicule or criticism; this may be the case, for example, with a mother who is fully aware of her anger toward one of her children but is ashamed to admit it, or with a woman who is afraid to tell the worker about a recent abortion. Or the client may have refrained from talking about his feelings because he has not recognized their significance or importance: a man may know he is ashamed of having had tuberculosis, but he never speaks of it to the worker because he does not realize the way in which it is relevant to his employment failures. Or the client may be truly unaware of his feelings because they are not part of his conscious thought: a mother may not even be aware, for example, of the strong feelings of hostility she is harboring toward her child.*

It is a great temptation when a worker can read a client's thoughts to do so out loud. There are occasions when this is necessary—either because the client is quite unable to bring his thoughts into the open but will be relieved if the worker does so for him, or because there is therapeutic justification for bringing them out even though this may make him uncomfortable. Far more often skill lies in finding ways of enabling the client to bring out the hidden material himself. Where full awareness is present, this often occurs without any specific prompting, as the client becomes more secure with the worker in response to a sustaining approach. If, however, it is obvious to the worker that the client is struggling with the question of whether to speak of something or not, he may want to handle this hesitation directly by commenting that he knows it is hard sometimes to speak freely but hopes, as the client becomes more comfortable, he will be able to do so. Or the worker may say, "I know it is hard to talk sometimes, but I can only help you with the things you can bring yourself to talk about." Or, "Can you tell me what

---

* We are talking here not of *memories* but of reactions to current life. The uncovering of hidden *memories* is part of the process of genetic understanding rather than of the current person-situation gestalt.

it is that makes it so hard for you to talk about this?" Or, "I have a feeling that you may be afraid I will criticize you. Is there anything I've said that makes you feel this way?" Or, "I'm not here to criticize you but to help you."

At other times, when the worker is fairly sure of what the client is withholding, he may be able to make comments which refer tangentially to the anticipated content, thus inviting the client to talk about it but still not facing him with it directly. It is possible, for instance, to give reassurance of acceptance in advance of the client's communication. "It isn't always possible, you know, to feel love for a difficult child." Or, "Sometimes mothers, even though they try not to, do dislike a child." Or, "Sometimes a person is so desperate about a pregnancy that they feel they have to do something about it." Often one can use the procedure of calling the client's attention to discrepancies between fact and feeling, or overemphasis, or inconsistencies, as these may point toward important feelings. Sometimes this can be done merely by repeating the revealing statement in a questioning tone.

On the less frequent occasions when it is actually advisable to put the matter into words for the client, this can be done tentatively, making it possible for the client to maintain his defenses if he needs to do so and also safeguarding him from agreeing too readily to a possibly incorrect interpretation when the worker is not certain of his perception of the client's thinking. Occasionally, a direct, unqualified interpretation is helpful, but for this the worker should be very sure of his ground.

As in the simpler process of spontaneous catharsis, when feelings are brought to expression, the worker has several choices as to his next step. He may turn to sustaining procedures, trying immediately to allay the client's anxiety or guilt; he may seek to involve the client in further understanding of the dynamics or of developmental aspects of his reactions; or he may concentrate on their immediate consequences in the client's current life.

Closely related to the process of helping a person become aware of feelings and thoughts is the process of encouraging him to recognize and consider inappropriate, unusual, or problem activities or reactions. The worker calls the client's attention to the fact that she has several times called Mary "Janet." Or he comments on the oddity that the client continuously works overtime without extra compensation for a boss he says he hates, despite the fact that he could easily get another job. This is a very important procedure and one that is often neglected by inexperienced workers to whom speed seems more essential than safety. Again, the more the client can think for himself, the better. When his attention is called to irrational or unproductive behavior, if he is capable of so doing he is very likely to go on himself to consideration either of the consequences of his behavior or the reasons for it. The worker who omits this step and rushes on to an explanation or interpretation deprives the client of the chance to seek this out for himself. Furthermore, the risk of an inaccurate or inadequate explanation is always greater when the worker trusts his own insight instead of the client's.

Another facet of this process in which the client thinks about his own responses comes into play when the worker helps him to use external realities to correct distortions in his ideas. A boy who is excessively fearful of a school test is reminded of his successes in previous tests. A girl who says she has no one to invite to a party when she has told the worker of many friends is asked to think over the many people she actually knows. A wife who has taken unnecessary offense at a remark of her husband is asked to think of what else he might have meant. Here, too, the temptation is to rush into consideration of the reason for the distortion—to dynamic or genetic understanding of it. But it is wiser first to try the simpler form of correction, by invoking external reality. For some people this will suffice; for others, deeper understanding may not be practical or advisable. When deeper consideration is both necessary and advisable, reality testing provides important diagnostic information and also serves as a base from which to proceed. "I wonder what makes it so hard for you to believe you can do well when you have such a good previous record?" "Have you noticed how you persist in thinking your husband is trying to hurt you even when what he says doesn't necessarily add up to that?"

] *Reactions to the Worker and to Treatment*

The last subdivision of this type of treatment involves the client's thinking about the *treatment process* itself: about the worker in his treatment role and about his own reactions to the worker and to treatment or to agency rules and requirements. In a sense this is a special case of the client-situation gestalt, for the worker is one aspect of the client's situation. (If one prefers role language one can say that the worker is a part of the client's role network, though some of us do not find this particularly felicitous phraseology.) But just as there are times when the client misperceives other aspects of his situation, so there are times when he distorts or fails to understand casework and the caseworker. Here, too, previous life experiences may lead him to imagine hostility where it does not exist, to anticipate criticism, to fear domination, or to expect inappropriate gratification of dependency wishes. Or the client may simply lack knowledge of the nature of the casework "situation."

There is a tendency to think that there is something mysterious about the casework relationship, something that makes it fragile and untouchable except by the very expert. In fact, it is no more complicated than—but just as complicated as—any other relationship. In the type of reflective discussion we are considering, attitudes and responses to the caseworker are handled in the same way as other attitudes and responses. Where distortions or misunderstandings exist, the worker tries to straighten them out by demonstrating the realities of his behavior toward the client and the actual nature of treatment.[5] If the client accuses the worker of disinterest because he refuses to give him more time, the worker may explain that his time has to be scheduled, that it is not a matter of lack of interest and that they can go on with the same discussion in their next interview. If the client thinks the worker is angry, it is well to find out what he is basing this conclusion on. If he has misinterpreted a remark, the worker can indicate what he really meant and reassure the client that he is not angry. (We are assuming here that the worker is truly not angry. When, as occasionally happens, he *is* angry, the only way to handle it is to admit it and either explain why, or apologize, or do both.) If the client expects advice and is disappointed at not getting it, a simple explanation of why the worker doesn't think it will help may clear the air. Clients do not need long and theoretical explanations of treatment processes, but when they ask for information or when misunderstandings arise, it is not only appropriate but necessary that they be told enough about the nature of casework to enable them to participate constructively in the process. Participation in treatment is a role to which they are unaccustomed and which they may need to have explicitly defined.

The client needs, furthermore, to express and even at times to become aware of his own reactions to the worker and the treatment process. In general, it is very important to encourage clients to express their feelings toward the worker. If they are angry at being kept waiting, their annoyance should be aired or at least acknowledged. If they are dissatisfied with treatment and think it is a waste of time to come for interviews, the dissatisfaction should be brought into the open so that the reasons for it can be discussed and misunderstandings straightened out. If they fantasy that the worker is interested in a personal relationship with them, this, too, must be brought into open expression. Details of how this is done, of course, are guided by the worker's diagnostic understanding, and timing needs to be carefully watched.

The same principles hold here as in the other subdivisions of this type of treatment. The more the client can say things for himself, the better. Explanations and interpretations should be used sparingly, and chiefly when the client is unable to speak for himself, yet seems ready for understanding. Sometimes acceptance or reassurance about content has to be given before the client can acknowledge his thought. When the client has expressed his reactions, the worker makes a choice of the type of treatment procedure with which to continue.

It is sometimes held that caseworkers should not bring the client's thoughts about them to the surface except in intensive psychological treatment. Nothing could be further from the truth! It is not infrequently necessary to do just this in the most matter-of-fact, practical work. All casework depends in part upon establishing and maintaining a sound relationship between client and worker. Obstacles to such a relationship can occur in any form of treatment and can best be removed by recognition and discussion. We mentioned earlier the sustaining steps that must often be taken to convince the hard-to-reach client of the worker's good will. It is equally important in such cases to bring the client's distrust into the open so that misconceptions can be explored and, when possible, corrected. Hard-to-reach clients have often had very bad experiences with other social workers or with people whom they mistakenly thought to be social workers, or their neighbors or friends have had such experiences. It is natural that they should expect and fear similar treatment from the current worker. Realistic discussion can be a first step in opening up the possibility of a more constructive casework relationship.

It has taken a good many pages to describe the treatment processes involved in logical or reflective discussion of the person-situation configuration. This is not inappropriate, however, for the type of understanding we have examined is a central part of casework treatment with all types of clients and problems. In a great many cases, more extensive understanding is either unnecessary or inadvisable. Not infrequently, a limited use of techniques that promote dynamic or genetic understanding is added to the person-situation techniques, while occasionally, treatment involves the use of such techniques in a major way.

] *Environmental Work*

Before we turn to consideration of these other types of reflective discussion, however, it is important to emphasize that the four sets of procedures so far considered are just as germane to environmental work as they are to direct work with the client. An unfortunate tendency exists to think of work directed toward the environment as "manipulation" and therefore rather different in nature from contacts with the client. Actually the contrary is true. The skills needed for bringing about changes in the environment on the client's behalf are in most respects identical with those employed in direct work with the client. The range of procedures is somewhat different but the greater part of the range is common to both approaches.[6]

It is a grave mistake to assume that environmental work is simple and does not involve the same subtle understanding of people that direct work with clients requires. Many a failure in the effort to modify or use the environment is directly due to this type of oversimplification. In work with collaterals, contact does have to be established, and sustaining procedures can be of great value. The client is not the only person who may be afraid of criticism: so may be the teacher, the public assistance worker, the nurse, the landlord. Their way of handling their feelings may be defensive hostility, which leads them to attack either the worker or the client. They, too, may require assurance from the worker that he understands the problem they are up against and has not come to criticize; they, too, will respond better if they feel the worker is interested in their point of view and is willing to listen to the headaches the client has caused them. They, too, need encouragement concerning the efforts they have already made to deal with the situation.

Procedures of influence also have a place in environmental work, particularly when the worker is trying to modify the way in which another person is acting toward his client. Reenforcement and suggestion play a large role in such activity, with advice sometimes of value, and advocating and intervention occasionally necessary. Ventilation and catharsis are sometimes useful when the person being interviewed has a great deal of emotion about the client or the situation in which he and the client are involved. The landlord resolved to report a boy who has broken a window to the police may need to express a good deal of feeling about this and other misdeeds of the child-client before he is ready to consider a less punitive course of action. So, too, may the nurse or the teacher who has had to put up with an "acting-out" child or a landlord who sees the money he should have received as rent going into an Easter outfit. It goes without saying that intervention between a client and the natural consequences of "acting out" is itself a matter for careful diagnostic evaluation of both the internal and external aspects of the situation. Overprotection of the client may tempt him to further delinquency.

As in direct work, procedures for reflective discussion are of the greatest value with collaterals wherever they can be used, particularly in the process of helping one person to understand another. Often such understanding is brought about simply by telling the person about some aspects of the client and his life. At other times the worker may enter into the reflective process with the interviewee in much the same way as with a client, though the scope of the contact is more limited, often indeed a single interview. Often worker and "collateral" are actually thinking together to arrive at a solution in which the interviewee is involved.

The worker is less likely in such contacts to use procedures which involve thinking about the *self*, though this, too, can occasionally take place. On the other hand, it is often necessary to straighten out the relationship between the caseworker and the "environmental" person. The worker's intent or attitudes may need to be clarified before effective work can proceed. Naturally the details of achieving this type of understanding vary with the context in which they are being applied. The worker is less likely to bring the interviewee's reactions into the open, but he must be all the more sensitive to them and skillful in finding tactful ways of conveying his own true attitudes and role to the interviewee.

All that we have been saying, then, about sustaining work, directive procedures, ventilation and reflective discussion of the person-situation gestalt applies to work with people in the client's milieu as well as to contacts with the client himself—to indirect as well as direct treatment in the Mary Richmond sense. (On the other hand it is unlikely that the collateral will become involved in discussion of dynamic or genetic aspects of his reactions.) In contrast, a set of procedures not used in direct work with the client is included in environmental treatment. These procedures involve the direct marshalling of resources and services on the client's behalf. Sometimes these are services of the agency by which the worker is employed: financial assistance, visiting homemakers, medical care. Or other community resources may be brought to bear on the client's situation: day care, employment counseling, recreational facilities, educational resources, opportunities for group experiences, and the like.

While the client can do much to modify his own environment and whenever possible should be encouraged by the worker to find ways of bringing about needed changes himself, he cannot always do so. There are times when the client's problem is due to factors which are either completely beyond his control or beyond his current ability to modify. Basic needs for food, clothing, housing, and medical care may be unmet because of lack of money or a job, or, in the case of a child, because the parents are unable to carry out their responsibilities. Such needs can be met by the varied resources of the agency in which treatment is being carried on or by referral to another social agency or community resource in which the worker acts as an intermediary between the client and the second agency.

Intervention in the environment is also sometimes necessary to remove or lessen situational pressures that are causing strain for the client. The worker may, for example, arrange for the care outside the home of a physically or mentally handicapped child whose mother is no longer able to bear the burden of his care, or work out plans for the entrance of a senile parent into a nursing home when his care has become too much for his relatives to continue. Sometimes the pressure is in the form of a person in the environment, such as a school teacher who has taken a dislike to a child. The caseworker, by acquainting the teacher with the facts of the child's background, may be able to modify her reactions. If this is not possible, however, it may be necessary to discuss with the school the possibility of transfering the child to another classroom. A similar procedure is the work the medical social worker often does with doctors who have become discouraged about the possibility of helping certain patients because of their critical or hostile attitudes.

Sometimes the worker uses the environment to accomplish psychological objectives identical in nature with those we have been discussing under direct treatment. Relatives, friends, teachers, and doctors are sometimes in a far better position than the social worker to give sustaining help to a client. Often they do so spontaneously, but the caseworker can also motivate them to take this type of responsibility. Particularly with extremely anxious people, it is sometimes most helpful to enlist the interest of a friend or relative who likes the client and has a warm nature with a good deal of common sense and capacity for equanimity. It is surprising how often such people can be found if the worker is alert to the possibility and is not so tied to his desk that he never makes contact with them.

It is often true, too, that the worker is not the person in the best position to exercise direct influence in the client's life. A friend or relative, a club leader, doctor, clergyman, lawyer, or teacher often carries more influence with the client, is better qualified as an adviser in a particular area, and can be enlisted in the client's interest. Sometimes a visiting homemaker can take on an educational function that is in part advisory and in part a matter of increasing a woman's understanding of the practical problems of running a home. This was the key, for instance, to the resolution of a marital problem that was threatening to end in divorce for a very young, immature wife, whose failures in home management not only irritated her husband but also re-enforced her emotional childishness, discouraging her from grow-ing into a more adult role in any aspect of her marriage. The visiting homemaker's work went hand in hand with the direct efforts of the caseworker to help her to mature.

Similarly, people other than the worker, particularly other professionals, may be better able to help the client understand certain aspects of his situation.

After the client has discussed a problem with the appropriate medical, religious, educational or vocational expert, however, he may well need the caseworker's help in assimilating the infor-mation he has obtained and deciding upon his own course of action. While it is true that the client can sometimes take full responsibility himself for such consultations and does not need help from the worker in arranging them, the consultations are often more productive when the worker has helped in the selec-tion of the person to be consulted and can orient him in advance about the client and his problem.

Work on the client's behalf in and through the environment is at times a very important part of work with problems of per-sonal adjustment. It is a form of treatment employed in many cases, and in some it plays a decisive role. Any worker who is inept in applying his basic understanding and skills to work in the environment is seriously handicapped in his efforts to help clients with intra- or inter-personal problems.

NOTES

1. See Rosemary Reynolds and Else Siegle, "A Study of Case-work with Sado-Masochistic Marriage Partners," *Social Casework*, *40* (December, 1959), 545–551, for discussion of the use of re-flective or "logical" discussion along with other techniques. Sidney Berkowitz also implies the use of such techniques in his article "Some Specific Techniques of Psychosocial Diagnosis and Treatment in Family Casework," *Social Casework*, *36* (November, 1955), 399–406, though it is not directly spelled out. Gordon Hamilton, in the revised edition of *Theory and Practice of Social Casework*, uses the term "counseling" (p. 250) to designate many of the techniques referred to in this chapter. Under the term "logical discussion" brief reference is also made to this type of procedure as one of the techniques of supportive treatment in the 1953 classification of the committee of the Family Service Association of America and in the 1958 report of the staff com-mittee of the Community Service Society of New York.

2. For an excellent discussion of the use of this procedure with schizophrenics, see Margaret M. Heyman, "Some Methods in Direct Casework Treatment of the Schizophrenic," *Journal of Psychiatric Social Work*, *19* (Summer, 1949), 18–24.

3. For illustrations and further discussion, see Laura Farber, "Casework Treatment of Ambulatory Schizophrenics," *Social Casework*, *39* (January, 1958), 9–17; and Frances H. Scherz, "Treatment of Acting-out Character Disorders in a Marital Prob-lem," *Casework Papers*, *1956*, Family Service Association of America, New York, 1956.

4. Miriam Jolesch refers to this type of work in joint interviews with marital partners in her article "Casework Treatment of Young Married Couples," *Social Casework*, *43* (May, 1962), 245–251. She advocates the use of individual interviews initially, with joint interviews introduced when the clients have gained

enough self-understanding in individual interviews to be ready to examine their interactional patterns.

5. Good illustrations of this can be found especially in articles on work with schizophrenics and with the "hard-to-reach." See Margene M. Shea, "Establishing Initial Relationships with Schizophrenic Patients," *Social Casework, 37* (January, 1956), 25–29; Alice Overton, "Serving Families Who Don't Want Help," *Social Casework, 34* (July, 1953), 304–309; and *Casework Notebook,* Family Centered Project, Greater St. Paul, Community Chests and Councils, Inc., St. Paul, Minn., 1957.

6. Articles are rarely written on environmental treatment as such but good examples of the treatment procedures involved are often embedded in discussions of the total treatment of individuals who need casework help with problems that either involve unusual environmental pressures or deprivation, or require special adaptation from the environment for their amelioration. The following fairly recent articles describe a wide range of treatment through the environment:

Ruth D. Abrams and Bess S. Dana, "Social Work in the Process of Rehabilitation," *Social Work, 2* (October, 1957), 10–15.

Celia Benny, "Casework and the Sheltered Workshop in Rehabilitation of the Mentally Ill," *Social Casework, 41* (November, 1960), 465–472.

Berta Fantl, "Preventive Intervention," *Social Work, 7* (July, 1962), 41–47.

Mary L. Hemmy and Marcella Farrar, "Protective Services for Older People," *Social Casework, 42* (January, 1961), 16–20.

Fern Stewart Mauk, "Helping the Unemployed Father," *Social Casework, 43* (October, 1962), 422–427.

William B. Neser and Eugene E. Tillock, "Special Problems Encountered in the Rehabilitation of Quadriplegic Patients," *Social Casework, 43* (March, 1962), 125–129.

Lydia Rapoport and Kate S. Dorst, "Teamwork in a Rehabilitation Setting: A Case Illustration," *Social Casework, 41* (June, 1960), 291–297.

Kermit T. Wiltse, "The 'Hopeless' Family," *Social Work, 3* (October, 1958), 12–22.

VII

Reflective Consideration of Dynamic and Developmental Factors

WHEN A PERSON'S BEHAVIOR is so strongly influenced by intra-psychic forces of which he is not fully aware that he cannot act or even perceive realistically, consideration of the person-situation configuration may not suffice to enable him to deal adequately with his problem. If he is capable of developing understanding of these intrapsychic forces, it is desirable to help him to reflect on the dynamics of how they work, and at times also on their historical development. Often, but not necessarily, both types of understanding are involved. Considerable dynamic understanding can be developed, however, without going into the early life experiences which have shaped the present personality.

When we consider dynamic factors with the client, we are helping him to pursue intrapsychic reasons for his feelings, attitudes and ways of acting, the influence of one characteristic of his personality upon another—in other words, how his thoughts and emotions work. Often the client himself is aware—sometimes definitely and sometimes vaguely—of his unrealistic or inappropriate behavior. He himself may forge into the question of "why" without any prompting from the caseworker. At other times, the worker takes the first step by calling the inappropriateness or inconsistency to the client's attention. "Have you noticed that you don't have trouble in being firm with Betty but seem to be so afraid to be firm with Joe?"—to a mother who does not realize that her difficulty in disciplining her son springs from her desperate fear of losing his love. "I wonder how it is that you can be so understanding of the children and yet seem unable to try to understand your husband."—to a woman who is ordinarily very perceptive of other people's feelings but does not want to lessen the conflict with her husband because she fears the sex relationships he would want to resume if they were on good terms. "What do you suppose makes you keep on working for him if you dislike him so?"—to a man who constantly gets into fights with his employer.

Sometimes the client does not recognize the problem behavior; in other words, it is ego-syntonic and must become ego-alien if the client is to be motivated to try to understand and modify it. A mother who continually got into tempestuous fights at the table with her son saw her reactions only in terms of his slow and sloppy eating habits, which she felt made such scenes inevitable. After a substantial period of patient listening, rational discussion, and suggestions, the worker responded to the heated description of a stormy session with the comment, "You are like two children battling each other, aren't you?" The remark obviously carried a value judgment, for adults do not consider it a compliment to be told that they are behaving childishly. It carried force with this client because a strong relationship had been established between her and her worker which made her value the worker's good opinion. The fact that the worker rarely took a position of this sort gave it added significance. Sometimes the client, in response to such a stimulus, begins himself to think about reasons for his reactions; at other times, further comment is needed: "There seems to be something between you and George that we need to understand—what thoughts come to you about it?" In this situation the client went on first to the realization that she prolonged the scenes at table for the pleasure she derived from hitting her son and later to the discovery that she had identified her son with her husband and was taking out on him anger she did not dare to express directly to her husband.

A client will seek dynamic understanding of his thoughts or actions only when he feels some dissatisfaction with them, recognizes them as unprofitable or in some way as inappropriate or ego-alien. Until this attitude exists, dynamic interpretations will fall on deaf ears. When it does exist or has been brought into being, the client will often be able to arrive at understanding with relatively little use of interpretation by the worker.

Almost any aspect of the personality that is either conscious or near-conscious may come under scrutiny in this type of procedure. Occasionally, unconscious matters may come through, but in general casework is not designed to uncover unconscious material.* A very common area in which understanding is sought is that of defensive behavior, such as avoidance, defensive hostility, and the various mechanisms of turning against the self, projection, intellectualization, rationalization, suppression, inhibition, and isolation. "Have you ever noticed that sometimes people get angry when they are scared?" "I wonder if you weren't pretty edgy about having that talk with your brother-in-law, and in a way hit him before he had a chance to hit you." "Have you noticed how often you go off into this kind of theoretical discussion when I'm trying to get you to think about your own feelings toward Mary?" "You know, it's good that you try to learn so much about children, but sometimes I wonder if it isn't a way of avoiding letting yourself realize what strong feelings you have when Johnny acts this way." "Do you think your wife was really mad, or were you so angry yourself that you kind of expected she would be? What did she actually say at the beginning?" "Do you think that you are feeling depressed because you are really so mad at Fred but feel you can't let it out? Sometimes, you know, you can turn those angry feelings against yourself and then you feel depressed."

Initially defense mechanisms often have to be explained to clients because they are not familiar with the way they work and cannot be expected to arrive at this kind of understanding entirely on their own. Subsequently, however, clients are frequently able to spot their own use of a particular defense. One of the goals of this type of treatment is to enable them to do this for themselves.

The greatest care is necessary in work with defenses, however,

---

* See Chapter VIII.

for they are self-protective mechanisms used by the personality to ward off anxiety. They should not be abruptly "broken through," but rather "worked through" when evaluation indicates that the individual is able to bear the anxiety involved. For the most part, interpretations should be made tentatively, and certainly in an atmosphere of acceptance, which often needs to be put into words.[1]

Important as defense mechanisms are, they are by no means the only part of the personality under scrutiny in the process of dynamic understanding. Often certain superego characteristics need to be thought about, especially the oversensitivity of the severe conscience. The client who is too hard on himself may be helped by knowing that he is suffering from his own self-criticism rather than from the too-high requirements of others. The person who feels deeply hurt by the discovery of imperfections in himself may be helped if he recognizes that the demand for perfection is a function of his own personality. "Have you noticed how upset you get whenever anyone makes the slightest criticism of your work?" "You hold very high standards for yourself, don't you?" "I think you are harder on yourself than anyone else would be."[2]

One of the hazards of helping a person to become aware of superego severity is that the worker himself may appear to the client to be too lax in his standards. It is extremely important to avoid this; and great care must be taken not to seem to be sponsoring antisocial behavior. If the client does, nevertheless, react in this way, his reaction must be brought into the open and discussed, with the worker making it clear that he is not opposed to standards as such but to unrealistic or harmful severity of conscience.

In one of the cases read for the classification study the worker showed particular skill and adaptability to the client's needs in an instance of this sort. The client was the mother of a child who had been sent to the agency for treatment because of school failures inconsistent with his intelligence. She was a very religious woman who set very high standards for herself and who initially found treatment difficult because the need to recognize that she might be contributing to her son's troubles shattered her faith in herself as a good mother. Every attempt at developing her understanding was taken as a criticism from which she cringed. One of her underlying problems was her effort to suppress and inhibit all hostile impulses; in this she was not completely successful, and she felt extreme guilt over her failures. When the worker tried to reduce her self-condemnation, she thought the worker was trying to undermine her faith and principles.

One day she brought a Bible to the interview, and seemed quite agitated. When the worker asked her gently if she had brought the Bible for a special reason, she opened it to the famous letter of Paul to the Corinthians on love, reading particularly the verse, "When I was a child, I spake as a child, I felt as a child, I thought as a child; now that I am a man I have put away childish things," and she cried as she finished it. The worker said it was a beautiful letter and asked if she had ever thought of why it was written. Did she think perhaps Paul might have observed that many people brought into adulthood feelings and thoughts from childhood? Perhaps he wished to counsel men to put away these feelings and behave like adults. No one could quarrel with the ideals of love, charity, and understanding. Religion and psychiatry have the same goals; the only question is how to achieve them.

As the client still seemed confused, the worker put her thoughts in terms of gardening, a known interest of this client. "If you had a garden and weeds were choking out the good plants, you could cut off the tops of the weeds and the garden would look good, but the roots would still be there. Wouldn't it be better to pull out the roots? It would be harder but the results would be better. The same thing is true for human emotions," she went on to say. "Many of us try to hide our difficulties and stamp them down, but this takes energy that could be used for better things. It seems worthwhile to try to uproot the difficulties. The only method I know for uprooting them is to understand and face things that are painful and intolerable. I'm not arguing against the goals of religion, but sometimes I question the way it goes about attaining them." The client was silent for several minutes, and then said she was greatly relieved and that she had had no idea the caseworker had such deep understanding of her feelings.

A similar difficulty can occur under almost opposite circumstances. The client whose control of his impulses is tenuous may have great anxiety about a possible breakthrough of his hostile or sexual impulses if he allows himself to become aware of his desires. With such clients it is extremely important for the worker to make clear the distinction between recognizing a desire or wish and carrying it out, and to make explicit his position that he is not trying to encourage the client to act out his impulses but rather to recognize them so that he can control them more effectively. If this type of approach is to be used, however, careful diagnosis must have indicated that the client will not be unable to control his impulses if he becomes aware of them.

Excessively strong needs of the personality—especially dependence and, sometimes, narcissism—must also sometimes be understood when they are causing trouble for the individual. Insight can also be gained into unrealistic beliefs or persistently distorted perceptions as they influence behavior in harmful ways. One man in the cases read was unaware of his belittling of all women and of the way in which this was affecting his behavior toward his wife.

An important step in the process of dynamic understanding is the client's bringing reason and judgment to bear upon the characteristic of his personality and its functioning that has been brought to his attention. It was not enough for the religious mother to see that she was trying to handle her anger by suppressing it; she had to be able to think about what she was doing, to bring her own judgment to bear upon it. She had to be convinced that her way of handling her feelings was unsound before she was ready to try to give it up.

The client's reactions to the worker are a fruitful source of dynamic understanding. As defense mechanisms or personality characteristics such as fear of criticism or excessive dependency come into play in the client-worker relationship, they can be used to enable the client to see the inner workings of his personality in action. He can then use this understanding to recognize similar dynamics operating in other life experiences.

A case often flows back and forth between consideration of the person-situation configuration and consideration of personality dynamics. After a piece of dynamic understanding has removed or lessened some of the deterrents to realistic and appropriate perception and response, discussion usually returns to the person-situation realm, where progress can be made in relating better to other people. Even in those cases where reflecting on the dynamics of behavior is a major component in treatment, however, discussion never rests for long exclusively in that realm. Often dynamic understanding is needed—or possible—only fleetingly in the course even of lengthy treatment. It is always accompanied by sustaining measures, and may at times be supplemented by procedures of direct influence.

There is a close relationship between the procedure of promoting reflective consideration of internal dynamics and one of the subdivisions of person-situation consideration—that of encouraging the client to reflect upon his own feelings and reactions. The difference is that in the latter procedure no effort is made to understand the *way in which* a given feeling or way of behaving operates in the functioning of the personality. Attention goes directly to the consequences in reality, rather than to the inner workings of the psyche. *Awareness* of inner feelings is often the prelude to the pursuit of *understanding of the dynamics* of the behavior when such feelings cannot be sufficiently accounted for by the reality situation. Also it often happens that defenses prevent the client from recognizing feelings, beliefs, and attitudes that are causing difficulty in his life, and it may then be advisable to lead him to think about the operation of these defenses in order to enable him to become aware of the obstructed material. That is, the worker must turn to consideration of dynamic factors, resuming thereafter the effort to help the client understand the effect of his feelings or reactions on his situation.

Dynamic understanding is frequently achieved without going into the derivation of the personality characteristic under discussion. For this reason, consideration of the dynamics of intrapsychic factors is more common in casework than is consideration of the genetic, or historical, aspects of their development.

Encouragement of reflection upon genetic material is usually undertaken in an episodic way in casework, certain themes being explored as it becomes apparent that factors in the client's development are blocking improvement in his current social adjustment. The procedure is used to help the client become aware of the way in which certain of his present personality characteristics have been shaped by his earlier life experiences, and sometimes to modify his reactions to these experiences. It is sometimes necessary because certain "dysfunctional" characteristics cannot be overcome except by insight into experiences which contributed to their formation. The term "contributed" is used advisedly because casework never reaches all the determinants of a given phase of behavior. The ability to reach causative factors is a relative matter in any case. Even analysts readily acknowledge that, in addition to constitutional factors, early preverbal experiences which cannot be reached even by analysis are potent in preparing an initial "personality set" that profoundly influences the way later infantile and childhood experiences are received by the individual.[3]

In Chapter I we pointed out that the factor of reenforcement is extremely important in personality development. Harmful infantile experiences are sometimes overcome by health-inducing later ones, but often, unfortunately, events serve to confirm and reenforce the child's misconceptions or distorted generalizations. We have also referred to the balance of forces in the personality and to the way in which lessening the strength of damaging tendencies in the personality may enable healthier components to take the ascendancy in controlling and directing personality functioning. The purpose of encouraging the client to reflect upon his early life experiences is to bring about such a change in the personality. In general, casework does not attempt to reach unconscious infantile experiences but rather conscious or near-conscious later childhood and adolescent events, which can be considered genetic in the sense that they are contributory developmental experiences.

We must not assume that every time a client talks about his past life we are engaging in the process of developing genetic understanding, for most of the time this is not the case. Considerable exploration of the past is often part of our effort to arrive at diagnostic understanding. On the basis of such understanding, the worker may decide about the advisability of seeking to help the client arrive at a particular segment of genetic understanding. Second, a great deal of the client's talk about his past is for the purpose of catharsis. He may get considerable relief from telling the worker about painful events in his life and from expressing anger or grief about them. Third, the client very often brings in his past to justify his present feelings, attitudes, or behavior. He is not really trying to gain understanding for himself but rather to explain to the worker why he reacts as he does and, often, why he feels that he is right, or at least should not be blamed, for so reacting; in other words, the past is used as a defense of a present position. This type of defense is sometimes of great importance to the client, for it protects him from overly severe self criticism; it should be handled with great care and not be thoughtlessly or prematurely stripped away. Fourth, talking about the past can serve the purpose of evading thinking about the present. And finally, the client sometimes has the impression that the past is what the worker is interested in, and he talks about it in order to please the worker.

There are other times, however, when the client cannot modify unhealthy and unprofitable ways of acting except as he comes to understand some of their historical sources. Some clients quickly and spontaneously seek this kind of understanding. Others need help from the caseworker before they are ready and *able* to do so. (Apparent readiness needs to be carefully distinguished from real readiness. The current sophistication about Freudian ideas makes intellectualization about childhood events a particularly popular form of defense.)

Sound movement into consideration of genetic factors follows much the same pattern as that just described for moving into the dynamics of psychological functioning. The client's attention is drawn to inappropriate or inconsistent behavior. Sometimes he himself makes the choice of seeking dynamic or genetic understanding, reacting in one way or the other to the worker's pointing up of his problem. At other times the worker takes the lead in steering his thinking toward his earlier life. "Have you had feelings like this before?" "Does this make you think at all of similar things that have happened to you?" Or, more specifically, to a mother who is very upset by her son's just average school report; "How was it for *you* in school?" Or to a man who is unduly upset in mentioning his brother's failure in school; "You haven't told me much about your brother—what was he like?"[4]

Often in previous general exploration of the client's earlier life, or as the client has talked about his childhood for other reasons, the worker will have obtained clues to areas in the client's life that may be of significance in understanding a particular reaction. These clues should certainly be used in guiding the client's associations. A woman who was unreasonably resentful of what seemed to her neglect by her husband had earlier mentioned to the worker that her father had paid very little attention to her as a child. When she complained at length about her husband's neglect of her, the worker responded by asking her more about her father. The client, simply by thinking of the two parallel situations in juxtaposition, saw the similarity and asked if she could be carrying some of her feeling toward her father over to her husband.

But sometimes the worker must make the connection. A mother was unreasonably angry with her adolescent daughter for borrowing her costume jewelry. The worker was already aware of this woman's deep hostility to her mother and suspected that it was being displaced on her daughter. She also knew that as an adolescent and later the client had been required to carry too much of the financial burden of the home, so that she had been deprived of many things she wanted. The worker ventured the comment, "I wonder if Joan's taking your things that way doesn't arouse the same feelings you had as a girl when your mother didn't let you get pretty things for yourself." This touched off an outburst of feeling about the client's deprived adolescence, followed by the realization that she had been taking out on her daughter the stored-up feelings of her own childhood.

Two different procedures are involved in these illustrations. One is motivation of the client to think about his earlier life so that he will understand the present. The other is the actual making of the connection between past and present. Sometimes the client is fully aware of the early experiences and little or no anxiety is involved in recalling them; the problem is simply to enable him to recognize the influence of past on present. At other times the early feelings or experiences are to a degree hidden from view, for reasons which directly parallel the reasons for hiding *current* feelings and reactions (see Chapter VI). There may be fear of criticism of things that are perfectly well remembered, or an event may not be regarded as significant or pertinent to the interview, or memories may have been suppressed or repressed because of their painfulness. (Casework rarely brings truly *re*pressed material to light, although it deals with a great many *sup*pressed memories.)

There are times when the recollection of an event and recognition of its influence in current life may not be enough. Rather, the past event itself may need to be thought about and reevaluated so that the feelings about it are modified. If a woman who is very resentful that her father did not provide adequately for his family can be helped to realize that his failure was due to a combination of illness and national unemployment rather than to weakness of character or unwillingness to carry his family responsibilities, the amount of hostility she displaces upon her husband, a hard-working, conscientious individual who does not earn as much as she would like him to, may be substantially reduced. A woman who had felt that her parents discriminated against her by not letting her go to college was helped to recognize that she herself had not shown any interest in college. She thus saw that her parents might not have been discriminating against her but were perhaps unaware of her interest in further education. This recognition, in turn, not only led to a reduction of the client's hostility toward her parents and enabled her to have better current relationships with them, it also substantially reduced her feeling, which had carried over into all her adult relationships, that she was not loved and was somehow unworthy of love.

Before moving into the reevaluation process, it is often necessary to allow considerable ventilation of initial hostile feelings, partly because of the relief the client obtains from such an outpouring and from the worker's continued acceptance of him despite feelings about which he may feel quite guilty, but also because he will probably not be ready to reconsider his earlier relationships until he has had an opportunity for catharsis. If the worker attempts the reevaluation process prematurely, the client is apt to resent it, thinking that the worker is unsympathetic, is criticizing him, or is siding with his parent.

Obviously, however, reevaluation is useful only when the client has really misconstrued the earlier situation. Many times the early reality has in fact been extremely painful or even traumatic. Under such circumstances catharsis, plus sympathetic acceptance by the worker and realization of the way in which early events are unnecessarily influencing current life, is appropriate.

The relationship with the worker can also often be used as a source of genetic understanding. When the client is clearly reacting to the worker in terms of attitudes carried over from early life, the worker should, if consideration of genetic factors is deemed appropriate, help him to recognize what he is doing. "Do you think that you fear criticism from me as you did from your father?" "Do you see what you are doing? You are trying to get me to urge you to study just as your mother used to do. Then you will be angry at me for 'nagging,' just as you used to be angry at your mother." Obviously interpretations like these would be appropriate only after the client has achieved some measure of understanding of his feelings toward his parents. Sometimes such transference interpretations are necessary to straighten out the relationship with the worker so that treatment can proceed. They are also of great value in helping the client become aware of similar transferred reactions in other parts of his current life. The client is, so to speak, caught in the act. The worker—assuming he has sufficient self-awareness to be conscious of his own part in the interplay—is observing the client's reaction directly in a controlled situation. He is in an excellent position to make an accurate, convincing interpretation.

The same general principle holds here as in other kinds of understanding: the more the client can do for himself, the better. If he sees connections by himself or questions the accuracy of his understanding of earlier events, fine! Otherwise, the more the worker can limit himself to starting the client on an appropriate train of thought by a question, suggestion, or tentative comment, the better. Interpretations, when they are necessary, should be made tentatively, unless the worker is absolutely sure of their accuracy. In every form of understanding the worker should endeavor to minimize the client's dependence on him and encourage his ability to think for himself.[5] Flashes of genetic work occur in many cases which are mainly focused on the person-situation configuration, without a sustained effort to reach developmental material. Indeed we may think of both dynamic and genetic procedures as aids for the purpose of proceeding with person-situation understanding where such understanding is temporarily blocked by intrapsychic influences. And as with reflection upon dynamic factors, episodes of thinking about genetic factors are followed in treatment by a return to the person-situation configuration as soon as the new understanding has cleared the way for better perception and handling of current affairs. A strong foundation of sustaining work provides the client with the necessary confidence in the worker's good will and competence. When anxiety mounts as a result of some of the memories, feelings, and connections that are uncovered, sustaining procedures may be needed to carry the client through a difficult period of work. Procedures of direct influence and environmental procedures are usually not prominent when either genetic or dynamic understanding is being promoted, but they are not necessarily entirely absent.

The techniques discussed in this and the preceding chapter are not essentially different. In order to promote consideration of dynamic or genetic matters as a major part of treatment, however, the worker must, in addition to being skilled in all the other casework processes, be thoroughly familiar with the workings of the personality—of unconscious as well as of conscious factors— and with the way in which the personality develops and early life events find continued expression in the personality of the adult. The worker must be particularly sensitive to the nuances of the client's feelings, have considerable security when dealing with anxiety, and awareness and control of the nuances of his own reactions. He must also be free of the need to probe into his client's life to secure vicarious satisfaction either of his own curiosity or of his appetite for power, or for other narcissistic gratifications.

NOTES

1. Annette Garrett in her article "The Worker-Client Relationship" *Ego Psychology and Dynamic Casework,* Howard J. Parad, ed., (in Family Service Association of America, New York, 1958, pp. 53–54, 59–60) discusses this point in her section on transference and interpretation.

2. See Lillian Kaplan and Jean B. Livermore, "Treatment of Two Patients with Punishing Super-Egos," *Journal of Social Casework*, 29 (October, 1948), 310–316.

3. For elaboration of this point, see Phyllis Greenacre, ed., *Affective Disorders: A Psychoanalytic Contribution to Their Study*, International Universities Press, New York, 1953.

4. For illustrations, see Lucille N. Austin, "Dynamics and Treatment of the Client with Anxiety Hysteria," in *Ego Psychology and Dynamic Casework*, Howard J. Parad, ed., Family Service Association of America, New York, 1958; and Hank Walzer, "Casework Treatment of the Depressed Parent," *Social Casework*, 42 (December, 1961), 505–512.

5. A very useful discussion of the timing and methods of interpretation is to be found in Ralph Ormsby, "Interpretations in Casework Therapy," *Journal of Social Casework*, 29 (April, 1948), 135–141.

VIII

Casework
and the
Unconscious

WE HAVE REFERRED SEVERAL TIMES to the tantalizing question of how much casework deals with unconscious material. The question has many aspects. The caseworker certainly needs to know a great deal about the unconscious: its nature and the generally recognized ways in which it plays a part in the mental life and behavior of the individual. Such knowledge is essential both for diagnostic understanding and for treatment of problems of inter-personal adjustment,[1] for the unconscious as well as the conscious is always involved in such problems.

It is not in diagnosis alone that the worker touches the unconscious, for it is also invariably involved in treatment. The client's reaction to the worker is influenced by unconscious as well as by conscious factors. Whether or not transference reactions are brought into the open, they are operative and in turn are affected by the worker's behavior. Sustaining procedures often speak more to the unconscious than to the conscious. The client may not be able to tell you how he has come to trust the worker, but somehow something within him has said, "This one I can trust"—or "This one I can*not* trust." The unconscious often reveals itself by tone of voice or gesture, signs to which the worker must be attuned, for often he must recognize fear, hostility, and distrust before the client himself comes to know the meaning of his own feelings, or else, he must sense the greatly feared positive feelings toward him which the client may cover by outward hostility.

Furthermore, the worker's comments often are directed to the unconscious even though no unconscious material is openly discussed. One of the cases read for the study of classification offers a very interesting instance of the use of this procedure. The client involved was a woman with a very high degree of repressed infantile hostility. Unconsciously she still wanted to destroy anyone who thwarted her, but she was very much afraid of this primitive desire. She had covered it up with a cringing, whining, self-abasing personality and was strongly overidentified with suffering in other people. Although her destructive impulses were well under control, her fear of hurting others was so strong that she constantly felt responsible for other people's suffering and overly responsible for the ills that befell her children. She had had an extremely traumatic childhood in which, during the war, she had witnessed the destruction of members of her family, including a younger brother, at a time when infantile death wishes can be expected to be strong. The underlying problem in this client's case was thought to be too severe to respond to casework directed toward genetic understanding. But an effort was made to give her some relief from the constant guilt aroused by her unconscious wishes and her unconscious belief in their magical power.

The work was strongly sustaining, in the hope that a consistently giving and accepting relationship with the worker over a long period of time would to some degree counteract the effects of the client's early life, at least during a period in which her daughter could be given help to withstand her mother's negative influence on her growth. The sustaining process was combined with some directive work particularly concerned with handling the daughter, as much reflective consideration of the person-situation configuration as she was capable of, and a great deal of catharsis about both past and present. The client had a quick mind and a good sense of humor on which the worker capitalized. One day, the client was commiserating at length about the men who had been wounded and imprisoned in Cuba. Her whole demeanor, as she spoke, implied that she felt responsible for their suffering. The worker, with a twinkle in his eye, said dryly that of course she would need to feel especially bad about this because she was there herself in the forces which captured them when they landed. The spontaneous response—"No, I was not"— was followed by a slight rueful smile of recognition and a lightening of the whole tone of the interview. Subsequently, the phrase, "Like in Cuba, I suppose," could be counted on to interrupt similar self-castigating episodes. Later, in talks about her daughter, the client's childhood jealousy of her brother and consequent guilt over her harmful wishes toward him were discussed in terms of the mistake children make of thinking that their wishes will actually cause harm to happen. In none of these interviews was the client's own repressed hostility brought to the fore. Nevertheless, the worker had spoken, as it were, to the unconscious, and a shift seemed to occur in the client's unconscious belief that her own deadly wishes would cause her daughter to commit suicide.

This case, parenthetically, was a remarkable illustration of the way in which the unconscious can create its own environment. The client's daughter had somehow become aware of her mother's underlying fear, and sensed that to threaten suicide was the most successful way both to hurt her mother and to express her own great hostility to her. The mother's unconscious behavior, by eliciting the daughter's threats, had created a situation which raised the possibility that she would once again feel responsible for the death of a child.

The technique of speaking to the unconscious is often used in work with adolescents or young adults of the same sex as the worker, where identification with the worker is encouraged in order to strengthen femininity or masculinity—in effect to say to the client's unconscious, "You don't need to be afraid of growing up. It is good to want to be a sexually mature adult," and thus to counteract fears engendered in the unconscious by unloving or restrictive parents.[2]

] *Unconscious or Preconscious?*

The question in need of clarification, however, is whether the caseworker brings unconscious material to consciousness. This is a controversial subject and one of considerable importance for casework, for it has implications both for the education of caseworkers and for professional responsibility. In discussing it, we are referring to work with adults, *not* to work with children. With children the line between unconscious and preconscious is much harder to draw.[3]

Much of the confusion on the issue stems from the fact that there are different formulations about the unconscious and the preconscious in psychoanalysis itself. Before going into these differences, it may be well to recall the kind of content that casework does reach. We have indicated that much of casework is concerned with thoughts that enter consciousness easily when the client's attention is turned to them. But we have also referred repeatedly to the client's discussing "hidden" feelings, vague and obscure thoughts and memories, of which he had not been aware. We have noted that clients can become aware of defenses of which they were not previously conscious and that they can recall childhood experiences which they seemed to have forgotten. Certainly they often become aware of feelings and thoughts, especially ego-dystonic feelings and thoughts, which they not only had never before put into words but had never allowed themselves consciously to experience.

This area of hidden thoughts is neither freely accessible nor stubbornly inaccessible. In psychoanalysis it seems to constitute a no-man's land that is sometimes assigned to the unconscious and sometimes to the preconscious, so perhaps it is small wonder that caseworkers too are confused. Freud himself was none too consistent on the subject. For the most part he wrote as if he were restricting the preconscious to content that needs only "attention cathexis" to become conscious, that is, to thoughts which the individual can bring into consciousness merely by turning his attention to them—thoughts that are completely accessible. All else seemed to be considered part of the unconscious, held from consciousness by countercathexis, or by the "censor" which would not allow material that would be offensive to the other parts of the personality to emerge. Even in his 1915 article on the unconscious,[4] however, Freud was not entirely satisfied with this simple division of the sheep from the goats. "Study of the derivatives of the unconscious," he said, "will altogether disappoint our expectations of a schematically clear division of the one mental system from the other."[5] And further, "A very great part of the preconscious material *originates in the unconscious, has the characteristics of the unconscious and is subject to a cen-sorship before it can pass into consciousness.*[6] Another part of the preconscious can become conscious without any censorship." The existence of a *"second censorship, located between the sys-tem's preconscious and conscious, is proved beyond question."*[7] Freud here seems to be referring to the very kind of content that emerges in response to casework techniques. Until comparatively recently, however, little attention has been paid in analytic litera-ture to this notion of preconscious content that is not readily accessible. The tendency has been to consider such material as part of the unconscious, some of it at least being referred to as "derivative" unconscious material.

This tendency may have been due to the fact that *unconscious* was defined not only in terms of its inaccessibility but also by cer-tain functional qualities. Unconscious content was said to operate by means of the "primary process," conscious content by the "sec-ondary process." The primary process is characterized by mobil-ity of the psychic energies, dominance of the pleasure principle and striving toward gratification discharge, absence of a time sense, the use of displacement and condensation in thinking, non-recognition of contradictions, and so on. The secondary process is characterized by less mobility of the psychic energies, dominance of the reality principle and the capacity for delayed discharge, a sense of time, recognition of contradictions, and the preeminence of other logical modes of thought.

Meanwhile, however, another tendency has existed in analytic writings to distinguish between *unconscious* and *conscious* pri-marily in terms of relative accessibility. Kubie, for instance, limits the preconscious to "borderline processes of which we are unconscious but which can be made conscious relatively easily merely by taking thought."[8] E. Pumpian-Mindlin writes, "Pre-conscious material is that of which we may not be fully aware but which can be easily recalled. Unconscious material however consists of all that which not only can not be recalled 'at will' but also cannot be recovered except through special means, e.g., free association work in the analysis itself or spontaneously under unusual circumstances 'in a flash' so to speak."[9] The assumption was widespread that unconscious material could in general be reached only by free association, hypnosis, or the use of drugs which suspended the operation of the repressing forces.

It seems to have been more or less taken for granted that the qualities of being ruled by the primary process and of being inaccessible usually occurred together. Perhaps because their techniques gave analysts ready access to both preconscious and unconscious material, their attention was not called to the theoretical question of whether a given piece of content emerged in response to free association or independently of it.

In more recent years, with the emergence of more concern about the nature of the ego—especially in the work of such theorists as Hartmann, Kris, Lowenstein, and Rapaport—interest has turned to the preconscious. Kris comments on three problems that arise concerning the accessibility of preconscious material:

> First, not all preconscious processes reach consciousness with equal ease. Some can only be recaptured with considerable effort. What differences exist between the former and the latter?
>
> Second, preconscious mental processes are extremely different from each other both in content and in the kind of thought processes used; they cover continua reaching from purposeful reflection to fantasy, and from logical formulation to dreamlike imagery. How can these differences be accounted for?
>
> Third, when preconscious material emerges into consciousness the reaction varies greatly. The process may not be noticed—the usual reaction if the preconscious process is readily available to consciousness. But emergence into consciousness can be accompanied by strong emotional reactions. How may we account for these reactions?[10]

Kris then proceeds to say that there appear to be mobile energy discharges in such preconscious activities as daydreaming, that such dreams play the same role of wish fulfillment as night dreams, that they may be ruled by the pleasure principle and that they utilize nonlogical thought processes in much the same way as the unconscious. He goes on to point out that a good deal of creative thinking goes on without conscious awareness during the "elaboration phase," and when it emerges into consciousness may even appear to the individual as something that comes from without—inspiration. He draws attention also to "preconscious lapses" of memory—temporary withdrawals from consciousness of content that can later be recovered without special techniques.

Kris finally suggests that three conditions may exist for eliminating "the countercathexis between preconsciousness and con-

sciousness": full cathexis of neutral energy, or attention; ego
syntonicity in the intersystemic sense, or freedom from conflict
between id and superego; and ego syntonicity in the intrasystemic sense, or harmony among the various ego functions.[11]

Rapaport, drawing upon a number of other writers, goes even
further, suggesting hierarchical series in which the various qualities of the primary and secondary processes exist in varying
degrees. "Different degrees of difficulty are encountered in making various daydreams conscious, in holding on to them once
they are conscious; this indicates that a countercathectic energy-
distribution controls the transition from preconscious to conscious
processes."[12] Again, "It is likely we deal here not with only two
but with a whole hierarchy of such controlling energy-distribu-
tions. At any rate, it seems that consciousness is not an all-or-
none proposition; rather there exists a continuous series of its
forms."[13]

These writings provide a most useful theoretical explanation
for the empirical findings of casework about the emergence of
hidden material. We do not use free association, hypnosis, or
drugs, but we do repeatedly have clients talk about matters of
which they have not previously been aware and of which pre-
sumably they could not have become conscious without the
intervention of the caseworker. Is it not possible that casework
promotes the emergence of the less accessible part of the preconscious by meeting the three conditions laid down by Kris?
Sometimes we merely increase the hypercathexis of this content
by drawing the client's attention to it. At other times we increase
its ego syntonicity through an accepting attitude and "eductive"
interviewing methods, either reducing the conflict between the
id and the superego by guilt-reducing comments, or else lessening the intra-ego conflict, as, for instance, by explaining that
contrary emotions, such as love and hate, can exist side by side
without the logical necessity for assuming that the presence of
the one indicates that the other is not genuine.

A few years ago the author attempted to explain the basis for
the emergence of hidden material in casework as follows:

> The term "unconscious" refers to memories, thoughts, and
> fantasies which, upon entering consciousness, were so anxiety-
> creating that they were automatically repressed, and material of

a similar or even greater anxiety-producing potential which was never even allowed to reach consciousness. These consist of memories, thoughts, and fantasies representing infantile destructive and sexual impulses and wishes, material concerning matters strongly prohibited or invoking punishment by parents especially in preschool years, later traumatic events, and derivatives so closely related to these matters that to recall them would involve danger of a break-through of the associated material. If casework deals with unconscious material at all it is only in a minor way with these derivatives.

The term "preconscious" covers a wide range of memories, thoughts, and fantasies. It includes, first, material that differs in no way from conscious material except that it is not at the moment the subject of attention. Second, it applies to material that has relatively little cathexis, either because it originated very long ago or was not very important to the person. Third, it refers to suppressed material—that is, ideas that were so anxiety-arousing that by more or less conscious choice or effort they were pushed out of consciousness. Fourth, it refers to material that has never been fully conscious but would arouse anxiety comparable to that of suppressed ideas if it entered consciousness. There is a vast amount of content in these last two types of preconscious material and it is primarily this content, I believe, that casework deals with in . . . developing self-awareness.[14]

The anxiety referred to is created by the intersystemic and intrasystemic conflicts noted by Kris. "Suppression" is a term analysts sometimes use for the force—the countercathexis—that operates between certain parts of the preconscious and the conscious. Our casework experience, in other words, is consistent with the formulations of Kris and Rapaport, and greatly illuminated by them.

] Levels of Consciousness in Casework Treatment

There was a period in the late forties when many of us believed that casework in "insight development" has as its aim the bringing of true unconscious material to consciousness. I am inclined to think that for the most part we were confusing "unconscious" with "*not* conscious" and were actually dealing with preconscious suppressed material. The Family Service Association of America committee study of classification (referred to in Chapter IV) attempted to locate illustrations of cases of such "insight development" in a wide range of family service agencies but reported finding none. Frequent sampling by myself and others of material from psychiatric and family agencies in which such cases might be expected to be found has confirmed my impression that very few cases in casework agencies uncover unconscious material in the strict sense of that term. In those few that do there is almost always a special condition: either the worker is operating directly under psychiatric supervision and consulting regularly and frequently on the case, with help from the psychiatrist on details of treatment, or he has secured special training from psychiatrists beyond his casework training. In the cases read for my classification study—and I asked particularly for illustrations of the agencies' "deepest" work—the goal of bringing clearly unconscious material to the surface was found in the cases of only two workers. On inquiry, I learned that one of the workers involved had originally had at least partial training as a lay analyst and the other was an experienced caseworker nearing the end of a long personal analysis who said that she often discussed the case with her own analyst. Occasionally a psychiatric agency offers direct psychoanalytic supervision to caseworkers. A few workers who have left agencies for private practice have associated themselves with analysts who "control" their work; others have gone through a definite course of training for this work where such a course is available to non-medically trained personnel. There is no reason why caseworkers who secure such added preparation should not go on to the practice of what is essentially psychoanalytic therapy. (Not psychoanalysis proper.) But it should be recognized that casework training has not in itself prepared them to do this, though it may have given them an excellent base from which to proceed. Certainly, a basic requirement for work with the unconscious would be a successful personal analysis.*

Caseworkers occasionally mistakenly think that a personal analysis in itself qualifies them to do psychoanalytic therapy. The ordinary psychoanalysis is a therapeutic procedure designed to rid the

---

* This is not a requirement of casework training, though many caseworkers have by their own choice undertaken it. For a similar point of view, see Lucille N. Austin, "Qualifications for Psychotherapists, Social Caseworkers," *American Journal of Orthopsychiatry*, 26 (1956), 47–57.

patient of neurotic symptoms and character disturbances which are causing malfunctioning. It often achieves these goals, and with it a much-to-be-cherished maturing of the personality, but such success does not mean that the particular features essential for deeply probing therapeutic work have necessarily been achieved. Furthermore, analysis alone is no preparation for this type of work. Intensive study of the unconscious and of therapeutic procedures in addition to close supervision by an analyst during a training period are minimum additional requirements of preparation for such work. Certainly even a moderately successful personal analysis is of professional value to the caseworker. It lessens hostilities and personality distortions that may interfere with realistic perception of the client and freedom to relate to his needs in a therapeutic way. It deepens the worker's understanding of the workings of the personality and of the unconscious. Yet despite the fact that it unquestionably adds to the therapeutic capabilities of anyone who undertakes it, the basic aptitude for therapeutic work varies so greatly that some workers who have not undergone analysis are superior to others who have had its benefits.

If the central focus of casework is conscious material and the various levels of preconscious material, by what means do we avoid going more deeply than we are prepared for into the unconscious? This becomes a real issue only in those types of treatment which involve dynamic or genetic content or promotion of self-awareness in the person-situation configuration. One's first consideration in using these processes is a diagnostic one: How strong are the forces of repression and suppression in this person? If, as in psychosis, the repressing forces are weak and material that would normally be unconscious is already breaking through, the worker must be extremely careful not to set in motion a process that will accelerate the breakthrough. He can help the psychotic or near-psychotic client to understand matters of which he is already aware; such understanding can sometimes be very helpful in combination with constant effort to strengthen the client's relationship to reality and to bring about greater control of his id impulses. But in work with the psychotic, the caseworker should not become involved in the pursuit of hidden material, for such pursuit may lead to a breakthrough of unconscious matter with which the worker is not equipped to deal.[15]

Except with psychotic or near-psychotic individuals, one does not need to be afraid of breaking into the unconscious as long as casework techniques are adhered to. Except where the ego is seriously impaired, the forces of repression provide a strong barrier to the unconscious. Casework customarily uses a number of procedures that tend to *avoid* overcoming repression. Most of these are well known. The once-a-week interview discourages too great intensity and regression in the transference and keeps the client's investment in introspection at a lower level than would more frequent interviews. The seating of the client face to face with the worker at a desk maximizes the reality elements in the relationship, rather than promoting extensive transference reactions. While the worker often understands some of the unconscious significance of dreams and symbols, he interprets them in ways that refer to conscious and preconscious material rather than using them as means to beckon unconscious memories to the surface. Reporting of dreams is generally discouraged, though sometimes when the client does bring them in their manifest content can be profitably discussed.

An illustration of how dream content may be used without interpreting its unconscious significance to the client occurs in the following: A client dreamed that a man fell by her window, and that she then saw him smashed dead on the ground, with arms and legs cut off. The dead man got up and kissed her with "a kiss of death." The dream occurred during a period when the client was extremely angry at a man with whom she was living but who would not marry her. The dream so upset her that she had to go to sleep with one of her children because of an impulse to throw herself out the window. Much of the meaning of the dream was clear. The client wished that her lover would die, and in both the symbolism of the dream and afterward in reality, she wanted to kill herself as punishment for her wish. She was all the more frightened by the dream and by her own subsequent impulse because she came from a culture in which dreams were taken very seriously and were thought to portend the future. It was important to lessen both her continuing anxiety and the magical quality with which she invested dreams. The worker spoke of dreams as childlike wishes, and of the very good reasons the client had for feeling a great deal of anger toward her friend. He then explained how in dreams our minds operate like children's in thinking that a wish can actually take effect: hence the client's need to punish herself. He was able to relate this discussion to earlier discussions about the wishes of her small children, pointing out the naturalness of their sometimes wishing that certain people were dead, and then reacting with fear of punishment. He did not pursue the latent meaning of the dream by asking for associations or by commenting on the obvious symbolic significance of the man's passing her window and the cut-off arms and legs.

The use of "eductive" interviewing is perhaps the most important factor distinguishing casework methods from those designed to elicit unconscious mental content. This distinction is not always as clearly understood as it should be, but the difficulty is in part a semantic one. Caseworkers sometimes maintain that they do use free association because they encourage their clients to speak as freely as possible. Actually, by this they usually mean that they are giving their clients permission and encouragement to talk about whatever is troubling them. They are not making it a condition of treatment that the client tell them everything that comes into his mind. But it is precisely this condition that distinguishes free association. In free association the patient really is not free to select what he says; he is *bound* by the obligation to share all his thoughts. All patients at one time or another violate this rule, but when they do the content is brought all the more forcefully to their attention, and they return to it again and again until it has to be blurted out. Until it is, they know they are violating the fundamental analytic rule and feel guilt and embarrassment which only make more trouble for them.

Now the casework client, filled with hostility toward his worker, is under no obligation to say out loud the thought that crosses his mind—you look like Mrs. Astor's pet pony! The analytic patient is. The client does not feel forced to speak of matters of which he is deeply ashamed, nor is he required to produce seemingly irrelevant or nonsensical thoughts. The patient must. *Permission* to speak freely and the *obligation* to say whatever comes to mind are very different things indeed. This voluntary selection of communications not only excludes from the casework interview the very leads that are nearest to the unconscious, but equally important, it also removes one of the dynamics that produces the regressive transference so important in analytic work. The patient who is under obligation to speak and does not do so feels like a disobedient child. If he speaks against his will, he still feels like a child who has been forced to do something unpleasant or to confess a fault or misdoing to a parent. This feeling promotes the regressive transference which helps the client to relive his early childhood and infantile years with the analyst and provokes the repressed memories of fantasies and experiences that have contributed to his illness. Casework does not seek to establish this type of transference.

] *Casework and Other Professions Practicing Psychotherapy*

This discussion leads naturally to the question of the relationship between casework and other professions practicing psychotherapy. It should be clear by now that there are fundamental differences between psychoanalysis and casework, despite the fact that modern casework is based upon psychoanalytic personality theory and has many principles in common with psychoanalysis. Similarly, casework also differs from those forms of treatment usually designated as psychoanalytic therapy or psychoanalytic psychotherapy.[16] These are forms of treatment which, although they do not attempt as complete an analysis of the unconscious as is characteristic of psychoanalysis itself, do explore unconscious material to varying degrees. The range of treatment among these therapies is very great.[17] Some are close to full analysis while others, insofar as the extensiveness of their work in the unconscious is concerned, are close to casework. This group of therapies embraces many different points of view. It includes some of the work of Freudian-trained analysts with patients for whom full analytic exploration of the unconscious is either unnecessary or inadvisable, some of the treatment carried on by schools of thought such as Horney's in which it is believed that it is unnecessary to go into infantile fantasy life as fully as Freudians do, and the work of therapists who are Freudian oriented and have undergone some discipline in work with the unconscious but have not secured full analytic training.

The general term "psychotherapy" is sometimes used specifically to designate these various types of treatment. When so used to refer to treatment which relies upon the uncovering and understanding of previously unconscious material, it distinguishes these therapies from casework. In common parlance, however, the word is not so restricted. Both psychiatrists and psychologists commonly use it indiscriminately to refer to any type of psychological treatment carried on under their auspices. It is very important also to understand that psychiatry and psychoanalysis are by no means identical professions. Psychiatry diagnoses and treats various forms of mental disturbance according to the disciplines of a variety of schools of thought. Relatively speaking, only a very small number of psychiatrists have completed psychoanalytic training. American psychiatry was slower than casework to study and accept the Freudian point of view, and to this day many psychiatrists use Freudian ideas only superficially, if at all. When conducted by the latter type of psychiatrist, treatment referred to as psychotherapy not only does not involve work with the unconscious but often is not even based upon understanding of the unconscious. On the other hand, there is a large group of psychiatrists who, like caseworkers, have found psychoanalytic theory extremely useful and have studied and used it in various ways in their treatment, but who also, like caseworkers, have not had specific training in the direct handling of unconscious material. Some of the work of this group is very close to casework in its general boundaries, though it usually does not include much work with the environment. There is also considerable variation among psychiatrists in the emphasis they place on directive versus rational techniques.

Among clinical psychologists—those psychologists most likely to be practicing psychotherapy—similar variations exist. Some have assimilated Freudian concepts in a fashion parallel to their psychiatric and casework colleagues. A larger group has tended toward eclecticism, with Freudian concepts contributing in varying degrees to the blend. Other psychologists follow Rogerian methods, and a very small group, mostly Europeans, are fully trained lay analysts.

When the term "psychotherapy" is used in a broad sense covering all these variations in treatment, it is obvious that it can equally well apply to casework when casework methods are brought to bear upon psychological problems[18] (as is always the case when the overt problem is one of interpersonal adjustment).

The caseworker should be oriented to these variations in treatment in the related professions both for the purposes of collaborative work and for referrals. When one is considering whether to refer a client from a caseworker to a psychiatrist for "psychotherapy," one needs to be informed both about the nature of the client's needs and about the kind of treatment that will be available. If referral is for the purpose of enabling the client to make use of deeper treatment than casework can offer, one must make sure that the psychiatrist to whom the referral is being made is actually offering this type of treatment. Obviously such treatment cannot be provided in a clinic offering fifteen-minute appointments once a month, or with a therapist whose competence does not include psychoanalytic psychotherapy.

This is not to say that one would not make referrals to a psychiatrist or clinic that does not offer some form of psychoanalytic therapy. Particularly in psychoses, psychosomatic illnesses, and some severe neuroses, a careful decision must be made as to whether treatment under medical rather than non-medical auspices may not be more advisable. Some patients get more security from a medical doctor; for others, physical and psychological care must be so closely coordinated that simultaneous treatment under separate auspices is not advisable; for others, the risk of further breakdown may be so great that accessibility of hospital care is important and only treatment under medical supervision is advisable; and psychiatric care will enable still others to take advantage of the possibilities offered by modern psychopharmacology, especially the use of tranquilizing and energizing drugs.

Variations in psychiatric training are also important in choosing agency consultants and instructors for schools of social work. Since the caseworker who identifies himself in point of view with this book needs considerable knowledge of Freudian theory and draws upon Freudian treatment principles, the more thoroughly the consultant or instructor is trained in this point of view, the more helpful he will be. Casework is certainly not, however, a "branch" of psychoanalysis. It has developed its own blend of treatment, resting in part on its own special knowledge, values, responsibilities, and place in society. It is responsible for deciding for itself what body of psychological knowledge and theory will best enable it to fulfill its purposes. When the choice falls, as it has in recent years for most of casework, upon psychoanalysis, it becomes the duty of caseworkers and consulting or teaching analysts to work out together what content will be of value for students and workers. In the end, casework must be responsible for itself.

NOTES

1. An excellent discussion of the worker's need to understand the unconscious is found in Ner Littner's "The Impact of the Client's Unconscious on the Caseworker's Reactions," in *Ego Psychology and Dynamic Casework*, Howard J. Parad, ed., Family Service Association of America, 1958, pp. 73–87.

2. An illustration of this procedure with adults can be found in Yonata Feldman, "A Casework Approach Toward Understanding Parents of Emotionally Disturbed Children," *Social Work, 3* (July, 1958), 23–29.

3. Jeanette Regensburg and Selma Fraiberg deal with this question in the pamphlet *Direct Casework with Children*, Family Service Association of America, New York, 1957. Fraiberg discusses specifically some differences between work with adults and with children, recommending substantial additional training for caseworkers doing "psychotherapy" with children. She uses

the term "psychotherapy" in the restricted sense which parallels the use of the term "psychoanalytic therapy" in this book. See her p. 21, and pp. 143–145 of this chapter.

4. Sigmund Freud, "The Unconscious" (1915), in *Collected Papers*, vol. IV, The Hogarth Press, London, 1949, pp. 98–136.

5. *Ibid.*, p. 122.

6. *Ibid.*, p. 124. Emphasis added.

7. *Ibid.*, p. 125. Emphasis added.

8. Lawrence S. Kubie, "Problems and Techniques of Psychoanalytic Validation and Progress," in *Psychoanalysis as Science*, E. Pumpian-Mindlin, ed., Basic Books, 1952, p. 91.

9. E. Pumpian-Mindlin, "The Position of Psychoanalysis in Relation to the Biological and Social Sciences," in *Psychoanalysis as Science*, E. Pumpian-Mindlin, ed., Basic Books, 1952, p. 146.

10. Ernst Kris, "On Preconscious Mental Processes," *Psychoanalytic Quarterly*, 19, 4 (1950), 542.

11. *Ibid.*, p. 556.

12. David Rapaport, *Organization and Pathology of Thought*, Columbia University Press, New York, 1951, p. 718.

13. *Ibid.*, p. 719.

14. Florence Hollis, "Personality Diagnosis in Casework," in *Ego Psychology and Dynamic Casework*, Howard J. Parad, ed., Family Service Association of America, 1958, p. 85.

15. See Paul Federn, "Principles of Psychotherapy in Latent Schizophrenia," *American Journal of Orthopsychiatry*, 1 (April, 1947), 129–144, and "Psychoanalysis of Psychoses," *Psychiatric Quarterly*, 17 (1943), 3–19, 246–257, 470–487.

16. See also Lucille N. Austin, "Qualifications for Psychotherapists, Social Caseworkers," *American Journal of Orthopsychiatry*, 26 (1956), 47–57.

17. For Freud's thinking about variations from pure analytic techniques, see *Lines of Advancement in Psychoanalytic Therapy* (1919), v. 17 of *Standard Edition of the Complete Psychological Works of Sigmund Freud*, Hogarth Press, London, 1955, p. 168.

18. A usage followed by Nathan W. Ackerman in "The Training of Caseworkers in Psychotherapy," *America Journal of Orthopsychiatry*, 19 (January, 1949), 14–24, and by many others.

For discussions of the place of casework in psychotherapy see Annette Garrett, "Historical Survey of the Evolution of Casework," *Journal of Social Casework, 30* (June, 1949), 219–229; and Gordon Hamilton, "Psychoanalytically Oriented Casework and Its Relation to Psychotherapy," *American Journal of Orthopsychiatry, 19* (April, 1949), 209–223.

IX

The
Client-Worker
Relationship

BASIC TO ALL CASEWORK TREATMENT is the relationship between worker and client. Three aspects of this relationship are of particular significance: it is a means of communication between the two people involved in treatment; and it is a set of attitudes, and a set of responses, expressed in behavior. Since attitudes and responses are basic ingredients in communication, we will take up these two aspects first.

] Realistic Attitudes and Responses

What attitudes and responses exist between worker and client? We customarily think of them as being of two kinds: realistic and unrealistic.[1] Unrealistic attitudes and responses are called transference and countertransference. Realistic attitudes, appropriate to the situation, will differ among clients in accordance with variations in the significance the treatment situation has for them. Almost universally, when a person comes for help with interpersonal problems, he experiences some anxiety. This is because he usually has some awareness that the problem lies partly within himself. Even when he has defended himself against recognizing this, it is still present underneath and a realistic cause of anxiety. Characteristically he also experiences discomfort about entering into a dependent relationship. To come for help signifies weakness, despite the fact that the recognition of the need for help and the decision to come for it require strength. One is acknowledging that another person is wiser or stronger and taking the first step in allowing oneself to come under the influence of another unknown or little known person. Such feelings are almost universal, but the intensity with which they are experienced will vary. Anxiety will be greater, for instance, when the client is consulting the worker about matters in which he has a vital interest than about peripheral matters; it will also vary with the degree to which the client consciously or unconsciously believes himself to be at fault, and with the intrinsic nature of the matters about which he must talk.

Many other types of client reaction can be realistic responses to varying circumstances. If the client has been either overtly or subtly pressed to apply for treatment, he may feel anger as well as anxiety. The desire to use casework help to bring about change, particularly internal change, will vary greatly, depending not only upon whether or not the client has come for help voluntarily, but also on the nature of the changes which he may anticipate, the degree of satisfaction he has in his present ways, and the fixity of the ways of behaving that he may have to give up.

What the client knows about the agency or casework will also affect his initial attitudes. If he has heard favorable reports about the agency or an individual worker, he will anticipate a sympathetic, skillful reception. A previous bad experience or negative reports of others will lead him to expect the worker to be critical or hostile or dominating. Community, ethnic, and class attitudes toward casework may affect his feeling as to whether coming for help is a respectable or a degrading thing to do, and will condition his expectation of what treatment itself will be like. The less well-educated client who has not previously experienced casework help will usually tend more to expect advice and a somewhat authoritative approach, than will the college graduate who because he is apt to have at least a speaking acquaintance with modern dynamic psychology will anticipate a more sympathetic and thought-provoking approach. The latter, however, may have even more doubts concerning the competence of the caseworker than the former, particularly if he is sophisticated about psycho-analysis and comes to casework because he either cannot afford analysis or is not yet ready to commit himself to it. From the client's point of view these are all realistic responses, in the sense that they are either appropriate reactions to the actual situation or else to reality as it is seen by the client's group.[2]

As soon as client meets worker, the latter's physical appearance and manner set new reactions in motion. A young worker may find an adult distrustful of his skill, particularly if this is not counterbalanced by obvious superiority in education, but may find himself more trusted than an older worker by an adolescent who expects greater understanding from peers and near peers than from his seniors. While class differences, including general education, may increase the confidence of the blue-collar worker in the professional ability of the caseworker, they may also make him fearful of being misunderstood and misjudged and may increase feelings of anxiety and resentment concerning a situation in which he feels inferior and dependent. Sex differences also arouse different realistic reactions. A man often finds it initially difficult to turn to a woman for professional help, the extent of this attitude varying with people of different backgrounds. A particularly pretty, handsome, or vital worker may arouse feelings of sexual attraction, though there be no seductiveness in his or her actual manner. The appearance of the worker's office and experiences in the waiting room will add their bit to the client's reactions. And all these responses take place independently of what the worker actually does!

What the worker says and the way he acts when he says it are obviously the next set of reality factors affecting the client's realistic responses. Before jumping to the conclusion that a client is displaying either transference reactions or subjectively conditioned resistance, it is very important for the worker to make certain that he is not actually saying or doing something that is giving the client a realistic basis for certain responses. Workers *are* sometimes hostile, or at least critical or disinterested. Some workers, out of their own needs, act in a superior, overly impersonal way. Some enjoy a subtle type of domination which puts the client in an unnecessarily dependent or inferior position. Some reveal their desire to be loved or at least admired and appreciated. Some are unconsciously seductive. Some are late for appointments, forgetful about doing things they have promised, and so on. Even the best of caseworkers will exhibit occasional "untherapeutic" reactions. Caseworkers too are affected by mood changes, health, events in work or private life quite outside the particular treatment situation, and other factors. Who of us at some time—on a hot day or when short of sleep or under the influence of an antihistamine—has not caught himself in a yawn that could not be entirely concealed from the client? (It's usually a repetitious client, too.)

This brings us to the realistic aspects of the *worker's* part in the treatment relationship. The worker's responses are not the natural reactions of one man on the street to another. The worker begins with such natural responses, of course, but they are subject to other influences which are the product of his purpose and training. His perception of the client is not that of the average person, his attitudinal response to the perception is different, and his overt behavior is different. A person who is trained as a therapist never sees a client's or patient's behavior as an isolated event. He has become attuned to the reasons for client responses, the kinds of life histories that lie behind different response tendencies, the defenses people use to cope with anxiety. He reacts not simply to the client's overt behavior but to a complex that includes possible reasons for the behavior, and the knowledge that, even if they are not apparent, reasons do exist, whether in life experience or in constitution. The stimulus, that is, is different since the worker, like everyone else, reacts not just to what is, but to what he perceives, or better, apperceives. To the well-trained worker the cue "anger" may read "defensive hostility" or "anxiety"; the cue "defensive" may mean "overly severe superego." If the client's response is thus read, the worker's response automatically is different from what it would otherwise be.

A worker's reactions are also modified by the fact that in his training and experience he has been exposed to the observation of a great deal of human suffering. He has lived with his clients through disappointment, sorrow, physical suffering, death, crippling frustration; he has been closely associated with the torture of mental illness; he has read and listened to life history after life history in which the distortions of the adult personality could be traced step by step to misfortunes, deprivations, mistreatment, mishandling, and misunderstandings in childhood. Unless he has remained untouched by these experiences, he cannot but respond with more spontaneous understanding and acceptance than he would have had he not become a caseworker. Herein lies one of the answers to the question often put to therapists: "How can you be so unspontaneous? Don't you get worn out controlling, or concealing, your natural reactions?" The point is that the natural, spontaneous reaction itself is different from that of the untrained person because both perception and judgment have been modified by training and experience. Let me hasten to add that none of us ever reaches the perfection of understanding and acceptance just implied, but that does not negate the fact that the typical worker has progressed markedly in that direction.

Even when the worker fails to achieve understanding and acceptance and instead feels hostility, criticism, or some other anti-therapeutic emotion, he tries to keep from translating it into speech or action. He does this for two reasons: because he knows it will hurt the client and this he does not want to do, and because his purpose in being with the client is a therapeutic one and he knows that to show his own feelings will defeat that purpose. The fact that he has been trained to become aware of his reactions makes it easier for him to control their expression than would otherwise be the case.

Although the responses of the caseworker to the client usually do have a predominantly positive flavor of sympathizing, accepting, liking, and wanting to help, worker responses that are not therapeutically useful even though they may be realistic nevertheless occur in varying degree. There may be irritation at the client who is hostile and attacking, or who is resistive and thwarts the worker's therapeutic intent (or aspirations). Despite training, there may be residues of dislike of the client whose behavior runs counter to the customs or mores of the worker's own class or ethnic group.[3] There may be particular resentment of the client who mistreats another person, child or adult. An especially attractive client may arouse erotic reactions. Very commonly there is realistic anxiety about ability to help: the client may be confronted by almost insoluble problems, and may sometimes be so seriously disturbed that his problem is beyond the worker's skill. Threats of suicide often arouse the worker's anxiety. Occasionally a psychotic or near-psychotic person arouses realistic fear of bodily harm. Sometimes, despite the worker's efforts to prevent these responses from affecting his work with the client, they do show themselves in one form or another; when they do, they become part of the reality to which the client is reacting and must be taken into account before the worker judges that the client's responses are due to transference.

] *Unrealistic Attitudes and Responses: Transference and Countertransference*

A client's unrealistic reactions spring from two sources so closely related that it is often impossible to separate them. When we speak of transference reactions, we usually mean that the client displaces onto the worker feelings or attitudes that he originally experienced in early childhood toward a member of his family—most often but not necessarily his father or mother—and responds to the worker as if he were this person. A similar phenomenon can occur with displacement from later important associates. These are clear and specific transference reactions. Less specific is the client's bringing into treatment any distorted way of relating to people that has become a part of his personality, whether or not he identifies the worker in a direct way with early family figures. All of these unrealistic reactions can be positive or negative (in the sense of warm or hostile), and they may represent id, ego, or superego aspects of the personality.

The worker is also sometimes unrealistic in his reactions to the client. He, too, may identify the client with an early or later figure in his life, or may bring into the treatment relationship distorted ways of relating to people that are part of his own personality. Although a very important part of the worker's training consists in developing awareness of these tendencies in order to keep them at a minimum, they are never completely overcome and may therefore be part of the reality to which the client is reacting. The term "countertransference" is rather broadly used to cover not only these unrealistic reactions of the worker but also realistic responses, such as those discussed earlier, that are "counter-therapeutic."

] *Problems of Communication Between Client and Worker*

The nature of the feelings and attitudes that exist between worker and client profoundly affects communication between them. If the parent of a schizophrenic child is trying to describe the child's unreachableness to a worker who has negative countertransference attitudes to mothers and blames them for all their children's difficulties, the worker may fail to understand the mother's communication, interpret it as rejection of the child, and fail to be alerted to this and other danger signals that point to the child's serious illness.

If the client, on the other hand, has identified the worker with an insincere, manipulating mother, he may construe the worker's efforts to communicate acceptance and encouragement as flattery with an ulterior motive. While this type of misinterpretation can sometimes be overcome by repeated demonstration of the worker's sincerity and lack of desire to manipulate, the process can ordinarily be greatly accelerated by bringing the client's distrust out into the open so that it can at least be recognized as a factor in the relationship and reacted to by the worker, and perhaps be understood in dynamic or genetic terms.

Another source of distortion in communication is the assignment of different meanings to symbols. All communication, verbal and nonverbal, makes use of symbols, but if the two people trying to communicate do not assign the same meaning to the symbols, the communication will obviously be distorted. The most blatant example of such distortion is the misunderstanding that can easily occur when the client has only a partial understanding of English. More subtle are differences in choice of words, which may be dependent upon class, education, ethnic background, age, region, and other variables. Not only does the worker need to understand the full significance of the client's words, but he must also be able to express his own ideas in words that will accurately communicate his meaning to the client.

This does not require, however, that he adopt the client's vernacular as if it were his own: to do so introduces into the relationship an element of falseness that is anti-therapeutic. The client whose background differs greatly from the worker's does not expect the worker to be like himself, and might not come to him for help if he were. But there is a middle ground in which at key points words can be introduced that particularly express the worker's meaning in the client's language. With most people, simple nontechnical language is the most likely to be clearly understood.

Not only words but actions are symbolic of feelings and attitudes. Facial expression, tone of voice, inflection, posture, gestures all convey meaning, meaning that varies according to different background factors that must be understood by the worker if communication is to be accurate.

] The Client-Worker Relationship in the Dynamics of Treatment

Thus far, we have been describing the elements that go into the relationship between client and worker. What part do these elements play in treatment?

We must first distinguish between the basic therapeutic relationship and special uses to which elements in the relationship can be put. On the worker's part, no matter what the form of treatment, the attitude must be a positive one, with concern for the client's well-being, liking, respect, and acceptance of him as an individual, and a wish for him to be happier or at least more comfortable. For himself, it must include confidence in his skill and in the possibility of its effectiveness in aiding the client. The more free the worker is of countertransference of any sort, the more likely it is that the client will sense that he can trust the worker to influence him.

The client will need to have enough capacity to perceive the worker in these terms to keep himself coming for treatment, not only physically in the room, but participating in the process. This means that no matter how great are the transference and other unrealistic components of his attitude toward the worker, he must be able at least part of the time to perceive the worker as a person to be trusted. Sometimes in the early weeks of treatment the client is kept coming only by external forces or by his own distrusting desperation. The first task of treatment, then, is to find a way of communicating cues to the real nature of the worker's attitudes so that the client will gain some confidence in the worker as a therapist. With practically all clients there are periods in treatment when the realistic view of the worker is obscured by unrealistic reactions, but the client is carried over such periods by his previous positive perceptions, of which some part of him continues to be aware.

The worker's good will and warmth toward the client are demonstrated in large part by sustaining procedures. Variation in the use of these techniques with different clients does not mean that the worker actually has stronger positive feelings toward certain clients than toward others, but rather that some clients consistently need to have the basic therapeutic attitude demonstrated to them more clearly than other clients do or that a particular client is passing through a period of anxiety in which he especially needs to be aware of the worker's good will. When the client has strong transference feelings toward the worker, sustaining procedures will usually promote the positive side of the transference and will take on added significance to the client, for he will feel as if he is receiving reassurance or love from someone who was important to him in early life. Consistent emphasis on sustaining procedures tends to create a dependent type of parent-child relationship in both its realistic and its transference components.[4]

Techniques of direct influence depend for their effectiveness in considerable part on the client's confidence in the worker as an expert or, particularly in advocating and intervention, as a person of authority. The worker using these techniques must also have this self-image if the client is to take him seriously. One of the troubles young workers encounter in the field of child welfare, where they may have to advise foster mothers who are many years their senior and experienced with children while they themselves may have had mainly book learning, is that they quite rightly lack confidence in their comparative competence and inadvertently communicate this fact to the foster mothers. Often an emphasis on directive techniques is combined with stress on sustaining procedures. In combination, these techniques encourage and gratify a positive, dependent, relationship of either the real or transference type.

Considering the person-situation type of reflective discussion we turn to the possibility of modifying the relationship by bringing it into discussion. In the types of treatment previously considered, the worker's attitude is really *demonstrated*, even though this takes place through words. It is not in itself discussed. But now the client's reactions to the worker are brought into the open and he is invited to test them against what the worker presents as the reality of the situation between them. In the process the worker becomes better informed about the client's reactions, and if they are unrealistic has an opportunity to judge whether they are due to misunderstandings or distortions on the client's part. In either case the worker has an opportunity to straighten the matter out and to establish a therapeutically positive relationship.

The nature of the worker's activities in helping the client think about the person-situation configuration often conveys to the client a picture of what the worker is like; at least, it shows what he is *not* like.[5] The fact that he refrains from advice or condemnation and encourages the client to think for himself may establish him as different from parents who have had a destructive controlling influence on the client. This may encourage strong positive feelings toward the worker based on the reality of the relationship. Sometimes this reflective discussion is buttressed by demonstration of sustaining attitudes and by a mild form of direct influence which encourages pleasurable, psychologically healthy activities discouraged in the past by restrictive or hostile parents. This particular combination of procedures is sometimes known as a "corrective relationship." Usually the client has at first regarded the worker as a parent substitute, anticipating, because of transference reactions, that the worker will respond to his verbalizations and behavior as his parent would have done. When the worker reacts differently, the effect of the early parental situation is in a measure corrected.[6] The client, responding to the worker as he would to a parent, is now accepted as he was not by his true parent and given, so to speak, a liberal emotional education instead of the restrictive one he originally experienced.

While the second edition does not efface the first, it can do much to counteract it.*

Not infrequently in present day casework, in which the character disorder is more common than the neurosis, the client's difficulty may spring not so much from oversevere as from overindulgent or inconsistent parents. In such cases the corrective feature in the relationship may be that the worker comes to represent a pattern of more realistic, in the sense of stronger, ego controls than the individual has previously experienced. Sometimes the main therapeutic task is helping the client to refrain from unwise "acting-out" behavior that constantly causes him trouble and defeats his own purposes. In this type of corrective relationship it is most important that the client see the therapist as someone who does not stand for an overly restrictive life and is not disapproving, but rather is interested in helping him learn not to defeat his own ends by activities that inevitably boomerang. The work with Miss Emerson discussed in Chapter II illustrates this kind of relationship.

An important facet of the corrective relationship is the effect it can have on the client's self-image. We know that children often see themselves as their parents see them. If the client has an unrealistically dismal picture of himself and the worker holds a more optimistic view, he can convey his attitude to the client in many ways. In the context of a transference, the experiencing of such an attitude in the worker can powerfully affect the client's self-image. It can be even further strengthened if through genetic work the client can become aware of the source of some of his self-devaluation and can come to understand the dynamics of how certain experiences have given him an unrealistic picture of himself.

The factor of the self-image is present in a special way in almost all treatment. It is related to the worker's professional

---

* The "corrective relationship" is to be distinguished from the "corrective emotional experience" used by Franz Alexander, in which the therapist actually plays a "role" artificially constructed to meet what he judges to be the corrective needs of the patient. It is rather the presentation of a consistently therapeutic attitude toward the client in which the worker is realistic in enlightened terms, represents adult reactions (in the sense of both privileges and responsibilities), and is continuously accepting of the client and his needs.

security and optimism. While he can never know in advance the actual outcome of a phase of treatment, the worker does foresee the possibility that as a result of treatment the client will be more comfortable or more effective, or both; if there were not some hope of this, there would be no justification for continuing the contact. Such therapeutic optimism can be perceived by the client and for him has the meaning that someone believes in him and his possibilities, sees him as better than he sees himself. Even in the absence of the type of transference and life experience upon which corrective-relationship treatment is based, the worker's optimism affects the client's self-image and is an important therapeutic element in treatment.

Another fairly universal factor in successful treatment of more than superficial intensity springs from the client's tendency to identify with a worker with whom he has a positive relationship. Clients often say, in describing a difficult current happening in their lives, "I tried to think, 'What would Mrs. ——— (the worker) do about that?' and then I said ———." And what they then say is often close to what the worker has said to them under similar circumstances. This phenomenon is sometimes described as the worker's "lending the strength of his ego" to the client. It is an imitative sort of learning—similar to a child's learning from imitation of the parent with whom he identifies—that can be incorporated in a lasting way into the client's personality. Such learning depends upon the existence of positive reality feelings toward the worker, feelings often reenforced by a positive transference.

When we turn to discussion of the use of the treatment relationship in developing dynamic and genetic understanding, we come to an area of casework about which there is not universal agreement. There *is* agreement that casework's handling of the transference is different from that of psychoanalysis, but opinions differ on whether relationship phenomena should be used in casework as a source of self-understanding. These questions have already been discussed at least in part in previous chapters, but they need to be brought together here.

Undoubtedly, the therapist-client relationship, particularly in its transference aspects, is markedly different in casework and in psychoanalysis. In casework, for reasons already outlined, it is certainly less intense. Unconscious relationship components are not brought into consciousness. Since free association is not used, the client is under no compulsion to verbalize all his thoughts about the worker. And, perhaps most important of all, the general way of conducting treatment does not encourage extensive regression in the transference. To put it more concretely: the casework client does not become as deeply immersed as the analysant in the unconscious fantasy that the worker is his parent. While he reacts to a certain extent as though this were so, the cathexis of the idea is not nearly so strong as it would be in analysis. Likewise, since he is not encouraged to regress—to feel and, within the treatment hour, to behave as a young child or even an infant—the client in his relationship with the worker does not re-experience the phenomena of his early childhood in anything but a very fragmentary way. He is more apt to re-experience the reflections of these earlier reactions as they appeared in his later childhood and adolescent relationship with his parents. As Annette Garrett put it in her excellent paper on the transference in casework,[7] the caseworker does not encourage the transference neurosis.

Some caseworkers, fearful of going too deeply into the transference, have taken the position that transference reactions should not be interpreted for purposes of aiding the client's self-understanding, but rather discussed only as necessary for the maintenance—or restoration—of a positive relationship. Such a position arises, perhaps, from our lack of clarity about the various elements in the transference as it appears in casework, particularly about the fact that there are ego-dystonic preconscious elements in the transference just as there are in all other phenomena, and irrational components affected by later childhood experiences than those of infancy and very early life. There is in reality no more "danger" in touching these elements as they appear in the transference than there is in commenting on them in other communications.

Among the procedures used in reflective consideration of dynamic and genetic content, then, are those that help the client to understand dynamically some of his transference and other unrealistic responses to the worker and the way in which these responses repeat earlier reactions to parents and other closely related people. The client can then put this self-understanding to use in recognizing similar reactions as they occur in his current life outside of treatment. He is then in a position to correct distortions and to respond to people more realistically. We deprive the client of a potent source of help in his struggle toward realistic living if we neglect to use the vivid experiences that occur between him and his caseworker.

NOTES

1. Annette Garrett points out the importance of this distinction in her paper "The Worker-Client Relationship," in *Ego Psychology in Dynamic Casework*, Howard J. Parad, ed., Family Service Association of America, New York, 1958, pp. 53–54, 59–60.

2. Variation among groups, especially among different classes in their attitudes toward and expectations of treatment agencies, has been a subject of interest in recent years and is often touched on in articles on work with delinquents and the "hard-to-reach." For the most part these articles are speculative and impressionistic rather than definitive, but they do serve to alert us to attitudes that may exist in these groups of clients. Also of interest on various aspects of group determinants of client expectations and responses are F. C. Redlich, A. B. Hollingshead, and Elizabeth Bellis, "Social Class Differences in Attitudes Toward Psychiatry," *American Journal of Orthopsychiatry*, 25 (January, 1955), 60–70; Leslie Schaffer and Jerome Myers, "Psychotherapy and Social Stratification," *Psychiatry*, 17 (February, 1954), 83–93; John Spiegel, "Some Cultural Aspects of Transference and Counter-Transference," in *Individual and Familial Dynamics*, Jules H. Masserman, ed., Grune & Stratton, New York, 1959, pp. 160–182; and Marsha Worby, "The Adolescents' Expectations

of How the Potentially Helpful Person Will Act," *Smith College Studies in Social Work*, 26 (October, 1955), 19–59.

3. There are many warnings against this in the literature, going back at least to the twenties if not earlier. Mary Richmond dealt with it briefly in *Social Diagnosis* (Russell Sage Foundation, New York, 1917, pp. 97–98). To what extent recognition of this type of bias has modified it in graduate social workers is not known. The writer is not aware of studies in which the existence of such bias has been established as a significant factor in treatment, though it is often hypothesized. The study by August B. Hollingshead and Frederick C. Redlich, *Social Class and Mental Illness* (John Wiley & Sons, New York, 1958), indicated that the psychiatrists involved in the study not infrequently responded to their patients in terms of their subjective reactions to the patient's social class. This may or may not be equally true of caseworkers. Scott M. Briar's carefully designed doctoral study, reported in his article, "Use of Theory in Studying Effects of Client Social Class on Students' Judgments," *Social Work, 6* (July, 1961), 91–97, indicates that the judgments of social work students were influenced by knowledge of the client's class but did not find a consistent inverse relationship (as had been hypothesized) between the student's own responses versus his predictions of client's responses, and the distance in social class background between worker and client. It did find a slight tendency for students to assume greater similarity between themselves and the client when middle rather than lower class status was attributed to the client. The study did not attempt to evaluate whether the judgments themselves were or were not justified in view of the client's ascribed class status. It is possible that the great emphasis in casework training over the past thirty years on acceptance of differences and on self-determination for the client has acted as a safeguard against at least the grosser forms of class bias entering the treatment process.

4. For an illustration see Leopold Bellak, "Psychiatric Aspects of Tuberculosis," *Social Casework, 31* (May, 1950), 183–189.

5. John Spiegel puts this in the language of role theory in "The Social Roles of Doctor and Patient in Psychoanalysis and Psychotherapy," *Psychiatry, 17* (November, 1954), 369–376.

6. For discussion of this see Lucille N. Austin, "Trends in

Differential Treatment in Social Casework," *Journal of Social Casework,* 29 (June, 1948), 203–211; and Otilda Krug, "The Dynamic Use of the Ego Functions in Casework Practice," *Social Casework, 36* (December, 1955), 443–450.

7. Garrett, *op. cit.,* pp. 56–58.

Suggested Additional Reading

Elizabeth S. McCormick, Dorothy D. Mueller, and Phoebe Rich, "Management of the Transference," *Journal of Social Casework, 27* (October, 1946), 207–216.

William V. Silverberg, "Concept of Transference," *Psychoanalytic Quarterly, 17* (October, 1948), 303–321.

John Skinner, "Transference Interpretations in Psychotherapy," *Journal of Psychiatric Social Work,* 22 (October, 1952), 5–13.

Adolph Stern, "Transference in Borderline Neuroses," *Psychoanalytic Quarterly, 17* (October, 1948), 527–528.

Part Three

DIAGNOSIS
AND
TREATMENT
PLANNING

X

The Psychosocial Study

THUS FAR WE HAVE CONSIDERED the frame of reference concerning the nature of the individual and his situation upon which case-work treatment rests (Chapters I and II), and have discussed the various technical means by which the worker endeavors to bring improvement in a client's life (Chapters III through IX). We must now turn to the more specific question of how treatment is related to the needs of a particular individual confronted by an adaptational problem.

Treatment planning must rest, first, upon thorough knowledge of the means of treatment—their nature and consequences, and other factors that determine their suitability—and second, upon thorough knowledge of the individual who is seeking treatment—his current situation and the variety of factors that have contributed causally to his predicament. In other words, so that the various means of helping may be drawn upon in the most suitable way to meet the needs of a particular person, there must be painstaking social study, followed by a diagnostic formulation leading to the planning of treatment. This planning in turn will include both the goals and the procedures of therapy.

Many factors converge in the making of the series of decisions that determine a plan of treatment. This is by no means a single question that can be settled at the outset of work on a case. In some instances, especially in rather uncomplicated cases, the major outlines can be planned at the conclusion of an exploratory period, and these actually become the mode of treatment to be followed. More typically, only the early phases of treatment and perhaps some general guides can be foreseen at the outset, with later decisions being made on the basis of new material that emerges during the treatment process. Indeed, the way the client uses treatment in the early phases is one of the most important considerations in later periods. Major trends, to be sure, can usually be outlined further ahead than more detailed steps. Flexibility is, after all, an essential ingredient of all skillful treatment, making it sensitive not only to actual changes in the situation but also to new understanding that the worker gains as treatment proceeds. It must also be noted that the worker cannot wait until the end of the social study and diagnostic process to initiate treatment. In actuality treatment begins the moment the client meets the worker. But early contacts usually include a good deal of ventilation and support with only cautious use of other approaches until enough is known for treatment to take more definite direction.

The idea of planning treatment and treatment goals raises serious value questions in the minds of some casework practitioners.[1] If you truly believe in the importance of self-determination for a client, they say, how can you talk about *planning* treatment for him? Isn't this something that is up to him alone? Some thinkers solve the dilemma by seeing agencies as offering certain types of services which the client chooses either to use or to reject. This, however, does not really solve the problem, but only circumvents it, for it is the agencies that make the choices, deciding both what services to offer, and what constitutes eligibility for them. A client is not given a foster home for a child just because he wants one, nor is he allowed to choose the type of foster home his child is placed in, any more than he can decide that he should be given financial assistance. Certainly, it is not up to him to determine whether his superego needs strengthening or liberalizing, or whether he should be helped to see his children's needs more clearly or should work on the question of why, even though he does see them clearly, he cannot put the understanding he already has of them into constructive action.

The truth that lies in the extreme position, however, is that it is not only inadvisable but impossible to impose treatment upon a client. Except in certain aspects of protective work, when we may be doing something against the client's will—taking a seriously psychotic woman to a hospital, placing a child who is being badly mistreated, reporting a delinquent's parole violations to the court—the use of treatment always involves choices on the part of both the client and the worker. The worker can offer reassurance to his heart's content, but it will not become reassurance to the client until he is willing to accept it—to believe in it. The worker can suggest and advise, but it is the client who chooses whether or not to follow the advice. The worker can try to stimulate the client to think about his situation or himself; only the client can *do* it. Interpretations are futile unless the client is willing to consider their validity. During the course of treatment, methods often have to be changed from one approach to another simply because the client is unwilling to make use of the kind of help the worker has first offered or shows that he wants to use something the worker has not yet offered.

The worker, on the other hand, has the responsibility of deciding what treatment to *offer*. Just as he would be wrong to propose a foster home for a child who needs the care of a treatment institution, or to give continued financial assistance to a client whose financial problems are caused not by lack of income but by poor budget management, so he would be wrong to try to center his work with an actively psychotic client on the development of genetic understanding. The worker is responsible for what he offers, while the client inevitably exercises control over what he accepts. Thus, except for techniques of intervention, no treatment can be successful if the client lacks *motivation* to use it. Motivation sometimes exists spontaneously in the client. At other times, the creation of motivation becomes an early task of treatment during the exploratory period.

How then does the worker decide what kind of treatment to offer the client? Two preliminary steps are essential: the psychosocial study and the diagnostic process. They are so closely related that they must be discussed together. In this chapter we shall discuss the psychosocial study, going on in the next to consider problems involved in diagnosis.

In the social study—the shorter term commonly used to refer

to the psychosocial study—the caseworker collects the facts upon which the diagnosis will be based. It is extremely important to be clear about the difference between study and diagnosis. Social study is client-centered. It is a process of observation and classification of the facts observed with the purpose of securing as much information as is needed to understand the client and his problem and to guide treatment wisely. Diagnosis, on the other hand, is an opinion—a professional opinion. It represents the *thinking* of the worker *about* the facts, and will be strongly influenced by the frame of reference he uses to guide him in understanding their meaning. Mary Richmond once quoted[2] an apt statement from Dr. Richard Cabot: "In social study you open your eyes and look, in diagnosis you close them and think." If these two processes are not kept separate in the worker's mind, he is in great danger of skewing the facts to fit the theory, asking questions in such a way that answers fitting a priori assumptions are bound to emerge. This is not to say that during the study process the worker will not be formulating the diagnosis in his own mind. Indeed, preliminary formulations help him know what areas need further exploration. Nevertheless, if the worker is clear about the difference between the two processes, he will guard against "contamination" of one with the other and make a clear distinction between his facts and his opinions.

A diagnosis can be no better than the facts it rests on.[3] The major social study period comes, of course, at the beginning of treatment, primarily in the first five or six interviews, but significant material which either confirms or modifies the original impressions is constantly being added throughout treatment.

The fact-gathering process receives its impetus and direction from two sources: the client's desire to tell about his difficulties and the worker's desire to understand how they came about and what capacities exist for dealing with them. When the problem appears to be one of interpersonal relationships, the current tendency in most casework settings is to follow a fluid form of interviewing which combines these two sets of interests. By encouraging the client to follow trends of thought related to his problem as they come naturally to his mind and by leading him to develop them further, the worker gains access with relative ease to the elaboration of significant matters. At the same time, the worker must fill the inevitable gaps in this type of exploration by directing the interview along lines which the client does not spontaneously introduce./ He can do so with relative ease when such matters are "adjacent" to subjects the client is discussing or flow logically from them, or he can explore them at points at which the client has temporarily exhausted his spontaneous productions and is ready to follow the therapist's lead. "You have never told me much about your father." "Set me straight on your schooling—where were you when you finished?" "You haven't told me much about your work—what do you do and how do you like it?" The caseworker needs to take a fairly active part in the gathering of information, for we do not depend on free association to lead eventually and inevitably to significant material. Clients cannot of themselves know what information is needed, nor can they free themselves without help from reluctance to discuss painful material which may be highly relevant to the understanding of their troubles. A great deal of ineffectual drifting and failure to formulate suitable treatment approaches results when the caseworker is too passive, especially in early interviews.

We see, then, that although the worker does not follow a set pattern for social study interviews, he does have in mind very definite ideas concerning the type of information he wants to obtain about the client and his situation. What he wants to learn will inevitably be influenced by his frame of reference, that is, the theories he holds about the causation of difficulties in social functioning and about appropriate casework treatment methods. In problems of interpersonal adjustment, the caseworker who is following the frame of reference presented in this book will want to know about the client's current functioning and current situation, about those aspects of his past life that might throw light on his current problem, and about his behavior within the treatment interviews themselves. Thus, starting out with what the client sees as his problem, its cause, what he has tried to do about it, and his thoughts about how he can be helped to resolve it, the study will move on to analysis of present and past factors that may be contributing to the current dilemma. Some clients move naturally into talking about significant aspects of their past life. Others may need a brief explanation of why telling about the past is important. The order in which these two areas of past and present are explored varies with both client and worker preference, and is less important than the nature of the content to be inquired into.

Since the worker is charged with responsibility for seeing whether problems exist beyond those initially presented by the client, there must be some exploration, however brief, of all the major areas of current functioning, the areas in which the client plays his various life roles—as husband or wife, parent or child, employer or employee, family member in the wider sense, friend, acquaintance, and so on. In areas in which problems appear, it is important to inquire not only about the details of the problem but also about the client's own participation in the difficulty. It is not enough for the client to say, "My wife is a spendthrift"; the worker needs to follow up with specific questions: In what way? What are the couple's actual expenditures in relation to income? Under what circumstances do unwise expenditures occur? How do they go about their money planning? By getting detailed accounts of what happens in the client's household when there is conflict about money, the worker can evaluate to what extent overspending is actually occurring, what sorts of situations either within the wife or in the interaction between husband and wife touch it off, what purpose it may serve in the marital relationship, the part the husband's response to the overspending may play in its repetition, and so on. If initial evidence indicates that there is little or no basis for the husband's accusation, the worker must look for the circumstances under which the husband believes it to be true, what within himself or in the marital interaction touches it off, what purpose his unrealistic reaction serves, and so on. An important aspect of these explorations is their revelation of how the client tries to cope with whatever difficulty he is experiencing, knowledge that is especially useful in throwing light on the question of his ego functioning.

The same careful regard for details must attend the exploration of the client's past. It is not enough for him to say, "My mother always preferred my older brother." The worker must seek out the details, asking, "In what way?" "What makes you think so?" "Could you tell me more about that?"—and so on.

Throughout the interview the worker is also observing carefully the client's reactions in response to the treatment situation. How much does he demand of the worker and what is the nature of his demands? How sensitive is he to criticism? What defenses does he use? How accurately is he aware of the worker's reactions? To what extent and under what circumstances is he warm, hostile, remote toward the worker? These observations throw light particularly on the nature of the client's demands upon the world and on his ego and superego functioning.

An important area of the social study that should not be neglected is the client's physical health. The worker must be alert not only to what the client says about his health but also to other signs that might point in the direction of illness. Appearance, of course, tells a good deal. Other indications of illness which the client may not fully appreciate appear in references to poor appetite, tiredness, or trouble sleeping, as well as to mild symptomatology such as pain, swelling, rashes, indigestion, dizziness, and so on. It is known that certain physical conditions have characteristic effects on personality functioning, and alertness to them will often throw important light on the client's reactions. Quite aside from these constant effects, any illness is also likely to play a significant part in interpersonal difficulties. It frequently causes pain or anxiety;[4] it often increases narcissistic attitudes and provokes regression to greater dependence; it can be used as an escape from unpleasant responsibilities; it can change the self-image and distort relationships in family life between husband and wife and between siblings. The worker must also be alert to the effect of bodily changes associated with different periods of life—the uneven growth rate and the genital as well as secondary sexual growth changes of adolescence, reactions to the climacteric and to the physical changes of old age. Unusual physical features or disabilities also have direct bearing on social and inner functioning.

In recent years there has been growing emphasis upon the importance of not limiting social study to office interviews with the client only. It is now widely accepted that in cases of marital difficulty, for example, there are very great advantages in seeing both the individuals involved, for diagnostic purposes at least and whenever possible for treatment also. Some therapists refuse treatment altogether unless such interviews can be arranged. Others, of whom the writer is one, would certainly favor interviewing all persons involved in a major way in a problem, but would not insist on it if the client is strongly opposed or if the others concerned are unwilling to participate. If this type of interview is handled as a routine expectation rather than as a major issue the client usually accepts it as a natural procedure, unless there are special reasons for him to regard it with concern. If there are, it is important to understand them, for they are often of great diagnostic significance.

Without doubt the home visit also can yield important data[5] not only about the client's physical environment, but in the case of the wife and mother about an important area of her functioning. A woman's home points up many personality characteristics, especially the extent to which regressive or primitive oral and anal traits are prominent in her personality. First-hand witnessing of a client's interaction with children in the natural setting of the home provides other significant diagnostic data. In cases where environmental factors are of chief importance, or with the "hard-to-reach" family, home visits are essential. In other cases, it is well to grasp any natural opportunity that arises for an interview in the home as a means of widening the scope of the social study. Some caseworkers are now advocating the home visit as a regular part of the social study in all kinds of cases. It would seem wise, however, to experiment with the assets and liabilities of such a procedure before adopting it in a wholesale way. It is likely to focus the client's attention on the fact of social study per se, which often has the effect of arousing his expectations that at the end of a short period the worker will be able to offer a formula for the cure of his troubles. It also can lead to unexpected complications which may be difficult to handle, in terms of relationships with other people. This is not to question the value of home visits but rather to warn that the home visit as an exploratory technique is not yet fully understood, deserves further study, and has not yet proven itself of such overriding significance that routine use is warranted. Since everything that is done in the process of social study has its effects on treatment, it does not make sense to use techniques in the study-diagnosis process that in themselves might hamper treatment.

Another procedure under current investigation is the use of the joint interview—husband and wife, parent and child, or even a whole family together.[6] This approach also is undoubtedly of great diagnostic value. Actually observing the interaction between people throws a great deal of light on the complementarity or "discomplementarity" of their behavior, on discrepancies between their individual perceptions of how they act and how others respond and act, and on the situation as it appears to a trained outsider. It yields insights of value not only as part of diagnosis but also of great immediate usefulness in treatment. The work that has already been done with this technique has certainly demonstrated its value. As with the home visit, however, the extent to which it should be used and the circumstances that require it are still a matter of experimentation and study.[7] The interaction involved is very delicate; transference problems of high import for treatment arise. Both the immediate effects on the dynamics of treatment itself and the long range effects in terms of outcome must continue to be studied before discriminating guides will exist concerning the circumstances under which use of this technique will be advisable.

In addition to interviews with the client and his immediate family, it is also sometimes useful to consult, with the client's knowledge and on a very selective basis, other people who may be in a position to add to the worker's understanding of his client. When a child is involved, it may be particularly useful to talk with the teacher or nursery school leader. Often a contact with a doctor yields valuable medical information. Occasionally a clergyman, employer, relative, or friend can add to the understanding of a particular aspect of the client's problem. In seeing collaterals it is always important to gauge the potential effect of the interview on the client himself and on his relationship to the worker. Only under exceptional circumstances, principally of a protective nature, is it wise to seek information at the expense of arousing anti-therapeutic reactions in the client. This is not to say that contacts with other people should never be allowed to arouse any anxiety in the client. Anxiety frequently occurs, at least to a mild degree, but discussion with the client beforehand gives an opportunity for helping the client with his anxiety both before and after the interview with the collateral.

Obviously, reports of medical or psychiatric diagnosis or treatment, of psychological tests, and of treatment in other social agencies may be pertinent to the social study. These and other types of written material should be secured on a carefully selected basis during the social study period as well as later in the contact.

As the caseworker learns about the client and his life he inevitably begins to form opinions about the nature of the client's difficulty. Often it is by trying to formulate the diagnosis that he recognizes gaps in a social study, areas of information about which he must make further inquiry in order to arrive at a clearer picture of the client and his situation. This is good and necessary, but the worker must guard against allowing speculation to substitute for facts or to predetermine the way in which questions are answered. The best way to obtain a clear and accurate picture is to enable the client to have sufficient confidence in the worker so that he can speak fully and frankly.[8] ✗

NOTES

1. See Kenneth Pray, "A Restatement of the Generic Principles of Social Casework Practice," *Journal of Social Casework, 28* (October, 1947), 283–290, for a statement of this point of view.

2. Mary Richmond, *Social Diagnosis,* Russell Sage Foundation, New York, 1917, p. 347.

3. As background for this chapter, readers should be familiar with chapters III, IV, and V in Richmond, *Social Diagnosis, ibid.,* and with chapters VII and VIII in Gordon Hamilton, *Theory and Practice of Social Casework,* 2nd ed., Columbia University Press, New York, 1951.

4. For an interesting discussion of this, see Mark Zborowski, "Cultural Components in Response to Pain," *Journal of Social Issues,* 8 (1952), 16–30.

5. See Marjorie L. Behrens and Nathan W. Ackerman, "The Home Visit as an Aid in Family Diagnosis and Therapy," *Social Casework, 37* (January, 1956), 11–19.

6. See the following:

Emily C. Faucett, "Multiple-Client Interviewing: A Means of Assessing Family Processes," *Social Casework, 43* (March, 1962), 114–120.

Bernard H. Hall and Winifred Wheeler, "The Patient and His Relatives: Initial Joint Interview," *Social Work, 2* (January, 1957), 75–80.

Celia Mitchell, "Family Interviewing in Family Diagnosis," *Social Casework, 40* (July, 1959), 381–384.

Viola W. Weiss, "Multiple-Client Interviewing: An Aid to Diagnosis," *Social Casework, 43* (March, 1962), 111–114.

7. See Frances H. Scherz, "Multiple-Client Interviewing: Treatment Implications," *Social Casework, 43* (March, 1962), 120–125.

8. Of interest here is Frances B. Stark, "Barriers to Client-Worker Communication at Intake," *Social Casework, 40* (April, 1959), 177–183.

Suggested Additional Reading

L. L. Geismer and Beverly Ayres, "A Method for Evaluating the Social Functioning of Families Under Treatment, *Social Work, 4* (January, 1959), 102–108.

Merton Gill and others, *The Initial Interview in Psychiatric Practice,* International Universities Press, New York, 1954.

Howard J. Parad and Gerald Caplan, "A Framework for Studying Families in Crisis," *Social Work, 5* (July, 1960), 3–15.

Alice L. Voiland, Martha Lou Gunderlach and Mildred Corner, *Developing Insight in Initial Interviews,* Family Service Association of America, New York, 1947.

XI

Diagnosis

DIAGNOSIS IN CASEWORK is undertaken to answer the question, "How can this person be helped?" Its objective is the formulation of treatment plans: content, aims, and procedures. The process of diagnosis begins at the first moment the caseworker sees the client, and by the end of the exploratory period, which ordinarily takes five or six interviews and during which the worker is actively engaged in the psychosocial study, a working diagnosis on which the early phases of treatment can be based should be reached. Diagnosis is always tentative, however, and open to enrichment and correction as fuller knowledge of the client emerges; reevaluation and, if it is indicated, reformulation of the diagnosis and treatment plan are therefore a constant part of ongoing treatment.

In diagnosis, the worker attempts to estimate the client's capacity to make use of the varying modes of casework treatment in overcoming the difficulty by which he is faced, making this estimate in accordance with the answers provided to various questions: What is the problem? What are the causative factors? What needs to be modified *in the situation,* how modifiable is it, and by what means? How able is the client to modify the situation? What does he want to modify and to what degree is he motivated to this end? What does the client need to modify *within himself,* how able is he to do this, and by what means? The diagnostic process itself consists of three major steps: assessment, the establishment of dynamic and etiological interrelationships, and categorization.

] *Assessment*

In assessment the worker "weighs up" the facts to see where the trouble lies. In so doing he uses two tools: a system for organizing or classifying the facts for the light they can throw on certain areas important for treatment planning, and a set of norms against which the facts are measured in order to reveal unusual or atypical factors that may contribute to the client's difficulty. The assessment process actually begins as soon as the client is first heard from and continues hand and hand with the fact-gathering process.

ORGANIZING THE FACTS

As the worker listens to the client, he constantly asks himself questions such as, "What is the reality by which this person* is confronted? Is this a realistic or exaggerated or distorted reaction? If it is not realistic, what might account for it? What does this tell me about the circumstances that provoke such a response? What does it tell me about the kind of person I am dealing with?" In other words, to what extent is this difficulty a matter of external deprivation, frustration, or provocation? To what extent is it a matter of unusual or excessive needs or demands? How much is it due to inadequacies or aberrations in the client's ego and superego functioning? The caseworker will be greatly helped in his assessment if he continuously orders his material according to a scheme which will help him locate the answers to these questions, some of which clearly refer to pressures or influences playing upon the client from his environment, and others to factors in the client's personality.

External pressures may exist in the form of active frustration, deprivation or inadequacies in any of the following areas:

    Housing
    Neighborhood conditions
    Income
    Employment

---

* Where the social study involves several people these questions must be asked from the point of view of each of them.

Education

Religious institutions

Medical treatment facilities

Social institutions (courts, police, social agencies, etc.)

Family relationships (parents, children, spouse, siblings, etc.)

Social groups (friends, peers, neighbors, etc.)

If a parent is concerned about his child, whom he sees as a problem, the worker needs to evaluate not only the way the parent is functioning as a parent but also the realities by which he is confronted. What is this son or daughter like to live with at the moment? Has the child withdrawn into himself so that he is hard to reach? Is he provocative in a hostile way, giving ample cause for parental anger? Is his behavior publicly embarrassing to his parents? If he is ill, how much of a strain does caring for him cause? Does it deprive the parents of sleep? Is his mother constantly running up and down stairs, or involved in all sorts of special cookery?

Obviously, in any sort of interpersonal problem, the worker must get as accurate a picture as possible of the pressures, or "presses," to which the client is responding before evaluating his behavior. Moreover, it is the exception rather than the rule to find the pressure in one spot alone; usually there are other people in either the immediate or wider family who are also contributing to the client's difficulty. Otto Pollak[1] has rightly called our attention to the pressures brought by grandparents, aunts and uncles, and other members of the wider family—or family of orientation—on the problems of children. Not infrequently these pressures occur in marital problems also.

Employment, housing, and neighborhood conditions are other possible sources of additional pressure in parent-child and husband-wife conflict. Certainly the realities of the school environment are of great significance for children. Social institutions such as the courts and police have causative as well as remedial meaning in problems of nonconformity.

Situational pressures in any of these ten areas may be mild or severe and may result from the failure of the environment to meet normal human needs or from actively frustrating or destructive conditions. It is only as the worker is fully aware of the nature and extent of such environmental presses that a balanced picture can be obtained of the interaction between the client and his environment. Obviously there will not be significant findings in all these areas in every case, but all are of sufficient importance to be within the attention span of the worker for any clues that active exploration is needed.

A dimension of the assessment that seems to lie midway between the external and the internal is the individual's physical condition.

As we noted in the previous chapter, the worker should take account of any diagnosed medical condition, the client's complaints, and his own observations, as well as any physical characteristics or disabilities that might be expected in view of the client's age, occupation, or way of life, bodily changes associated with different periods of life; and any unusual features or bodily disabilities.

When we turn to internal factors affecting the client's personality, the data should be so organized as to lead to answers to questions about the client's functioning, his strengths and weaknesses, and his potentiality for change. This understanding should of course be related to the frame of reference upon which we will rely in the diagnosis, but should also draw from the general body of theory those factors that are of special pertinence for casework diagnosis and treatment. A useful outline to keep in mind in evaluating the client's communication and the worker's observations would include four major divisions: libidinal and aggressive characteristics, ego characteristics, superego characteristics, and symptomatology.

The *libidinal and aggressive characteristics* most important in casework diagnosis and treatment planning include:

Narcissism
Dependence
Residuals of oral, anal, and phallic developmental stages
Capacity for mature love relationships
Ambivalence
Hostility
Aggressiveness

Sexual immaturities or deviance
Unresolved attachments or hostilities toward parents

The *ego* qualities of most significance for casework include:[2]

Perception
Judgment
Reality testing
Self-image
Impulse control
Ability as an executant
Thought processes
Identifications
Fantasies
Affects
Anxiety
Guilt
Defenses

In evaluating the *superego* the worker must consider both the general structure of the superego—its relative strength or weakness in the personality—and the quality of its demands, that is, the level of its demands and the consistency of the standards it supports.

By *symptomatology* is meant the specific signs that are generally recognized as characteristic of known neurotic or psychotic disorders, such as phobias, compulsions, hallucinations, depression, and the like. There often is an overlap between such symptomatology and the various ego qualities, but there is value in noting in a special way behavior that is widely recognized as a sign of a specific type of disorder.

The external situation and physical condition have purposely been placed before personality factors in this presentation because it is impossible properly to evaluate the personality except as it is seen in the context of the situation by which the person is confronted or, to put it another way, of which he is a part. One cannot judge whether a reaction of anger is normal or excessive unless one knows the provocation. How can one tell whether anxiety is excessive without knowing to what extent there are realities to account for it? It is one thing to be plagued by the fear of losing a job in normal times when one's performance is adequate, and quite another when there is a recession on and one's performance is marginal. It is one thing for a client to accuse his wife of belittling him when in actuality she does constantly criticize and devalue him, and it is another thing for him to be distorting her remarks, projecting on to them his own devaluated self-image. Feelings of depression may be part of a particular physical illness syndrome, a reaction to the loss of a valued friend, or, in the absence of any such provocations in reality, evidence of emotional or mental illness.

This disentangling of reaction from reality is a most complicated task. It is simplest when the worker can observe the externals directly, or can look at the situation in terms of his own general knowledge. For instance, the worker often knows what a given neighborhood is like, or how a particular doctor reacts to patients, or the eligibility procedures in the local public assistance agency. General knowledge of this type must, however, be used with caution. Sometimes the doctor, public assistance worker, or school principal has not acted in a specific instance in the way our prior knowledge has led us to expect. Direct observation is more certain. Here lies the great advantage of the worker's having direct contact with the principals in any interpersonal problem, and of the home visit and of joint interviews from which so much can be learned. It must be remembered, however, that even insights thus gained are not infallible and can sometimes give the worker a false sense of certainty.[3] Things that have been "seen with my own eyes" and "heard with my own ears" carry great weight, but they are also subject to misinterpretation by the worker because of his own countertransference and subjective judgments.

Another method of disentangling the objective from the subjective is to evaluate the circumstantial detail which the client himself uses to support his own opinions and reactions. Does the situation he describes bring the worker to the same conclusion? Insofar as the worker's own perceptions and judgment are realistic, he can then evaluate the client's reactions. The importance of self-awareness in a worker's training—so that his biases will be reduced or at least near enough to consciousness that he is alert to possible sources of error in his judgment—can easily be seen.

Repetitiveness provides another very useful clue in assessing behavior, for if an individual has a tendency to over- or under-react or to distort it will not occur in a single instance only but will show itself again and again. If the same type of seemingly unrealistic response arises several times, and particularly if in each instance it occurs in reaction to different people, the chance is very great that an atypical personality factor is involved. This is one of the ways in which past history is of particular value. As personality structure is shaped early in life, repetitive patterns will often show themselves very clearly in the life history. Specific symptoms of neurotic or psychotic disorders in the client's past are of course of great significance.

NORMS

Implicit in assessing behavior is the idea of norms. When we ask whether a given action or reaction of a client is realistic under certain circumstances we are really asking whether it is normal. (It is important to note here that we are not asking whether or not the *person* is normal but whether a given *action or reaction* is normal. These are very different things.) When we evaluate behavior in any way we inevitably compare it with a model of a "normal" or "healthy" reaction which we hold in our own minds. For the most part models used in casework are not clear-cut with definite outlines but rather are drawn with hazily shaded edges to accommodate the whole range of variations existing even within the norm. Furthermore, they usually lie somewhere between an "average" reaction (in the statistical sense) and a reaction considered "healthy" or "ideal" according to the frame of reference within which it is being evaluated. For instance, the average American woman who is forty years old and 5 feet 5 inches tall weighs 140 pounds. The ideal weight for this same woman is said to be about 123 pounds. When the modern doctor urges his middle-aged patient who weighs in at 150 to lose fifteen or twenty pounds, he is setting his treatment goal at a point midway between the ideal norm of 123 and the actual norm of 140. Similarly the caseworker carries in his mind a model of functioning that lies somewhere between the average and the ideal or healthy.

The "average" type of the model or norm derives from the

therapist's experience and from his observation—both professional and personal—of others and himself.[4] The "healthy" or "ideal" type of norm is a composite of his observations of people who function in a superior way and of ways of functioning which he believes to be superior. This type of norm is obviously influenced by the caseworker's scientific frame of reference and by the values of his profession; inevitably it is influenced by personal opinions and values as well. But the caseworker who is well acculturated to his own profession will try to eliminate from his diagnostic thinking and treatment goals personal norms that do not approximate those of his profession.

Just as one does not have a single ideal weight for all human beings, so one cannot have a single model of appropriate responses. What is adequate or normal or appropriate or realistic or healthy (or whatever term is chosen) will be influenced by many variables[5]—sex, age, class, ethnic background, religion, educational level, geographic location, social role. A man is expected to respond differently to frustration when he is functioning as a father than when he is at the poker table with the boys from the office. What is normal for a Protestant in certain respects may be abnormal for a Roman Catholic. Behavior indicative of normal virility for a highly educated man from a highly educated family might label a stevedore a sissy. Normal aggression for a person of one background is overaggressiveness for one of another. People of different backgrounds normally emphasize different defenses and have different norms for sexual expression and for the expression of aggression. Even the level of psychosexual maturity expected of men and women may vary in different cultures.[6] Certainly concepts of appropriate male and female ways of acting are very differently defined in different parts of the world. The superego and ego ideal are in large part the product of group-accepted norms and vary very greatly between people of different ethnic, religious, class, and geographic backgrounds. The caseworker must have wide knowledge of the major behavioral variations that lie within the norm for individuals of the varying backgrounds with whom he is dealing, and these factors must be taken into consideration in estimating how normal or abnormal the individual's behavior is.

When the time arrives for thinking of goals for treatment, the worker must again be alert to these behavioral differences. The client's aspirations for himself are likely to be in terms of the norms of his own culture unless he is trying to identify himself with a group other than that of his family of orientation. However, the fact that a certain way of functioning is the "mode" for a particular ethnic group or class is not in itself evidence that it is the most useful way of functioning either for the client's associates or for himself. We are well aware of the fallacy in a worker's trying to impose on the client his own way of doing things. It is equally fallacious to give blind allegiance to cultural pluralism.[7] Cultures can be sick too. We must steer carefully between these twin errors, neither introducing culturally foreign goals because of personal preference for them nor feeling inhibited from trying to motivate the client to changes in culturally conditioned ways of behaving when his social functioning and personal well-being will be improved by such change. In considering this question, however, the worker must always weigh in the balance the expectations, interpretations, and reactions of the client's associates as these are influenced by ethnic or class factors.

Certain role concepts developed by sociology and social psychology are of particular value for the light they throw on the way in which behavioral expectations—and hence, norms—vary with the position held by the individual. A father is expected to act differently from a son. A man functioning as an employee is expected to behave differently than he does in his role as father. This is a many-faceted idea: there is the way the individual actually performs in a given capacity, the way others expect him to perform, and the way he expects himself to perform, the last being one of the more subtle components of the superego. In addition, the individual quite normally expects others to act toward him in a way that is partially defined by the roles each occupies, so that he reacts to another person in terms of how that person's behavior toward him accords or fails to accord with his own role expectations. Astute diagnosticians have intuitively taken such expectations into consideration in evaluating behavior. There is value, however, in the caseworker's becoming familiar with these concepts so that he can use them consciously in understanding an individual's actions and reactions.[8]

This way of viewing behavior is also of great help in evaluating other people's responses to the client. Discrepancies between the reactions of different people with whom an individual is associated can often be accounted for either by actual differences in his ways of acting in their presence or by their different role expectations of him. Variations in role expectations may be of great significance in creating marital problems and may also account for the very different initial pictures husband and wife give the caseworker of themselves and of each other.

Role expectations, like behavioral norms, are influenced by many factors—ethnicity, class, religion, education, family (different family members having different degrees of influence), peers, and so on. In addition, each individual has his own variation of role expectations, a composite of many different influences. The worker's awareness of role as a factor in interpersonal relationships and as a component in the estimation of the "normalcy" or appropriateness of functioning will certainly enhance the assessment process.

To summarize, then, norms are indispensable in estimating the nature of both sides of the person-situation configuration. We use them constantly in locating the spots at which external pressures are strong and the ways in which the individual is reacting in an unhealthy fashion.

The assessment process provides the worker with a workable knowledge of the client's strengths and weaknesses, the pressures, gratifications, and potentials of his situation, based on a study of his current life, pertinent aspects of his past life, and his ways of acting in the casework interviews. The diagnostic process now moves from delineating "what" the trouble is to "why" it is. In this step we seek to understand cause and effect both in terms of current interactions and in developmental terms, that is, the effect of past events on current functioning. We try to learn to what extent and in what way the causative factors of the client's problem lie within the situation by which he is confronted or are the product of unusual needs within the client or of poor functioning within his ego or superego.

] *Diagnosis: Dynamic and Etiological*

Having discussed the various internal and external factors that the caseworker must evaluate in assessing a client's difficulty, we must now consider the relative importance in the problem of this aspect of the environment or that characteristic of the personality and the way in which the various features of environment and personality affect each other.

We are, in the first place, looking for coherent patterns. If there is high anxiety we seek to understand why, considering the various possibilities of current provocation, historical factors, and interrelationships within the personality itself. Is it fear of the superego or fear of a breakthrough of the instinctual drives or fear of external reality? Is it a recent development or a long-time pattern? If the latter, what developmental factors account for it? Is health a factor? What in the situation may be provoking the anxiety? What effect does it have on the client's functioning? What responses does it provoke from others toward him? The caseworker must seek to understand in similar fashion each aspect of the personality where dysfunctioning has appeared and each aspect of the environment as it contributes to the total problem.

Interaction between different facets of the environment must also be understood. Is the teacher critical of Johnnie because he is impudent, or because he is overgraded, or because his mother criticized her, or because Johnnie comes from a poor neighborhood, has poor clothing, and no privacy for study, or because he is big for his age and looks as though he ought to behave in a more grownup way than he does? Pete sees himself as a delinquent and begins acting like one. What part in his trouble is played by his neighborhood, his housing, the lack of decent recreation, his teacher's attitude, the curriculum offered by the school? Was he put in a "general" course because he wasn't bright enough for vocational high? Has he gotten to think of himself as a delinquent because he was taken into court for truancy?

Especially in problems of interpersonal adjustment, it is useful to view the person-situation interaction in a special way. In such interactions one individual is at the same time the other person's situation, and vice versa. The term "transaction" has recently come into use to describe the flow of currents between two individuals who are in close personal interaction. We suggested in an earlier chapter that this interaction is not a billiard-ball type of direct impact* of one force upon another.⁹ A better parallel could be drawn to football or lacrosse. When the ball is thrown from one team to the other it is first passed around within the opposing team according to its plan of play, and when it finally reemerges within the reach of the first team, its location, direction, and speed are only remotely related to the way it was originally thrown. In the same way the action of one person upon another takes effect only in the form in which it is perceived by the other. The first person may have used a complaining tone because he was tired, but if the "alter" perceives the tone as anger, he will react to it as such. His response, in turn, may be silence, or martyrlike murmurings, or explosive retaliation, depending upon his own personality, earlier experiences of the day that have set his mood, his perception of the first person, his notion of the requirements of the role in which he is functioning, and a variety of other things. The first speaker's next response is subject to similarly complicated influences.

If one studies a series of interactions—or transactions—as the caseworker inevitably does in interpersonal problems, he will find that certain characteristic patterns begin to emerge. It is as if the captains of the teams had caught on to the inner workings of the opposing team and each is now manipulating the other.† In 1949 the present writer called attention to this factor in the form of complementarity between marriage partners. More recent writings have pointed out similar patterns in interaction characterizing the behavior of whole families.¹⁰ Without question, casework diagnosis in cases of interpersonal conflict must include comprehension of the interaction between the main participants in the conflict. Such comprehension involves understanding of the way in which one person's behavior sets off or provokes certain responses in the other, the extent to which this is consciously or unconsciously purposeful, and the extent to which unrecognized complementary needs are being met in the process. In marriage conflict, certainly, the worker will make serious treatment errors if he is not aware of the factor of complementarity in such combinations as father-daughter mar-

---

* Apparently in some disciplines "interaction" did have this simpler connotation, and "transaction" was adopted to signify the richer conception.
† This phenomenon is also referred to as role reciprocity.

riages, mother-son marriages, marriages in which there is some degree of reversal in masculine-feminine patterns, sado-masochistic marriages, certain marriages of alcoholics, and so on.[11] He will often find that serious trouble has emerged in a family where a previously existing complementarity has been disturbed.[12] In such cases serious consideration should be given to the possibility of restoring the previous balance in the family. Marriage is not infrequently the means by which two neurotic or otherwise disturbed individuals are enabled through complementarity to function at a reasonably high level of personal satisfaction and social effectiveness.

A significant aspect of interaction is communication—the extent to which two people are able to convey their feelings and opinions to each other, either verbally or nonverbally. Such defenses as repression, suppression, and inhibition may interfere with the communication. Attitudes expressed verbally may be contradicted by nonverbal behavior (which is often unconscious or ego-dystonic preconscious). Words, tone of voice, gestures, and bodily behavior may be misinterpreted because of the internal needs or attitudes of the "alter." Defenses of projection, denial, and turning against the self are particularly likely to "distort reception." Even differences in the literal meanings of words exchanged between individuals using the same basic language will cause misunderstanding. Not only different classes and geographical regions but even individual families give special meaning to words.

Important as these "transactional" matters are, however, a word of warning is needed against overemphasizing them. There is a tendency among some caseworkers to seize upon any new idea as the last and only word in casework technique. Interaction or "transaction" is important, the dynamics of small groups are important, "dyads" and "tryads" are significant—but it is still *individuals* who are interacting. The whole may be greater than the parts, but it must not obliterate them. The "whole" and the "transaction" will, in fact, never be fully understood except as the interacting parts themselves are fully understood. Our growing understanding of interaction or transaction provides us at most with one further tool for understanding the individual and the situation of which he is a part.[13]

We noted earlier that previous life history is important in the assessment stage of diagnosis because it affords a good opportunity for noting repetitive patterns. It is also immensely valuable in helping us to understand causation in the developmental sense of how the person came to be the way he is. Early family relationships particularly help us to understand the level of psychosexual development, parental attachments, sexual identification, superego development, and the basis for the anxieties against which the ego is defending itself. Early family history can also give greater understanding of many qualities of the ego. Furthermore, sharp discrepancies in the way an individual functions at different times in his life provide excellent clues to the ways in which situational factors affect him.

A final note of warning is necessary against oversimplifying either the assessment or the dynamic and etiological parts of the diagnosis. Two phrases are heard over and over again ad nauseam in diagnostic discussions by caseworkers. They are, as the reader has probably guessed, "ego strength" and "oedipal conflict." "Ego strength" is an almost meaningless term, despite its use in the best psychiatric circles. The ego is not a composite force to be measured on a single scale; it is rather a series of functions and qualities of many different dimensions. Perception is accurate or inaccurate; judgment is sound or unsound; self-image is appropriate or inappropriate; only controls may be strong or weak. One may say about the ego as a whole that it functions well or poorly, but this description is not useful as a delineation of *which* aspects of the ego function well and which poorly, and when poorly, in what way.

The term "oedipal problem" is likewise almost meaningless. In nine cases out of ten the worker will note that the client has an oedipal problem. In about a third of these cases, however, the worker will have mistaken a primitive oral parental attachment to the mother or father for an oedipal one. In the remaining two-thirds the observation will be correct, but it will not be of much value if the worker regards it as the total answer to the problem and is satisfied to stop his diagnostic thinking at that point. It is only as the observation is related to other parts of the dynamic diagnosis that it takes on real meaning. Are its effects increased anxiety, sexual inhibitions, hostility to men or to women, reversed identifications? Does it show itself in transference reactions, in defensive hostility? Is perception distorted, self-image awry? Oversimplification is one of the worst traps into which the worker can fall.

The dynamic and etiological part of the diagnosis, then, represents the caseworker's effort to understand causative factors in the client's difficulty. It seeks to say why the total situation is as it is. It tries to establish interrelationships between the various factors which combine to create the client's discomfort or poor social functioning. It seeks to comprehend the interaction of the internal and the external, the sources of the present in the past, and the internal dynamics within the personality or among the environmental forces.

From the assessment and the dynamic-etiological diagnosis together should emerge a coherent picture of the client as a person, the qualities of his ego, the nature of his conscience, his ideals and aspirations, the extent of his maturation in his capacity to relate to others in all degrees of intimacy. Similarly, his situation should be understood in terms of its realities—its contribution to the problem and the potentialities it contains for amelioration of the problem. Together the assessment and the dynamic-etiologic diagnosis should define as clearly as possible the key points toward which treatment must be directed.

] *Categorization*

A third major step in diagnosis is categorization, the placing of a disorder—not a trait or characteristic but the whole disorder—in a known classification.[14] Such classifications have a variety of uses. They may be of value, for instance, in any statistical accounting of the type of work done by an agency, of the incidence of one type of difficulty or another, of the degree of successful treatment in one type of case as against another, and so on. For such purposes descriptive categories are useful, and casework employs a number of terms that describe the problems of clients, terms such as marital conflict, parent-child problem, unmarried mother, family breakdown, delinquency, unemployment, old age problem, and so on. These are essentially descriptive categories, centered around the symptomatic behavior resulting from the interaction of the person and the situation. They tell us something about the difficulty and can become the focal point for assembling data about the disorder. They are not, however, systematic categories, and they do not in themselves take us very far along either in understanding the nature of the client's difficulty or in making treatment plans.

When we turn to the environmental and social features of the problem, we can classify such aspects as ethnic background, class, income level, education, housing level, religion, occupation, family type, and so on. This is the kind of classification we used in assessment, and it is useful for scaling a number of separate factors. There is, however, no generally accepted set of categories that pulls together constellations of such factors into entities that can serve as a guide to treatment. This type of diagnostic category has to await the development of theory to the point of establishing causative and other dynamic associations between certain social and environmental features of characteristic disorders.

Categories for different types of personal interaction, especially family interaction, are currently being developed (in fact the term "family diagnosis" is coming into use).[15] It is conceivable that in time terminology may be devised to designate commonly found types of interaction.[16] At present, however, designations on a family level are largely descriptive and overlap to such an extent that one questions their usefulness. It is possible that too many variables are being grouped together in the quest for a system of family diagnosis. A family "profile" describing the main features of the family in normative terms might be more manageable.

For categorizing the physical side of the client's problem, it is customary to use lay descriptive terminology or to repeat the medical diagnosis, if one has been made.

The only well-developed categorical scheme of diagnosis used in casework is a combination of terms derived from psychoanalysis and psychiatry and used to designate certain major personality configurations. This system of clinical diagnosis has progressed considerably further than other categorizations employed in casework in the direction of being a "conditional-genetic" rather than a "descriptive" system of classification. These are terms Lewin[17] uses to distinguish between Aristotelian and Galilean methods of classification. In an interesting chapter in his *Dynamic Theory of Personality* Lewin points out that in Aristotelian classification things are grouped together on the basis of external or superficial characteristics, because they look alike or behave alike. This, it seems to me, is comparable to our "problem" classifications that categorize people as "unmarried mothers" or "delinquents" or "unemployed" without regard to the dynamics or the etiology of their behavior. In Galilean classification, on the other hand, distinctions are based upon "an essentially functional way of thinking," the conditions under which things occur or the causes of their occurrence.

Before the introduction of Freudian theory, psychiatric classification was largely Aristotelian, descriptive; and to a certain extent it still is, as for instance in the term "anti-social reaction" or "emotionally unstable personality." Increasingly, however, psychoanalytic terminology is becoming Galilean or "genotypical" rather than "phenotypical" again to borrow Lewin's terminology. This tendency is best seen in the designations for different neuroses and in the major distinctions between neurosis, psychosis, and behavior disorder. Within the general behavior disorder category itself such classification is just beginning to emerge. The classification currently advocated by the American Psychiatric Association[18] is a combination of Freudian-based terminology and the older descriptive categories. While symptomatology is part of the more genotypical diagnostic system, it is only one of the indices used. Predominantly, these categories rest upon common etiological and dynamic features, and thus can be particularly useful in the planning of treatment.

Contrary to a currently popular assumption, casework has not borrowed psychiatric terminology in wholesale fashion but rather uses only those terms which apply to conditions with which caseworkers are recurrently familiar and concerning which they have access to diagnostically discriminating data. The worker first attempts to arrive at the broadest discriminations. Is this client probably psychotic, or does he fall somewhere in the neurotic group; does there seem to be a character disorder, or are there evidences of antisocial or dissocial[19] behavior; or is this individual close to normal? If he does not fit clearly into any one of these classifications, between which major categories does his difficulty seem to lie?

The caseworker's right to diagnose psychosis is sometimes questioned on the grounds that such a diagnosis is a medical question. If, however, the caseworker did not arrive at his own opinion that this is or may be psychosis, how else would he know enough to refer the client to a psychiatrist for a medical diagnosis or to consult the psychiatrist himself for confirmation of his opinion? Should every client in every casework agency be seen by a psychiatrist to determine whether or not he is psychotic? If in the worker's opinion psychosis may be involved, psychiatric consultation is clearly a necessity.[20] Often the worker can go somewhat further and, subject always to medical confirmation, discriminate in clear-cut cases at least between major categories such as schizophrenia and manic-depressive psychosis. Where any organic factor is involved the caseworker has very little diagnostic competence, but he should have sufficient knowledge of symptomatology to recognize signs that should be reported to the medical consultant. *Definitive* diagnosis in psychosis cannot be made without knowledge of the psychological manifestations of numerous physical conditions which produce psychotic symptomatology.

As the writer has pointed out in an earlier paper,[21] the worker is not making a medical diagnosis simply by using the same terms as the psychiatrist. An opinion about the nature of a mental disturbance becomes a medical diagnosis only when it is expressed by a physician. Furthermore, such a diagnosis is designed for use in medical treatment; when the caseworker expresses such an opinion it is a casework diagnosis and is designed for casework treatment. A most important part of this casework treatment when either psychosis or borderline psychosis seems possible is either to refer the client for psychiatric care or to consult a psychiatrist about the advisability of such care and for medical confirmation of the casework diagnosis. If by joint agreement it seems advisable for the caseworker to carry the treatment, the diagnosis of psychosis will indicate that emphasis will be upon reality adjustments and sustainment. When a diagnosis is being transmitted from one agency to another it is essential, if there is any possibility of confusion as to whether a diagnosis is medical or casework, that the professional source of the opinion be made clear.

When neither psychosis nor antisocial or dissocial reaction is indicated but the cause of the problem seems to lie sufficiently within the client to indicate some type of personality disturbance, the next distinction to be made is most frequently between some type of character disorder and psychoneurosis. In most cases in which long-time treatment of interpersonal maladjustment is undertaken it should be possible for the experienced caseworker to make even finer distinctions, such as those among anxiety hysteria, conversion hysteria, obsessive neurosis, compulsive neurosis, and neurotic depression.[22] There is less standardized nomenclature for the various character disorders, but it should be possible to distinguish among three major types: (a) oedipal, phallic, or hysterical, closely related terms sometimes used interchangeably; (b) anal or compulsive, and (c) oral, impulsive, "acting out" or infantile, also more or less interchangeable terms. The terms "neurotic character" and "character neurosis" are also used to designate the oedipal and anal types. It is the exception rather than the rule, of course, to find "pure" types—people who fall exclusively within any given diagnostic category. Clinical terms represent focal points on several different continua, and most individuals show some characteristics of one category and some of another. When this is so, both should be mentioned with indication of where the greater emphasis lies.

When intensive work on interpersonal problems is being undertaken with individuals suffering from any type of personality disturbance there is great value in psychiatric consultation. The more severe the disorder appears to be, the more important such consultation is. Any sort of physical illness also calls for medical evaluation, even when in the worker's judgment the illness appears to be hysteria. Psychosomatic disorders should be given psychological help only under medical auspices or, if the work is of a supportive nature, in close coordination with medical treatment. If depression is present in any significant degree psychiatric consultation is of great importance, partly because the border between neurotic and psychotic depression is sometimes hard to distinguish, partly because medication may be indicated, and partly in order to have a medical opinion as to whether the severity of the depression makes hospitalization advisable. Deviations such as overt homosexuality, sadism, masochism, voyeurism, and drug addiction sometimes come to the caseworker and, like psychosis, call for immediate psychiatric consultation.

From time to time the value of the clinical diagnosis is questioned, for there is a tendency to feel that the dynamic-etiologic diagnosis is sufficient. But the clinical diagnosis has the additional value of designating a cluster of factors characteristically found together. For instance, the term "compulsive neurosis," when correctly used, immediately conveys certain information about a client. It signifies that the individual has reached the oedipal stage of development in his relationship to his parents but has not resolved the conflicts of this period and has regressed in substantial degree to ways of behaving characteristic of the anal or habit training period of development. It indicates that he has a severe superego to which he may be overly submissive on the surface but which he is unconsciously fighting. He usually is very sensitive to criticism and has strong dependency needs, though they may be covered over; he sometimes very much wants to please the worker and other parent figures but at other times is balky and is either outwardly negative to suggestions or subtly sabotages them. He is often perfectionistic, usually ambivalent, often confused in masculine-feminine identifications. He is apt to make heavy use of such defenses as intellectualization, rationalization, isolation, and reaction formation. He usually has had a strict upbringing by a parent or parents who loved him but imposed rigid training in habits and behavior. He may be strict in bringing up his own children, or ambivalent in training them, or else he may be strict on the surface but unconsciously promote vicarious acting out. Of course not all of these characteristics will be true of every compulsive person, but the presence of a few of them in the absence of contrary evidence will alert the worker to the probable diagnosis, and to the avenues to explore that will either confirm the diagnosis or contraindicate it.

As it takes firm shape the diagnosis becomes a sort of index to many things about the individual that have not yet become clear from what has been observed or said. It often enables the worker to anticipate reactions to contemplated treatment steps and to guide them accordingly. The worker knows in advance, for instance, that a compulsive client will be very sensitive to criticism; he therefore will be extremely careful to avoid remarks that could be construed as criticism until the client is sufficiently secure with him to respond constructively. Such foreknowledge can also help greatly in the control of anti-therapeutic counter-transference reactions. The intellectualism often found in the compulsive, for example, can arouse feelings of frustration and dislike in the worker. If, however, the worker can recognize this trait as a defense against the anxiety created by an oversevere superego and can see that he is really dealing with a scared little boy or girl afraid of a harsh mother, the dislike may well be quickly replaced by the desire to help.

In other words, if one knows enough about some characteristics of a person to designate his clinical diagnosis, one immediately has the key to a great deal of other knowledge that will be useful in the process of helping him. In the psychoneuroses proper, specific symptoms such as phobias, hysterical paralyses, obsessions, compulsive rituals, and evidences of depression are distinctively related to the different categories and quickly alert the worker to the possible diagnosis. Symptoms alone, however, do not establish a diagnosis. There are always several possible explanations of any symptom. It is only when a specific form of behavior can be shown to be part of a larger configuration characteristic of the disorder in question that any certainty can be felt about the diagnosis.

It is clear, then, that knowledge of the major outlines of the better established clinical entities and of their characteristic symptomatology can very greatly sharpen the worker's diagnostic thinking. One weakness of the dynamic-etiological diagnosis taken by itself is that it tends to see a little bit of this and a little bit of that in an individual without reaching a definitive delineation. It is when one tries to say whether the difficulty is primarily a character disorder or a neurosis, whether the client is a borderline schizophrenic or a severe hysteric, and so on, that incompleteness in the social study or lack of clear-cut evaluation of the facts becomes apparent. This assumes, of course, that the clinical diagnosis itself is not a glib designation based on superficial impressions. The greatest safety lies in seeking to arrive at both forms of diagnosis and using each to supplement the other.

There are indeed several dangers involved in the use of diagnostic categories. One is that of stereotyping, assuming that all people in the same category are exactly alike. Each person has many individual qualities that make him quite unlike his fellows, despite the fact that in the rough outlines of a personality disturbance he may have much in common with others suffering from the same disorder. Another danger to be guarded against is careless labeling, assuming a person belongs in a given group because of superficial qualities or overlooking other qualities that point in another direction—the old story of Cinderella's sister cutting off her toe to make the shoe fit.

Whenever a categorical scheme of diagnosis based on common dynamics and etiology rather than on descriptive features only is available, it can, if properly used, aid very greatly in understanding and hence in treatment. It is, however, only an additional tool to be used in conjunction with the assessment and the dynamic-etiological diagnosis, in which the features of the case are spelled out in terms of norms and in terms of dynamic cause and effect relationships.

It is surely apparent that there is no simple one-to-one relationship between diagnosis and choice of treatment. Diagnosis involves a many-faceted but orderly understanding of the client and his problem. In treatment planning, all that is known—strengths as well as weaknesses—is reviewed and evaluated for the purpose of learning how best to help.

As the contact progresses, the fund of knowledge grows and the worker repeatedly refers to it in making the decisions which either modify or implement plans made at the outset of treatment. The more orderly the ongoing diagnostic process by which assessment is made and dynamic understanding grows, the more wisely will the worker decide what treatment to offer his client.

NOTES

1. Otto Pollak, *Social Science and Psychotherapy for Children*, Russell Sage Foundation, New York, 1952.

2. For a somewhat different listing, see Sidney L. Green, "Psychoanalytic Contributions to Casework Treatment of Marital Problems," *Social Casework*, 35 (December, 1954), 419–423; and Isabel L. Stamm, "Ego Psychology in the Emerging Theoretical Base of Casework," in *Issues in American Social Work*, Alfred J. Kahn, ed., Columbia University Press, New York, 1959, pp. 80–109.

3. For an excellent discussion of "evidence," see Richmond, *Social Diagnosis, op. cit.*, Chapter IV.

4. Such "models" can be found in LeRoy M. A. Maeder, "Diagnostic Criteria—The Concept of Normal and Abnormal," *The Family*, 23 (October, 1941), 171–179; Talcott Parsons, "Illness and the Role of the Physician," *American Journal of Orthopsychiatry*, 21 (July, 1951), 452–460; and Otto Pollak, "Design of a Model of Healthy Family Relationships as a Base for Evaluative Research," *Social Service Review*, 31 (December, 1957), 369–376.

5. A number of excellent articles bearing on this subject have appeared in recent years:

Charlotte Adland, "The Attitude of Eastern European Jews Toward Mental Disease: A Cultural Interpretation," *Smith College Studies in Social Work*, 8 (December, 1937), 85–116.

Urie Bronfenbrenner, "Socialization and Social Class Through Time and Space," in *Readings in Social Psychology*, E. Maccoby, T. Newcomb, and E. Hartley, eds., Holt, Rinehart, and Winston, New York, 1958.

Berta Fantl, "Integrating Psychological, Social and Cultural Factors in Assertive Casework," *Social Work*, 4 (October, 1958), 30-37.

William V. Gioseffi, "Culture as an Aspect of the Total Personality," *Social Casework,* 40 (March, 1959), 115–119.

Robert Havighurst and Allison Davis, "A Comparison of the Chicago and Harvard Studies of Social Class Differences in Child Rearing," *American Sociological Review,* 20 (1955), 438–442.

Shirley Hellenbrand, "Client Value Orientations: Implications for Diagnosis and Treatment," *Social Casework,* 42 (April, 1961), 163–169.

Alex Inkeles, "Some Sociological Observations on Culture and Personality Studies," in *Personality in Nature, Society, and Culture,* Clyde Kluckhohn, Henry A. Murray, and David M. Schneider, eds., Alfred A. Knopf, New York, 1953.

Elizabeth G. Meier, "Social and Cultural Factors in Casework Diagnosis," *Social Work,* 41 (July, 1959), 15–26.

S. M. Miller and Elliot G. Mishler, "Social Class, Mental Illness, and American Psychiatry: An Expository Review," *The Milbank Memorial Fund Quarterly,* 37 (April, 1959), 174–199.

Jerome K. Myers and Bertram H. Roberts, *Family and Class Dynamics in Mental Illness,* John Wiley & Sons, New York, 1959.

6. See Margaret Mead, *Sex and Temperament in Three Primitive Societies,* W. Morrow, New York, 1935, and *Male and Female: A Study of the Sexes in a Changing World,* W. Morrow, New York, 1949.

7. For an excellent statement of this, see Louis Lehrman, "Science, Art, and Social Casework," unpublished paper, mimeographed, University of Pittsburgh Graduate School of Social Work, 1957.

8. For a list of readings concerning role concepts, see page 32.

9. For another discussion of this, see Roy R. Grinker and others, *Psychiatric Social Work: A Transactional Casebook,* Basic Books, New York, 1961, pp. 11–14. The author was amused to find, after using the billiard ball simile, that Grinker had expressed the idea in almost identical terms.

10. See Nathan W. Ackerman, "The Diagnosis of Neurotic Marital Interaction," *Social Casework,* 35 (April, 1954), 139–147; Florence Hollis, *Women in Marital Conflict,* Family Service

Association of America, New York, 1949, pp. 90, 97, and 209; Carol H. Meyer, *Complementarity and Marital Conflict: The Development of a Concept and Its Application to the Casework Method,* doctoral dissertation, New York School of Social Work, Columbia University, 1957; and Bela M. Mittlemann, "Analysis of Reciprocal Neurotic Patterns in Family Relationships," in *Neurotic Interaction in Marriage,* Victor W. Eisenstein, ed., Basic Books, New York, 1956, pp. 81–100.

11. See Marjorie Berlatsky, "Some Aspects of the Marital Problems of the Elderly," *Social Casework, 43* (May, 1962), 233–237; and Sue Vesper, "Casework Aimed at Supporting Marital Role Reversal," *Social Casework, 43* (June, 1962), 303–307.

12. For further discussion of this and related points, see Jeanette Regensburg, "Application of Psychoanalytic Concepts to Casework Treatment of Marital Problems," *Social Casework, 35* (December, 1954), 424–432.

13. See Grinker, *op. cit.*

14. For discussion of the problem of classification, see Samuel Finestone, "Issues Involved in Developing Diagnostic Classifications for Casework," *Casework Papers,* Family Service Association of America, New York, 1960.

15. Nathan W. Ackerman, and Raymond Sobel, "Family Diagnosis," *American Journal of Orthopsychiatry, 20* (1950), 744–753.

16. Two interesting but not markedly successful attempts to do this are found in Nathan W. Ackerman, *The Psychodynamics of Family Life: Diagnosis and Treatment of Family Relationships,* Basic Books, New York, 1958; and Alice L. Voiland and associates, *Family Casework Diagnosis,* Columbia University Press, New York, 1962.

17. Kurt Lewin, *A Dynamic Theory of Personality: Selected Papers,* translated by Donald K. Adams and Karl E. Zener, McGraw-Hill, New York, 1935, p. 11.

18. American Psychiatric Association, *Mental Disorders: A Diagnostic and Statistical Manual,* American Psychiatric Association, Washington, D.C., 1952.

19. The terms "anti-social reaction" and "dissocial reaction" are now used in the "Diagnostic and Statistical Manual" to replace the former terms "psychopathic personality" and "psychopathic personality with asocial or amoral trends."

20. Many cases involving psychosis or borderline psychosis are now referred to casework agencies. With proper precautions, including psychiatric consultation, considerable help can be given many of these clients by use of sustaining procedures, direct influence and discussion of current person-situation realities.

21. Florence Hollis, "Personality Diagnosis in Casework," in *Ego Psychology and Dynamic Casework*, Howard J. Parad, ed., Family Service Association of America, 1958, pp. 83–96.

22. The following are of particular value as guides in the "clinical" diagnosis: Franz Alexander, "The Neurotic Character," *International Journal of Psychoanalysis*, *11* (1930), 292–311; Franz Alexander and Helen Ross, eds., *Dynamic Psychiatry*, University of Chicago Press, Chicago, 1952; Helene Deutsch, *Psycho-analysis of the Neurosis*, Hogarth Press, London, 1951; O. Spurgeon English and Gerald H. J. Pearson, *Common Neuroses of Children and Adults*, W. W. Norton & Co., New York, 1937; Otto Fenichel, *The Psychoanalytic Theory of Neurosis*, W. W. Norton & Co., New York, 1945; Arthur Percy Noyes, *Modern Clinical Psychiatry*, 5th ed., Saunders, Philadelphia, 1959; and Herman Nunberg, *Principles of Psychoanalysis: Their Application to the Neuroses*, translated by Madlyn and Sidney Kahr, International Universities Press, 1955.

XII

The Choice of Treatment Objectives

WE NOW COME TO THE QUESTION of treatment planning—the purpose for which social study and diagnosis are undertaken. By this we mean the caseworker's formulation of the kind of help he will *offer* the client—the kind of treatment he believes will be of most value to him. As we have noted, however, treatment depends not on what the caseworker offers but on what the client is willing to accept and participate in. It involves the willing participation of both client and therapist, with the client's response to treatment throughout the contact being a most important indicator of his capacity and motivation.[1] We have also stressed that treatment is a very fluid affair, changing its direction and emphasis as it proceeds in response to new understanding, which sometimes confirms but at other times modifies the earlier picture.

The knowledge made available by the psychosocial study and the diagnosis is used in two ways. First, it supplies the basis for certain major preliminary decisions that must be made fairly early in the contact—usually around the fifth or sixth interview—and for details of the early stages of treatment. Second, it provides a fund of information which the worker will continue to draw on and use in treatment and treatment planning throughout his whole association with the client. Later content enlarges upon earlier content as it is compared with earlier content in the worker's mind. Knowledge attained early gives perspective to what comes later, and often is drawn on in helping the client to increase his understanding. Similarly, throughout treatment, diagnostic conclusions remain a backdrop against which necessary decisions about details of procedure can be made.

In thinking about the best way to help a client we must first envisage tentative goals of treatment and then assess the technical means by which the client can be helped to reach them. In the present chapter we will consider goals, moving on in the next to an examination of treatment methodology.

] *Goals: Intermediate and Long-Range*

When we speak of goals we really refer to a series of intermediate or sub-goals as well as to the overall or ultimate objective of treatment. This ultimate goal is always some type of improvement in the client's personal-social functioning, that is, in his personal sense of comfort or satisfaction in life and in his functioning as it affects the people with whom he is associated. It is a very unusual situation in which these two types of improvement do not go hand in hand, though the client may be primarily concerned with one more than with the other.

The long-range goal is, of course, related to the problem of which the client either is aware at the beginning of the contact or comes to recognize as treatment proceeds. Sometimes the client has a broad awareness of the nature of his problem at the outset of treatment. In the very first interview a mother may say, "I know there must be something wrong with the way I am handling Tommie." She does not know all that lies behind the trouble, but she sees that she herself is involved as well as Tommie, and at least implicitly recognizes that the goal of treatment includes modification of herself as well as of the child. Very often, however, in interpersonal problems, the client sees the trouble as lying only in the other person—child, husband, wife. This was the case, for example, with Mrs. Ryman, whose treatment we followed in Chapter II. An important part of treatment in this case was bringing Mrs. Ryman to recognize her own role in the marital conflict and working through her resistance to trying to understand and modify her own behavior. Occasionally the problem does lie primarily in someone else, but far more often it is a matter of interaction with need for change in the person seeking help, whether or not other people involved in the situation are also willing to change. Frequently, too, the very location of a problem appears to be in one area of functioning at the outset but in another after a few interviews. The client may see his problem as difficulty with a child, while the worker, listening to him describe the divergent ways in which he and his wife handle the child, may locate the trouble as also, or even primarily, in tension between husband and wife.

From the caseworker's point of view the ultimate goal in problems of interpersonal adjustment is not solely to find a solution to the immediate problem or dilemma but, whenever possible, to enable the client to achieve a better way of functioning at least in this one area of his life.

Some valuable work has recently been done on "crises" as one form of dilemma or predicament by which a person may be faced. Going back to Erich Lindemann's work on the Coconut Grove fire and the effects of this catastrophe on its victims,[2] Howard Parad and Gerald Caplan,[3] and more recently David Kaplan,[4] have pointed out the value of studying the exact nature of the crises by which individuals or families are confronted in order to understand the tasks they must undertake in order to surmount them. For instance, David Kaplan, in his analysis of the crisis of premature birth,[5] points out that there are four distinct psychological tasks by which the mother of a premature child is confronted, beginning with the expression of "anticipatory grief" in preparation for the possible loss of the child, and ending, if the child survives, with the task of understanding how a premature baby differs from a normal baby in its special needs and growth patterns. Similar analyses could be made of many situations by which clients are confronted, whether or not they can be called "acute situational disorders." An out-of-wedlock child, for instance, presents the mother with certain specific tasks whether or not her relationship with the child's father is a sign of personal maladjustment. The accomplishment of the tasks required by such situations is sometimes the final treatment goal; at other times it constitutes an intermediate goal in the pursuit of a generally sounder adjustment.

The intermediate goals of treatment are always way stations on the road to the ultimate aim, means by which it is hoped the final goal will be achieved. We speak of aiming to reduce the severity of the superego, or to strengthen the client's ability to assert his own needs, or to modify the tendency to project. Or we state that we hope to induce a mother to send her child to camp, or a husband to share his thoughts and feelings more fully with his wife. These objectives are sought only because they are seen as necessary for the achievement of an ultimate goal of improved personal-social functioning. They are closely related to the procedures of treatment and are often articulated in combination with them. A worker will say that he intends to "try to reduce anxiety by acceptance and reassurance and by getting the sister-in-law who lives nearby to visit daily," "try to reduce hostility to child by ventilation of mother's anger," "endeavor to get father to see he is displacing hostility to John from his own brother," "help mother to see that her failure to control Sidney is increasing his anxiety," "use corrective relationship to help Mrs. George reduce her tensions about sex," "try to get Mr. Brown to recognize his underlying hostility to his father," "face Mrs. Field with the consequences of her impulsiveness in an effort to get her to control it." None of these objectives is an end in itself, but rather a way station on the road to better personal-social functioning.

] *Goals and Motivation*

A factor as important as the nature of the problem in determining both ultimate and intermediate treatment goals is the client's motivation. Motivation involves, first, the client's own degree of discomfort with things as they are. Has he come in of his own volition or has he been urged or even coerced into seeking help? In the latter instance much will depend on the therapist's skill in enabling him to recognize that he himself may gain from participating in treatment. He may need to ventilate a good deal of feeling about the situation that precipitated the opening of the contact and the person responsible for his coming.

More important, he will need to gain some preliminary understanding of the nature of the treatment situation. Above all, he will need to be convinced of the worker's acceptance of him and interest in understanding and helping him for his own sake rather than to please others who are dissatisfied with him. And, except in certain protective situations, he will also need to know that the worker does not intend to impose help or change upon him but rather is there as an enabler, and only with his consent.

In sociological terminology we can say that the client becomes "acculturated to the role of a client," that is, he adapts himself to the treatment process, learning how to be a patient or client.[7] A first step in this "acculturation," and a crucial one for developing and maintaining motivation, is that of coming to appreciate the intent of the therapist and his basic attitude toward his client. The client must also learn what kind of participation is appropriate in interviews. This too begins in the first interview, which is in itself a sample of what treatment will be like and thereby makes its own contribution to the client's motivation to continue in the undertaking.

Another major component of motivation rests upon the client's values. Only if the parent believes that a child should do well in school will he become interested in improving his child's school adjustment. Only if he believes that a child should be happy and spontaneous, will he be disturbed by his child's excessive anxiety and inhibitions. Only if a wife believes in the ideal of an equalitarian marriage will she complain if her husband is dominating. Clearly, class and ethnic factors, as well as more individualized family and personal norms, enter into these values.

During recent years, moreover, there has been a reemphasis on the long-recognized fact that the worker's personal values, including those of his own class and ethnic background, enter into his judgments concerning treatment goals and that attention must be paid to the question of whether or not these are realistic in the client's terms. Certainly the worker's *personal* values must not be translated into goals for the client. His *professional* norms and values, on the other hand, inevitably and quite appropriately become a factor in treatment objectives. When a mother complains about an adolescent's behavior, the worker compares her description with a norm in his own mind. This norm is the product of his training—his accumulated experience, and that of his educators, of the range of adolescent behavior that can be tolerated without bringing harm to the child or his associates, and the relationship of the type of behavior shown by the child to later adult adjustment. The worker's evaluation should include, as well, considerations of class and ethnic background which influence role expectations and constitute part of any evaluation of norms. The objective of treatment then becomes an effort to narrow the gap between the initial situation and the worker's professional perception of socially and personally "healthy" functioning. It might take the form of helping the mother to see that her child was only showing normal adolescent growing pains, or else of helping her in various specific ways to respond more appropriately to real disturbance in the child. This type of evaluation is a constant part of the setting of treatment objectives. We invariably measure social or psychological functioning against professionally derived models of social and psychological health.[8]

It has long been recognized by caseworkers, and has recently been emphasized in role analyses, that the client initially comes to treatment with a good deal of trepidation and often with underlying resentment at having to take what is essentially a dependent position. This is true even when he comes of his own volition, with favorable knowledge of the agency and of the nature of the treatment. In a culture that values self-reliance as much as ours, it is not easy to admit that one cannot handle one's own problems. Fear of criticism and fear of the changes to which treatment may lead are often present too.[9] But it must also be recognized that anxiety is an important component in motivation.

We are accustomed to think of anxiety as something to be gotten rid of. Without it, however, motivation lags. With too much, on the other hand, there may be immobilization. The ideal therapeutic situation is one in which the client is anxious enough to want help and to keep coming for it, but not so afraid that fear interferes with his ability to use help.

Motivation is also affected by the client's appreciation of his problem and its ramifications. Most individuals tend in one way or another to minimize or to blind themselves to their difficulties. A husband remembers that he was grouchy last night but does not appreciate the fact that last night was only one of many and that he is slowly becoming disgusted with his marriage, while his wife is becoming withdrawn and despondent. His motivation for treatment may be very low unless in the first few interviews he can come to realize that his marriage is really breaking up and that his wife, despite her defensive appearance of disinterest, is deeply hurt because she still has a great deal of love for him. Not infrequently, when one partner's caring for the other comes to light during the exploratory period, the other will exclaim, "But I didn't know she cared any more—why didn't she tell me?" or "How could I have been so blind!" Following such realizations motivation may come to life. Their occurrence at any stage of treatment may mark the turning point from resistance to full participation, and may make possible intermediate treatment goals quite different from those thought feasible before.[10]

] *Goals and Causation*

A third important determinant of treatment goals is the *causation* of the problem—its etiology and its current dynamics. Here the worker draws on the formulations about dynamics and etiology made during diagnosis to arrive at intermediate goals of treatment. In a specific marital counseling case, for instance, the ultimate goal may be improvement in the marital relationship, or greater acceptance of a situation which basically cannot be improved, along with better adaptation to it, or some form of separation. The appropriateness and feasibility of any one of these goals will depend to a very great extent on the cause of the difficulty in the marriage and the modifiability of the causative factors. Thus, depending upon the causative picture, intermediate goals within the general objective may be a reduction of quarreling, or the giving up of an extramarital affair, or a trial period of separation. They may aim to enable the husband to increase his satisfaction in his work, to encourage the wife to control her provocativeness, or to help the husband reduce the extent to which he displaces feelings from his mother to his wife, or to aid the wife to out-grow childish inhibitions about sex. Formulation of such possible intermediate goals depends upon the worker's assessment of the nature of both the internal stress and the external pressures to which the client is responding, his evaluation of the functioning of various aspects of the client's personality—drives, ego and superego—and of the dynamic interrelationships between all these factors and the developmental features that explain them.

] *Intervening Variables*

The phrase *"possible* intermediate goal" is used advisedly, for the relationship between causation and treatment is not a direct, straight-line correspondence. Rather, there are a number of intervening variables.

MODIFIABILITY OF CAUSATIVE FACTORS

One is the modifiability of the causative factors themselves. Not infrequently the most important causative factor is not the one most likely to yield to treatment. The most direct cause of disturbance in a family may be the presence of a severely retarded child who, for the benefit of the rest of the children as well as the mother, should be institutionalized. Sometimes early work shows that it is impossible to enable the mother to agree to place the child. The objective then becomes improvement in the mother's household management and in her relationships with the rest of her family. Household or other help may free more of her time for them, and her perception of their requirements may be heightened so that she responds more adequately to their needs. Later, work with the other childrens' problems may lead to intrapsychic shifts that make it possible to return to the question of placement of the retarded child. Poor housing may be another factor that cannot be improved by treatment: a family's low income and crowded conditions in the city may make it impossible to do anything about their housing. Attention may be focused instead on the children's peer relationships and opportunities to build these up in the local settlement, and on health care and income management. Sometimes a marital and parent-child problem arises because of mental disturbance in one parent, which is not so serious as to require hospitalization but does make substantial modification of the marital relationship impossible. Though this major cause of the family's problem cannot be remedied, as an alternative it may be possible for the healthier parent to work on the problems of the children per se.

Sometimes the unmodifiable causative factor lies within the personality of the client himself. It may, for instance, be clear that a woman is overly dependent and that an excessive need to be cared for in a childish fashion leads her to involve herself in unwise relationships with men who give the appearance of strength but always have character defects that eventually cause her unhappiness and suffering. Her dependence may be so strong and deep-seated that it is impossible to reduce it, but the caseworker may be able to help her recognize her pattern and the consequences of her haste to satisfy her needs, in an effort to strengthen her perception and judgment to the point that she can find a more stable person to lean on. Or a mother may be overly protective of her child because she is thus attempting to control or compensate for unconscious wishes to destroy him, but her guilt and anxiety may be so great that it would be unwise to bring any of her hostility into the open. The underlying cause of the overprotectiveness may not be modifiable by casework methods, but other treatment goals may be set up, seeking either to protect the child from the mother or to enable the mother to modify her behavior toward the child.

Indeed, there is one whole group of causative factors which can never in themselves be changed—harmful developmental experiences. The individual's *reactions* to these experiences can be modified, but not the experiences themselves. Sometimes the client can reevaluate them in the light of more mature judgment, or can see that he has actually distorted the early picture. This was true, for example, of the woman who blamed her parents for not letting her go to college when, as she later came to see, she had never let them know that college interested her (see Chapter VII). At other times, however, even the reactions cannot be modified, but some control can be gained over their effects in current life.

It must be abundantly clear from the examples given that when we speak of the influence on treatment aims of causation or of modifiability we actually mean the worker's *thinking about* causation and modifiability. How he views these factors, rests not only on his individual perception and judgment but also upon the body of theory by which his conclusions are influenced. A worker viewing a client and his situation from the vantage point of a different theory might well come to different conclusions about causation and modifiability, and therefore envisage different treatment aims. Theory of causation and treatment goals are closely related.

OTHER FAMILY MEMBERS

Thus far we have been discussing treatment goals from a client-centered perspective. A further dimension must of necessity be added. It is the exception rather than the rule that the worker can be concerned with the welfare of only one person. The caseworker always has an overall responsibility to the people with whom the client is interacting and sometimes, as when he is dealing directly with several members of the same family, a very direct responsibility. This constitutes another variable intervening between causation and treatment. The worker must take into consideration the effect on others in the family of changes sought in the individual who for the moment is the focus of attention. This does not mean that he sacrifices the interests of one individual to those of another, but rather that it is his responsibility to bring into the treatment planning in both his own and the client's mind pertinent interrelationships between the client and other members of his family. Nor is this an intrusion into the integrity of the treatment process, for neither worker nor client can move wisely without giving full consideration to the interactions among family members. Complementarity exists in family relationships. A change in one part of the equilibrium not only brings changes in other parts but also results in "feedback," counterreactions that in turn affect the person with whom the change originated.[11]

Increasingly in interpersonal adjustment problems work is under way with two or more people in a family at the same time. The ultimate goals are often common to the several people involved, but the intermediate objectives usually vary. While the needs and ways of functioning of family members interlock, and certainly interact in a "transactional" way, they are by no means solely the result of such interaction: they are rather rooted first in the individual personalities. Treatment, whether in individual or in joint interviews, must make substantial use of interactions, mutual provocations, and misunderstandings among family members, but for full effectiveness it must be guided by diagnostic understanding of each individual. Otherwise, it will lack sufficient direction and specificity, and may even be seriously misdirected.

PERIPHERAL FACTORS

Before going on to an examination of the choice of treatment procedures, we must consider some additional variables—somewhat peripheral but nevertheless important—that intervene between treatment and the ideal objective of modifying or removing the causal factors in the client's difficulty.

An obvious one is time. If experience indicates that a certain type of change is likely to require a number of months of work and the client will be available for only a few interviews, it certainly makes no sense to embark upon a line of treatment that will have to be interrupted in midstream. A decision on this factor will be influenced not only by the special function of the agency, as in Travelers' Aid where contact is almost always limited to a short time span, but also by circumstances affecting the client. After six or nine months of treatment a client may have to move to another city. Themes may be emerging at this point about which treatment decisions must be made. If they cannot be developed profitably within the time available, they should be circumvented rather than opened up and dealt with inadequately.

Another variable affecting the nature of treatment may be the way in which the agency function is defined. The course of a case in which there are both parent-child and marital problems is apt to be very different, depending upon whether the client applies to a child guidance clinic or to a family service agency. A woman who is deciding whether to separate from her ill but very difficult husband may be offered very different treatment, depending upon whether she goes to the social service department of the hospital for the mentally ill where her husband is being treated or to a community mental hygiene clinic in her own section of town.

An agency's view of priorities in its function will often translate itself into other variables affecting treatment: offices that do or do not provide privacy or protection from interruption during interviews; caseloads that permit 45-to-60 minute interviews per week for each client who needs the time, or caseloads that are too large to permit adequate time; and so on. Casework that has as its objective a substantial change in individual functioning usually requires protected and regular interviewing time of considerable duration.

The availability of dynamically oriented psychiatric consultation is another variable that may influence choice of treatment aim and procedure. Work with types of intrapsychic problems in which considerable anxiety may be stirred up is usually not undertaken without consultation with an analytically trained consultant.

The caseworker's skill is an intervening factor of great importance. Different themes, aims, and procedures require different kinds of skill. It is essential that the worker define treatment aims and employ procedures which lie within his range of competence and, within these limits, treat with skill rather than venture in a clumsy fashion into forms of treatment where he is unsure. This requirement, however, must not be taken to mean that treatment skill is static and cannot be further developed in workers, but rather that development is achieved by gradual reaching just beyond the border of one's present ability and not by luring the client into deep and troubled waters to sink or swim along with the worker.

Ideally, of course, the client's need should be met by whatever form of treatment will bring him the greatest relief from his discomfort. This means either that the agency function should be sufficiently flexible to adapt to varying needs or that transfers should be made to other agencies that offer the required treatment. It also means that within agencies clients should be referred to workers whose skill is adequate to meet their particular needs. These are objectives toward which we should and do work. Meanwhile, however, the variables we have mentioned are realistic factors that must be taken into consideration in setting treatment objectives, and planning treatment strategy that will result in greater comfort for the client and improvement in his functioning.

Treatment goals, then, are arrived at jointly by client and worker, whether the process is implicit or explicit. It is often of very great value for the goals to be explicit, for the client will more surely move toward his objectives when he is conscious of what they are. Goals are finally implemented only when they are shared by both client and worker. The objectives of treatment must be thought of as fluid, changing with changes in the client's understanding of his own needs and in his motivation and as the worker's understanding of the client's needs and capacities develops. The response to treatment itself is a major component in these reformulations. While the ultimate goal is often seen at the beginning of treatment, intermediate and short-range goals are set as new phases of treatment emerge and may exist even within single interviews.

To have goals in mind is of the greatest importance in treatment. They not only enable the worker to avoid drifting along in a kindly, noneffective way, but also make it possible to avoid blind alleys. Conscious treatment planning serves the purpose of trial action. It compels the therapist to think through the possibilities and consequences of a line of treatment before undertaking it. Many pitfalls can be foreseen without the client's having to participate in the worker's trial and error. Well-focused and consciously planned therapy is more apt to be effective therapy.

NOTES

1. See Helen P. Taussig, "Treatment as an Aid to Diagnosis," *The Family, 19* (January, 1939), 289–294.

2. Erich Lindemann, "Symptomatology and Management of Acute Grief," *American Journal of Psychiatry, 101* (1944), 141–148.

3. Howard J. Parad and Gerald Caplan, "A Framework for Studying Families in Crisis," *Social Work, 5* (July, 1960), 3–15.

4. David M. Kaplan, "A Concept of Acute Situational Disorders," *Social Work, 7* (April, 1962), 15–23.

5. David M. Kaplan and Edward A. Mason, "Maternal Reactions to Premature Birth Viewed as an Acute Emotional Disorder," *American Journal of Orthopsychiatry, 30* (July, 1960), 539–547.

6. The subject of motivation is often discussed under the name of its opposite, i.e., resistance. In many ways these are two sides of the same coin: to "reduce resistance" is to "increase motivation." For discussion of resistance in early interviews, see Gordon Hamilton, *Theory and Practice of Social Casework*, 2nd ed., Columbia University Press, New York, 1951, pp. 52, 56–57, 80, 210. A useful discussion of resistance per se can be found in William H. Wilsnack, "Handling Resistance in Social Casework," *American Journal of Orthopsychiatry, 16* (April, 1946), 297–311. See also Beatrice Werble, "Motivation for Using Casework Services. I. Current Research in Motivation," *Social Casework, 39* (February–March, 1958), 124–130.

7. See Helen Perlman, "Intake and Some Role Considerations," *Social Casework, 41* (December, 1960), 171–177, and "The Role Concept and Social Casework: Some Explorations. I. The 'Social' in Social Casework," *Social Service Review, 35* (December, 1961), 370–381. See also letters to the editor appearing in subsequent issues following each of these articles and the article by Aaron Rosenblatt, "The Application of Role Concepts to the Intake Process," *Social Casework, 43* (January, 1962), 8–14. Also of interest is John Spiegel, "The Social Roles of Doctor and Patient in Psychoanalysis and Psychotherapy," *Psychiatry, 17* (December, 1954), 369–376.

8. See Lawrence S. Kubie, "The Fundamental Nature of the Distinction Between Normality and Neurosis," *Psychoanalytic Quarterly, 23* (April, 1954), 167–204.

9. See Hamilton, *op. cit.*, and Henry Maas, "Building Social Work Theory with Social Science Tools," *A Report of the Annual Meeting of the Research Department*, Welfare Planning Council, Los Angeles Region, Special Report Series, No. 41, 1950, including discussion by Frances Lomas Feldman.

10. For reports on research concerning motivation see Beatrice Werble, Charlotte S. Henry, and Margaret W. Millar, "Motivation for Using Casework Services," *Social Casework, 39* (February–March, 1958), 124–137; Lilian Ripple, "Motivation, Capacity, and Opportunity as Related to the Use of Casework Service: Theoretical Base and Plan of Study," *Social Service Review, 29* (June, 1955), 172–193; and Lilian Ripple, and Ernestina Alexander, "Motivation, Capacity, and Opportunity as Related to the Use of Casework Service: Nature of Client's Problem," *Social Service Review, 30* (March, 1956), 38–59.

11. For amplification of this point see Frances Levinson Beatman, "Family Interaction: Its Significance for Diagnosis and Treatment," *Social Casework, 38* (March, 1957), 111–118; Robert M. Gomberg, "Family-Oriented Treatment of Marital Problems," *Social Casework, 37* (January, 1956), 3–10; and Frances H. Scherz, "What Is Family-Centered Casework?" *Social Casework, 34* (1953), 343–349.

XIII

The
Choice of
Treatment Procedures

HAVING DISCUSSED THE OBJECTIVES of treatment, we are now ready
to consider the *procedures* most likely to be of value in reaching
these objectives under different circumstances and with different
personality configurations.[1] Many alternatives exist for helping
the client to move toward a given objective. Whether or not it
will be achieved depends not alone on the client's abilities and
motivation but to an equal degree on the worker's skill in
choosing the treatment procedures most congenial to the client's
personality, situation, and goals.

We have seen that objectives of treatment may involve modification not only of the environment but also of the individual,
for when the problem is one of interpersonal adjustment environmental change alone is seldom the total answer. Almost always
the major undertaking is some form of change within the person
seeking help, as well as within others of his family who may
also be interested in better relationships. Environmental factors
may nevertheless be contributing to the problem, or else may
offer avenues for alleviating its severity. Furthermore, problems
do not come singly. One can be ill or unemployed and at the
same time troubled in one's personal relationships. When such
a combination of external and internal pressures exists, the ob-

jective of internal change must be coupled with that of reducing external pressures or opening up opportunities that will be advantageous to the client in certain areas of his functioning.

] *Environmental Change: By Client or Worker*

In determining what procedures will be most effective in reaching goals involving environmental change, primary consideration must be given to two questions: (1) Is the environmental factor likely to respond better to the worker or to the client? (2) Will the client, with certain types of help from the worker, be able to assume responsibility for dealing with this factor in his environment himself? Once again, we are dealing with questions of modifiability and means.

It sometimes happens that while a patient could talk to a doctor himself about his condition, the worker's knowledge of both doctor and patient leads him to think that the client would not get the information needed for future planning if he asked for it initially himself. Not infrequently the worker, because of his status and role, can influence the environment in a way that the client cannot. At other times the worker's knowledge or skill in human relations may enable him to effect changes beyond the client's capacity to achieve by his own efforts.

Similarly, agencies have resources to supply the means of making up for environmental deficiencies that could not be overcome in any other way. In two fields in particular—public assistance and the provision of substitute care, such as foster homes, institutionalization, or adoption for children—agencies offer resources for changing the environment which the, client could not provide for himself or could obtain only with great difficulty.

Furthermore, factors within the client himself may make him unable or reluctant to act on his own behalf. Depression or great anxiety—the very state of mind that one is attempting to alleviate —may make it impossible for an individual to reach out for the comfort and support of relatives or friends, and this may have to be done for him. Sometimes, too, the expenditure of effort required is out of proportion to the benefit that would come from the client's acting for himself. It doesn't make sense for a man to lose a day's work to get a piece of information from his public assistance workers that the caseworker can get for him over the telephone.

Nevertheless, a very large part of the time it is possible for the client to bring about environmental changes himself, and direct work with the client to this end is the preferred form of treatment.

Having said this, we introduce another type of criterion into the decision: the set of social work values implicit in the assumption that, other things being equal, it is preferable to work directly with the client rather than indirectly by intervening in the environment. This criterion is also a factor in choosing among different direct treatment procedures. The caseworker's choice is usually influenced by his professional commitment to two principles: (1) that it is of primary importance to strengthen the client's ability to handle his own affairs (and this is chiefly a matter of improving ego functioning), and (2) that ends cannot be separated from means—that is, other things again being equal, the end of better ego functioning is most likely to be promoted by the client's having practice in doing things for himself rather than having them done for him.

Still another factor in such a decision will be the technical one of what effect the use of one mode of treatment or another in dealing with a particular aspect of a problem will have on treatment as a whole. For instance, it has been demonstrated that in order to convince the hard-to-reach client that the worker is really well disposed toward him and interested in helping rather than reforming him or his children for someone else's benefit, it is necessary to do practical things for him from which he can derive benefit and pleasure. With such a client the worker would welcome the opportunity to bring about environmental changes, whether or not the client might eventually have learned how to effect the changes himself. Learning to do for himself will come later in the contact; in the early stages of treatment, priority must be given to measures that will build a therapeutically useful relationship. Occasionally, too, the matter of timing enters into the decision. For the benefit of a child it may be important for a teacher to be seen immediately. Though it would be better for the child's mother to make the contact, it may take some weeks before she can be brought to do so, and under these circumstances, if the mother is willing for the worker to visit the teacher, this would be the advisable course to follow.

When it seems best to try to enhance the client's ability to deal with his own environment, the worker must decide what blend of sustaining procedures, direct influence, ventilation, or reflective discussion of the current person-situation interaction will be of the greatest benefit. To make this decision he turns to his diagnostic impression of his client's personality, evaluating his capacity in *relation to the particular task at hand.* Is the client's perception, judgment, and control or directive capacity sufficiently good that with help in understanding the situation he is confronted with he will be able to handle it himself? Is he immediately ready to do this, or are his feelings so deeply involved in the situation that he first needs to ventilate them as a prelude to clear thinking? When the pressure of underlying emotion is so great that it interferes with wise action or even consideration of action, ventilation may be required. When anxiety is high, or the self-image low, or the defense of turning against the self is crippling the client's self-confidence or causing him to behave in masochistic, self-damaging ways, a large measure of sustaining procedures may need to precede and accompany reflective discussion.

If the client's ego functions too poorly for him to use reflective discussion effectively, even when it is buttressed by ventilation and sustainment, will he be likely to respond favorably to the worker's taking a guiding role and using procedures of direct influence? To answer this question, the worker must assess the worker-client relationship at this specific point in treatment. Are the client's feelings toward the worker such that he will accept his influence? As we noted in an earlier chapter, the client's response will depend upon the degree to which his dependency feelings are directed toward the worker, the extent to which he believes the worker is well disposed toward him, and the extent to which he respects the worker as an expert whose advice can be relied upon.

Note especially that personality here is not being assessed in the abstract but in relation to the task or situation by which the individual is confronted. A person may be capable of rational consideration of one type of dilemma, but not of another; amenable to advice about matters concerning which the caseworker is regarded as an expert, but not amenable in others; overwhelmed by anxiety under some circumstances, cool and collected in others that to an outsider might seem just as threatening. The client's need for different treatment procedures is a shifting pattern requiring reevaluation in each interview as different topics arise for discussion. Without this constant reappraisal of needs and matching procedures, treatment would become automatic and stereotyped, and the client would not get all the help he is capable of using. Typically, the worker "feels his way along," testing within each interview whether the client is able to discuss his situation and his contribution to it reflectively, calling on sustainment, direction, and ventilation as need for these is shown.

Here again a social work value comes into play. Just as we earlier noted that the caseworker usually prefers to see the client deal with his environment himself rather than to act for him, we now find a preference for reflective discussion over direct influence, and for the same reason. An overall objective in casework is the increase of the client's ability to handle his own affairs. Thus the more he can learn to think for himself rather than depend upon the caseworker for direction, the better. Even when a good deal of guidance is needed early in treatment, it is hoped that the movement will be toward more self-direction as treatment proceeds. Similarly, the need for guidance in respect to one problem does not necessarily imply that it will be needed for other problems. The client's capacity to act must be evaluated anew with each problem as it arises, with opportunity for reflective discussion created again and again.

] *Internal Change: The Range of Possibilities*

When we turn from the objective of change in the environment to that of change in the person, the choice of treatment means becomes more complicated. All six forms of direct treatment are possibilities here, and a variety of considerations combine to influence the worker's activity at any moment and his emphasis on different elements in the total treatment picture. In the previous chapter we saw that the types of possible psychological change parallel the personality characteristics considered in diagnosis. Procedures, in turn, vary in their appropriateness for bringing about modifications in different characteristics of the individual. For the most part several types of procedure may be effective for any one type of change, with the specific objective itself one element in the final choice.

Distorted perceptions and impaired reality testing, for instance, can best be corrected, if they are not too severe, by reflective consideration of the realities of the person or situation that is being distorted. If this procedure proves ineffective, it probably means—except in psychosis, where something more serious is happening—that defense mechanisms are interfering with the process of perception. The client may then need to think about dynamic or developmental factors affecting his misperceptions. Poor judgment may be helped through reflective discussion of the situation, either alone or together with thought about the dynamics of the intrapsychic factors and conflicts that are interfering with sound judgment. A distorted self-image can sometimes be corrected by examination of external reality, as when a child who underestimates his ability is led to appreciate his actually very good school record, an approach often supplemented by sustaining procedures in which the worker adds the weight of his own estimate of the child's abilities to increase his confidence. At other times the self-image can be corrected only by dynamic or genetic procedures demonstrating the nature of the faulty self-image, the purposes it serves, and perhaps its source.

When strengthening of impulse control becomes a treatment aim, a variety of approaches may be used. Usually the core of treatment is examination of the consequences of weakness in this area of ego functioning. Not infrequently, however, direct influence is important, in the form of urging the need for better control. On the other hand, where there is *too much* control or rigidity, not only will direct influence in the form of sponsoring relaxation of controls sometimes be appropriate but consideration of dynamic or genetic factors is often of value. With children, indirect work may be most important, providing an environment that promotes a balanced combination of control and gratification.

When the reduction of anxiety is a major aim of treatment, sustaining techniques can be of great importance and in cases of severe anxiety may be the most significant element in treatment. The environment may be called into play by either decreasing reality pressures or providing reassuring contacts and experiences. Sometimes dynamic or genetic components may need to be considered to reach the causes of anxiety.

Closely related to anxiety is guilt—actually a special form of anxiety, described by Anna Freud as fear of the superego.[2] Catharsis may be of particular value in reducing it, especially if there is a basis in reality for the guilt feelings. The sustaining technique of acceptance—not to be confused with the case-worker's denying guilt when there is a factual basis for it—is always called for. Directive procedures, and more often reflective discussion of current life events, may help the client find ways of remedying the situation about which he feels realistic guilt. When there is little or no basis in reality for guilt feelings, sustaining techniques continue to be of importance. Discussion of current realities will sometimes enable the ego to overcome unrealistic guilt reactions; at other times only dynamic or genetic understanding will achieve this.

If defenses are to be modified, consideration of their dynamics is necessary; and sometimes thought can also be given to their development with profit.

Superego modification may be brought about by a great variety of means. With the overly severe superego, sustaining techniques may be particularly valuable. Direct influence is often useful. So is reflective discussion of the appropriateness of certain superego tendencies in the light of reality, as well as discussion of beliefs held by others of similar cultural background, or of different background when the source of the difficulty lies in a type of cultural conditioning that is inappropriate to the situation in which the individual is functioning. Dynamic and particularly genetic discussion may be of great value, too. With the too-lax superego or one with important lacunae, techniques of direct influence are sometimes appropriate, as is reflective discussion of consequences in reality. If a positive dependent relationship can be established, the milder forms of direct influence may be of considerable value. In extreme situations, actual intervention may be necessary. Again, with children, environmental procedures are most useful, providing for the child life experiences which will develop a well-balanced conscience.

If changes in the libidinal or aggressive aspects of the personality become the objective of treatment because they are causing dysfunction, the first approach to modifying them is usually to demonstrate their harmful effects in actual life. A narcissistic orientation presents great difficulties in treatment, although the individual may learn to control its more extreme manifestations. Dependent traits can sometimes be modified by a period of gratification through sustaining and directive techniques followed by gradual practice in thinking through decisions and courses of behavior in the current situation. Sometimes consideration of developmental factors can pave the way for more willingness to practice self-reliance. If ambivalence itself—the simultaneous existence of affectionate and hostile impulses toward another—becomes a theme of treatment, it is usually necessary to understand it dynamically and sometimes also genetically.

With aggressiveness and hostility, catharsis may be of value as are also consideration and reevaluation of the current realities which are provoking them. Certainly discussion of the ways in which such responses affect the client's current life situation is of primary importance. Aggressiveness and hostility are often closely related to difficulty in controls and to superego deficiencies, and like them sometimes respond to a directive approach; more characteristically, however, dynamic and genetic understanding that brings relief from pressure is more helpful than control alone. The problem is often one of too little aggressiveness rather than too much—that is, inhibition of aggressive impulses amounting to a lack of necessary assertiveness in everyday life. When this is the case, the milder forms of directive procedures are sometimes useful, reflective discussion of current person-situation interactions often helps, and sustaining techniques may serve to increase aggressiveness. It may be particularly helpful to such clients to reflect upon their unassertiveness in dynamic terms and in terms of the life experiences that have contributed to it.

It is very difficult for casework to modify sexual deviation. Sometimes it can be brought under some measure of control by either directive techniques or reality discussion, at least to the point of preventing behavior that is obviously damaging to others or to the self. Where the condition itself is not treatable, guilt and anxiety can sometimes be relieved by sustaining measures. But the dynamics and genetics of sexual deviation are usually too deep-seated to be reached by casework. Sexual immaturities, on the other hand, can often be modified a great deal. One way to do this is through the "corrective relationship," which, as noted in a previous chapter, is a combination of sustaining and mildly directive work, usually linked with reflective consideration of current realities. Consideration of developmental factors affecting such immaturities is often of very great value.

Unresolved ambivalent ties to parents are, of course, frequently involved in sexual immaturity. They also affect other areas of life, independently of their effect on sexual adjustment. Here, as with sexual immaturities, the corrective relationship, combined with reflective discussion of reality considerations, may be extremely useful. In other cases, genetic understanding can be developed with great effectiveness.

] *Dynamic and Genetic Understanding*

In the foregoing discussion of relationships between the objectives of treatment and the means to be used in seeking to reach them, discussion of dynamic and genetic considerations is frequently offered as a possible alternative—usually the last to be mentioned. This is not an accidental arrangement; it rather reflects the fact that these means of dealing with the problem are ordinarily not used if adequate improvement can be achieved in other ways. While intrapsychic content also receives attention in certain types of person-situation discussions where the client gains awareness of his feelings and thoughts about his current life, the consequences of his own actions on others, and current life provocations for his reactions, it is in the pursuit of dynamic and genetic understanding that intrapsychic content is most deeply explored.

Ordinarily it is not important for an individual to understand his inner psychology if he is able to overcome problems in his social functioning without such insight. In many matters of perception and judgment the client, if his ego in general functions realistically, will respond to help in understanding the current person-situation interplay without the need for either dynamic or genetic understanding of his own psychological processes. Where controls are defective or the superego is too lax, the difficulty usually does not lie in an intrapsychic conflict but rather in the relationship of the individual to the external world. Consequently, understanding of the dynamics of these inner interrelationships is usually not called for. It is true that such disturbances are frequently caused developmentally, but they are generally due to lacks in a child's upbringing rather than to influences that can be undone—or at least overcome—by reconsideration in adulthood. Insofar as treatment is possible, it consists of supplying in the present something that was lacking in the past. To accomplish this task, educational techniques and reflective discussion of current realities are the necessary procedures.

On the other hand, if the client's difficulty is rooted in tension or conflict between different facets of his personality, or if the destructive developmental experiences by which he has been influenced can be counteracted by insight concerning them, procedures useful in promoting dynamic and genetic understanding should be considered. The most usual type of conflict is between the ego and either a generally overly strict superego or one that sets up special prohibitions against aggression or pleasure. The ego then reacts with defense mechanisms which cause tension either between the ego and the unmet needs of the id or within the ego itself when it is torn between realistic responses to internal and external realities and unrealistic or inappropriate defensive responses. Common destructive developmental experiences include overly restrictive or repressive upbringing, parental deprivation or hostilities, which later are displaced on other personal relationships, parental fears and inhibitions passed on to children, unrealistic parental expectations, excessively close parental ties, and emotionally traumatic experiences which are not realistically assimilated and result in anxiety, fear, or guilt against which unhealthy defenses are set up.

But even in these types of problems, if the ultimate objective of improved personal-social adjustment can be reached without going into extensive intrapsychic exploration, it should not be undertaken. It is time-consuming for both client and worker, it involves hard work for both, and it is very likely to cause the client greater discomfort than other approaches. In those cases, where treatment objectives require that this type of understanding be fostered, it is usually only at a few spots in treatment that it need be undertaken; only in relatively few cases does it constitute a major component in treatment. It must be kept firmly in mind that the total treatment process is always a blend of many techniques; when the worker encourages consideration of intrapsychic components in the client's difficulty, it is always in addition to other treatment procedures.

] *Anxiety and Guilt as Key Factors*

We have indicated that certain characteristics of the client's personality are of key significance in estimating which treatment approaches he will be most able to use. Six characteristics have shown themselves again and again to be of primary importance: anxiety, guilt, object relatedness, impulse control, repression, and certain qualities of the thought processes or intellect.

Anxiety and guilt may be considered together, for guilt is one form of anxiety—in Anna Freud's words already cited, the ego's fear of the superego—and what is said about anxiety in general applies with equal force to guilt.

No single factor in treatment is more important than the worker's keeping his finger on the pulse of the client's anxiety. To begin with, he must be sensitive to the actual existence of anxiety and to the degree to which it is present in the client at any one moment. He must know the extent to which the client chronically carries anxiety around with him or is vulnerable to its arousal. What particular things in the client's present or past provoke his anxiousness? How does his anxiety show itself and how does he handle it? In particular, does it impel him to unwise acting out? Does it result in increased neurotic or somatic symptomatology? What defenses does he use against it? Is he immobilized? Will he run away from treatment?

When anxiety—or guilt—is either chronically very high, or

aroused because of the experiences the client is going through when he comes for treatment, a goodly measure of sustaining procedures is of particular value. If the anxiety is extreme, the worker may need to rely more than ordinarily on suggestion and advice and to be more active than usual even in leading the client to think about his current dilemma. Very rarely would a person experiencing extreme anxiety be able to deal constructively with any extensive inward explorations, unless the acute anxiety subsides.

Reflective consideration of intrapsychic content is by no means the only treatment procedure by which anxiety is aroused. Merely describing as part of the application process life events one is ashamed of may be a very painful, anxiety-arousing experience. Catharsis which involves the expression of emotions or desires of which the client is afraid may bring fear that talking will be a forerunner of acting. Guilt may be very easily aroused in a sensitive person by discussions which make him aware for the first time of the harmful effects of his own actions on others, or even of needs of his child or wife to which he has been blind. The individual with a very severe superego will feel guilt very keenly whenever matters come up in which he believes he is or was even slightly in the wrong. He anticipates that the worker will be critical, often projecting his own self-condemnation onto the worker; he fears loss of love, or the worker's disinterest; he may need to defend himself by projecting blame on others or by outright denial or by defensive hostility or even withdrawal from treatment. Similar sensitivity may exist in the very narcissistic person.

Even in the giving of suggestions and advice the worker must know his client's personality well enough to foresee the possible arousal of anxiety. In one case known to the writer the worker was greatly and rightly concerned about the severity with which an impulsive mother was in the habit of disciplining her seven-year-old son. Early in the contact she advised her against it and was gratified at the change in her client's handling of the child and his immediate improvement. Unfortunately, however, she had not made a careful diagnostic study of the mother nor thought ahead to the probable consequence of her advice. In the first place, the child had never been controlled in any other way. His initial reaction was to be very good, but he soon began to explore the limits of his new freedom and became increasingly defiant of his now disarmed mother. In addition to being impulsive, the mother had a great deal of compulsiveness in her makeup. A good diagnostician could easily have identified the clinical signs of this and would have known that along with her impulsiveness this mother had a very severe conscience and a great need, like a small child, to win the worker's approval. She tried very hard to be a good mother along the lines the worker suggested. In fact, however, after the initial good news of improvement in the child, she found it very hard to let the worker know that things were not going so well. Eventually one day "all hell let loose" and her anger against her son burst forth in a really dangerous way. Then, to justify herself, she had to condemn the child as uncontrollable by any other means and turn completely away from the worker and her advice.

In general the development of dynamic or genetic understanding involves more anxiety than do other treatment procedures, although it would not be accurate to say that this is *always* so. Certain themes, moreover, even when they are dynamically or genetically explored, may be fairly low in their anxiety potential, and therefore can be safely explored even in "fragile" personalities. A case in the group studied, for example, included a borderline schizophrenic woman who was able to see that her suspicious expectation of hostile attack from a woman in her current life was a displacement from a childhood experience in which she had actually been very badly treated by a harsh grandmother. Discussion of the circumstances not only did not arouse anxiety, but allayed it. Talking about the oppressive grandmother was not frightening, because the worker did not attempt to explore whether the client was partly at fault but rather accepted the situation as an externally caused and regrettable hardship. Recognition of the possibility of displacement also involved no blame for the client; instead it gave her a rational explanation for some of her fears so that she was able to look more realistically at the lack of evidence in the current situation to justify them.

Clients sometimes find great relief in talking about painful experiences in the presence of a sympathetic worker who is not overwhelmed by their ventilation. This process may help the ego to assimilate the memories, and to be less afraid of and more able to bear the pain involved, and to express the natural emotions of grief and anger associated with the experiences. Such verbal activity is similar to the play activities of children, in which they repeat painful and frightening experiences in an effort to assimilate them. When the happenings that are being aired are also responsible for some current reaction that is causing the individual trouble, he may in the very same interview also experience a sense of relief from talking about them. For instance, a person who in reality had very critical parents, with consequent feelings of distrust in his own ability, may obtain almost immediate relief from talking about their unjust criticisms of him, and by sensing the confirmation of the worker's agreeing that they were unjust, experience some freeing of himself from his earlier acceptance of his parents' views.

At other times, however, painful early experiences have been of such traumatic proportions that extreme anxiety would be involved in reliving them. In such cases there is usually strong resistance to recalling them, and this should serve as a caution signal to the worker. This situation often arises with people who suffered the extremes of persecution in the last war. Some of the things that happened to them could be assimilated only by very exceptional people and more often could be surmounted only as they could be walled off by suppressions and repressions which it would be unwise to disturb.

On the whole, a past experience that arouses anxiety concerning only the pain of reliving the experience itself is more easily borne than one that arouses guilt. If, for instance, the memory involves actions or even feelings and wishes which the individual thinks are shameful or wrong, his fear of his own and the worker's disapproval may be very strong. Guilt is frequently associated with childhood hostilities toward parents and others in families where such high value was placed on surface amiability that all anger had to be hidden. It is also associated in a great many people in our culture with childhood sexuality, current and past masturbation, and any types of sexual deviation. Both individual and cultural values are strong determinants here. For one person hostilities will be taboo; for another, lying; for still another, erotic responsiveness.

Despite these variations in the degree of anxiety aroused by different types of content, it is necessary to keep in mind that the effort to arrive at intrapsychic understanding tends to arouse more anxiety than other procedures. The reasons for this are several. These are types of self examination. The client does not lend himself to such treatment emphasis unless he has come to realize that there is something wrong with his way of functioning, something that requires inward examination. He may not have said it in so many words, but his very willingness to participate in a major way in the pursuit of self-understanding indicates tacit realization of it. He senses that there may be damage to his self-image. Once a person admits that he needs to look to himself for the cause of his troubles, he is laying himself open to criticism. He is likely to find that he had made mistakes, that he is distorting, or blaming others unnecessarily, or is inappropriately hostile, or childishly dependent, or what have you. His emerging picture of himself is almost certain to turn up some flaws of which he was previously unaware. All of these realizations cause discomfort and pain, particularly if the client has a severe superego. They also constitute a narcissistic injury. These discomforts, in turn, characteristically stir up anger at the worker —the bearer of evil tidings—which causes the client still further anxiety.

A second source of discomfort lies in the fact that to a certain extent in dynamic understanding, and to a much greater degree in genetic understanding, the client is bringing to consciousness memories and realizations that he has hidden from himself, or has at least refrained from talking about to others. These matters would not have been hidden away if they were not in some way painful. It may be the pain of earlier sorrow and frustration. Or the superego may be affronted, for the client may be defying parental threats in producing particular memories or becoming aware of certain feelings and attitudes. This source of anxiety is similar to that experienced by the patient in analysis (who feels it even more strongly) in relation to unconscious, repressed material. In analysis it is recognized as a principal source of resistance, and in casework a similar factor is involved.

A third source of anxiety is related to the client's capacity to control impulses of which he may become fully aware during the course of treatment. Realistically or unrealistically, there is often fear of a breakthrough of forbidden impulses and of translating wishes and desires into action.

Sustaining techniques, as we have seen, are of particular value in relieving anxiety, and there often are times in work on intrapsychic themes when this sort of relief is very important. Some anxiety, however, is a necessary accompaniment of work on many types of intrapsychic themes, particularly if the objective of treatment is to enable the client to understand and hence modify aspects of his personality. In such cases the therapist is confronted by a dilemma. For the client must be basically secure with the worker; whatever the exigencies of the moment, there must be a strong underlying conviction that the worker feels positively toward the client, respects him, and is endeavoring to help him. This conviction is inevitably obscured from time to time at difficult moments in treatment by transference elements and by projection of the client's own attitudes. Such distortions can be corrected, however, only if the actual relationship is a positive one and fundamentally perceived as such by the client. To achieve this basic relationship and keep it alive, sustaining procedures are necessary; on the other hand, it is often necessary to refrain from reassuring and comforting remarks in order to keep the client at work pursuing understanding of his difficulties.

To illustrate: a woman who tends to be overly critical of her husband, tells the caseworker about an incident in which this tendency was prominent and half apologizes for her disparaging words. The worker may either make a reassuring remark about her annoyance being understandable, or may comment more directly, "You do have a sharp tongue!" The latter procedure will not be very reassuring. It will increase rather than decrease the client's anxiety and, if the worker has correctly gauged her ego and superego qualities, will serve to motivate her to seek understanding of her over-reaction. Great care must be exercised in finding the balance by which to give enough warmth and security to nourish progress and protect the client from excessive anxiety, and at the same time to maintain a level of tension conducive to motivation toward self-understanding.

A source of anxiety that may be present in any form of treatment that has as its goal a change in personality is the fear of the change itself. Even though present ways of functioning may cause discomfort, they also have their gratifications. A known discomfort is often not as frightening as the uncertain result of change, for the known at least has been adjusted to and lived with a long time. The direct implication of the discovery of faulty functioning is that it must be modified. Sometimes such modification is immediately gratifying, but more often there have been secondary advantages in the faulty functioning. The new understanding often requires greater self-control, less expression of hostility, less blame of others, more altruistic and less narcissistic behavior. The client may desire change, but he is also uneasy about it and reluctant to give up comfortable self-gratifying ways. But now a new discomfort has entered the picture, because the ego has seen the unreasonableness of the old ways and the superego is no longer comfortable with them. This element, too, causes resistance as well as anxiety.

In order to be alert to the presence of anxiety in the client, the worker must have sound knowledge of the ways in which anxiety expresses itself. Occasionally it is shown physically, by trembling of body or voice, body tenseness, sweating or pallor, nervous gestures or excitement, and so on. Sometimes the client reveals it by posture or gesture, sitting on the edge of the chair or at a distance, wrapping his coat tightly or refusing to take it off. More often anxiety shows itself in increased use of the client's characteristic defense mechanisms. The intellectual goes off into theoretical, often contentious discussions; defensive hostility erupts in the challenge that treatment is not helping, with the implication that the worker is incompetent; rationalization, reaction formation, denial—any of the mechanisms of defense—will be brought into play in their characteristic role of attempting to protect the individual from experiencing anxiety. Avoidance may finally result in the client's skipping interviews altogether. If these signs are spotted early enough, they can alert the worker to the cause of the anxiety. He can then allow the client to withdraw from exploration of the anxiety-arousing content if it is not necessary or advisable to pursue it further at that particular point.

If it does seem wise to go on, the worker can proceed in a number of ways. Sometimes it is possible to draw the client's attention to his defensiveness. At other times, and this is often true with compulsive clients, it may be necessary to work first on the personality characteristic that makes the individual respond so strongly—with compulsive clients, the overly severe superego and perfectionism. At other times it is necessary to have a period of relaxation in treatment, the worker saying directly or in effect, "perhaps later you will feel more able to talk about this." And at still other times, when the worker has good reason to think that the client is close to talking about certain experiences but is afraid to do so, he may find ways of framing a question or comment that relieves guilt or anxiety before the frightening content is actually expressed. For instance, a worker seeking to enable a client to talk about his childhood masturbation may comment that most children do masturbate and often don't realize that it is natural and think it is very wrong. Has he had experiences like this, too? Here, guilt is allayed in advance.

One often finds that after a difficult piece of self-understanding, the client, in the next interview, stays on superficial, more or less self-congratulatory material. This relaxation is necessary, and the worker must not become impatient for further immediate progress. Often these periods are used for consolidation, with the client using the interview to increase his understanding of his current situation and his handling of it. Nothing is more important than that the worker keep his finger on the client's "anxiety pulse" and regulate treatment accordingly, finding a balance between relaxing and sustaining measures on the one hand and procedures pressing toward self-understanding on the other.

] *Other Important Personality Factors*

The other characteristics of the personality that are particularly pertinent in guiding treatment procedures, are less complicated than anxiety in their ramifications and therefore can be discussed more briefly. The capacity for mature object relationships is one such quality. It is measured in large part by the individual's ability to love others as well as himself, and to care about their needs as well as his own. This capacity, of course, is a matter of degree. Maturity in human relationships does not require that narcissism and dependence be completely given up. That would be neither possible nor desirable.

The person who has a very well-developed capacity for mature human relationships is likely to be pretty healthy psychologically, able to perceive realistically and to judge sensibly the most reasonable way to deal with his troubles. His difficulties tend to be either situational or the result of inadequate knowledge. Parents, for instance, often do not know what kind of behavior to expect of a three-year-old or of an adolescent. In the present state of lack of agreement about child-rearing practices among otherwise well-informed Americans, parents may be in conflict about how to deal with a child, even when they are fundamentally loving mature people. Young couples may not realize the amount of adjustment that may be necessary in learning to live together successfully. Rather serious conflict can arise, despite basically good object relationships. In such situations, reflective consideration of the needs of the other person, of the effects of the interactions that occur between them, and of the client's own feelings and the things that arouse them is usually the most appropriate treatment activity. Ventilation in an accepting atmosphere is also very helpful, along with other sustaining procedures. It is usually not necessary to go into dynamic or developmental considerations to any great degree, though this may occur in a fragmentary way.

At the other extreme, the individual who is greatly retarded in the quality of his object relationships often does not have sufficient concern for the welfare of others to be willing to look within himself for the cause of his difficulties. He is not sufficiently attuned to others to appreciate their feelings easily or to see the ways in which he provokes and hurts them. He is very unlikely to be able to put to good use treatment that requires much self-examination. He may be introspective, but it is a narcissistic or self-pitying type of introspection. He often can be reached only to the extent that he feels very strongly the worker's interest in helping him for his own sake. With such a client sustaining techniques are likely to be very much needed. Discussion of the effects of the client's own actions on other people is often very useful, especially if it can be related to his own self-interest. This latter qualification will also hold for encouraging him to think about the reactions and needs of other people.

Most clients fall between these two extremes. Those who are closer to the mature person in their object relationships and yet have intrapsychic conflicts and tensions will tend to make good use of treatment that gives consideration to the nature of these internal factors. Those who are less mature in this respect will respond better if the worker encourages them to think in realistic terms of how to make themselves more comfortable.

Another personality factor significant as an indicator of treatment is impulse control. Quite obviously the worker must safeguard the client's interests and those of the people with whom he is associated. The impulsive client will therefore need help in learning better control. If the treatment relationship is strong enough, the worker will often find direct suggestion or advice very useful techniques in helping the client protect himself from poorly directed impulsiveness. Whenever possible the client should be led into reflective consideration of his impulses before acting upon them, so that he will be helped to develop the habit of foreseeing consequences instead of having to experience them. As with the narcissistic individual, such reflection needs to be related to self-interest. If the impulsive client is to be encouraged to think introspectively, however, great care must be taken with the nature of the content he is encouraged to think about, particularly its anxiety-arousing or impulse-promoting potential.

A further treatment indicator of importance is the strength of repression. If the client produces easily material that would ordinarily be very hard to reach in casework, the question should be raised in the worker's mind as to whether this is a person who has less than the normal ability to repress. This is of course particularly true with the psychotic or borderline psychotic. With such individuals the worker should rarely turn to consideration of dynamic or genetic material, for this procedure will encourage the release of more intrapsychic content than either worker or client can handle. Rather the client should be directed to consideration of current realities and of how to adapt himself to them or to bring about their improvement.

A final treatment indicator has to do with the intellect. A

certain quality of mind is necessary for the constructive use of introspection. Work of this sort requires the making of fine discriminations, a capacity for straight logic, and the ability to recognize contradictions and inconsistencies. This kind of mental capacity is important also in discussion of the person-situation configuration, but intrapsychic phenomena are often more subtle and more elusive than the actual happenings of everyday life. It is important not to confuse this type of mental capacity with education. While education seeks to promote the basic capacity to reason, it does not always succeed; conversely, this capacity not infrequently exists in people who have not had the benefit of much formal education.[3]

At the same time, education and other cultural factors do have bearing upon the choice of treatment procedure. Little education and low class status tend to be accompanied by major environmental causative factors[4] which prevent the client from seeing his personal involvement in his own troubles. There are too many other places to put the blame, and it is very hard for the caseworker to demonstrate the intrapsychic problem to the client convincingly. As a result of these environmental factors, which cannot always be adequately cleared away, very few undereducated, economically hard-pressed individuals have been brought to the point of readiness for inward understanding. Consequently we have little experience upon which to base generalizations. If, however, intelligence is normal and external causation can be reduced to the point where internal factors can be clearly seen and shown to the client, there would seem to be no reasons inherent in educational and class status to make this type of treatment impossible.

Ethnic factors are extremely diverse in their significance for treatment. Certainly language differences of any major proportion are a deterrent to the kind of communication necessary for extensive intrapsychic exploration. Attitudes of personal reticence, distrust between races, a marked difference in experience and values between client and worker, difficulties in casting the worker in a therapeutic role—all are obstacles to treatment of any type and might be particularly obstructive to the pursuit of inward understanding. The degree to which these handicaps to treatment can be overcome obviously varies in different cases, but again, as in educational and class status, are not to be construed as insurmountable.

] Significance of the Clinical Diagnosis

Up to this point in our consideration of criteria for deciding upon methods and emphasis in treatment, we have been discussing impressions gained from the assessment and the dynamic-developmental aspects of the diagnosis. What relationships are there between the clinical diagnosis and treatment choices?

The clinical diagnosis is particularly helpful in quickly differentiating in a gross way between clients who may need and be able to use consideration of dynamic and genetic intrapsychic factors and those who are best helped by greater emphasis on current realities, supplemented by directive procedures and buttressed throughout by a good measure of sustainment. The clinical diagnosis after all is a kind of summarization of the characteristics of the individual, and hence a sort of shorthand for signifying in an individual the presence of the qualities we have been discussing.

We have already pointed out the obvious fact that if dynamic or genetic factors are to be dwelt upon there must be an intrapsychic problem of sufficient proportions to require understanding for improvement in social functioning. At one extreme of human adjustment, the person who is healthy enough to deal with his problems realistically with the help of environmental, sustaining, directive, and person-situation procedures does not need to explore dynamic and genetic factors extensively. At the other extreme, the psychotic and near-psychotic must usually be ruled out for extensive use of these procedures because their egos are weak in many of the qualities needed for the development of understanding of intrapsychic factors. In severe psychosomatic disorders it is also best to avoid any technique that will heighten anxiety and risk increasing the physical difficulties. Furthermore, the need for medical supervision makes such patients more suitable for treatment by a medically trained therapist than by a caseworker, if insight should be a major goal of treatment.

There has been a tendency to believe that the person with a

character disorder cannot use treatment requiring introspection. This generalization fails to take into account the tremendous range among character disorders. The recent publication by Reiner and Kaufman brings a systematic discussion of character disorders and their treatment to caseworkers for the first time.[5] These authors make it clear that character disorders can vary from the near-psychotic to the near-neurotic, and hold the point of view that even with serious character disorders a considerable degree of self-understanding can be achieved, if the client's motivation for pursuing self-understanding is built up in a period of preliminary treatment in which other techniques are used to develop a sound relationship with the worker, and a greater capacity for guilt. The proposition that different types of character disorder vary greatly in their treatment need is completely consistent with the formulations of this chapter. The near-psychotic individual with a character disorder, like other near-psychotics, needs treatment that is held close to the realities of everyday life and may also require considerable guidance and support. The likelihood of eventually developing dynamic or genetic understanding would be least in the oral type of character disorder and greatest in the phallic or oedipal type, but there is always also the question of severity within a category.

Obviously, the neurotic client is the most likely to need extensive self-understanding. Neurosis always manifests itself in both symptoms and social behavior, though it may show itself less patently in behavior than character disorders do. When the symptoms are severe, as in marked conversions, serious phobias or obsessions, or marked compulsive phenomena, psychotherapy under medical auspices is more advisable if extensive self-understanding is to be developed. But often this latter type of treatment is not available, or the client does not want or respond to it. Casework stressing examination of current interactions, accompanied by sustaining procedures and sometimes by environmental manipulations, may then be very helpful, or these types of casework may accompany and support medical psychotherapy.

When the neurotic symptomatology is mainly in the area of social adjustment, casework directed toward self-understanding should certainly be made available to the client. Here the individual characteristics we have just been discussing will determine the extent to which he can respond to these procedures. In general, the hysteric is more responsive than the obsessive compulsive, but here again the severity of the disturbance is of great importance. The extreme sensitivity of the compulsive client to criticism requires that great care be taken, especially in the early phases, not to cause him so much anxiety that his resistance becomes insurmountable. In people who suffer periodically from neurotic depressions, the question of degree is again of importance. In milder forms of this disorder, if care is taken to guard the anxiety level and if sustaining procedures are emphasized along with more taxing ones, exploration of certain themes along dynamic and genetic lines may be very beneficial.

] Treatment Procedures and the Problem

The reader may have wondered why we have not tried to relate treatment method to "problem." In the preceding chapter we indicated that the problem is a major determinant of the *objectives* of treatment. But that is a different matter from the choice of treatment *procedures*. From time to time one hears it said that we need a problem classification system that can be related to choice of treatment method so that one can say—for this problem, that treatment is needed. This is a gross oversimplification of the question of choice of treatment; it is comparable to looking for a patent medicine to treat skin eruptions.

The issue is complicated by the fact that the word "problem" is used in so many different ways in casework. Sometimes it designates the difficulty or disturbance the client complains about, whether it be the particular circumstance by which he is confronted or a quality within himself which he recognizes as painful or dysfunctional. At other times we speak of the problem from the point of view from which the worker sees it; then the word is more likely to include a causative connotation. At other times, as in the "problem classification" of Ripple and her associates, it is used to characterize certain major features of a case—location of difficulty plus location of its causation. But in any of these uses, the term "problem" represents too broad a concept to guide the worker in the fine differentiations that must be made in finding the most appropriate treatment *means* by which the type of change sought can best be achieved.

We have been endeavoring in this lengthy chapter to delineate the characteristics of people and their situations that indicate differentially to what extent the principal procedures of casework can be of value in treatment. We do not see this as an either-or choice between two major modes of treatment. Rather, the treatment of any person is an individualized blend of procedures, themes, and goals. The nature of the blend is not a matter of individual worker artistry or intuition, important though these may be. On the contrary, choice and emphasis follow definite principles and rest upon most careful evaluation of the nature of the client's problem, external and internal causative factors and their modifiability, the client's motivation, and pertinent aspects of his personality. In addition, there must be comprehension of the nature, effects, and demands of the different types of casework procedures and of the criteria by which the worker can match the client's needs and capacities with the particular combination of procedures most likely to be of value in enabling him to overcome, or at least lessen, his difficulties. It should by now be clear that the evaluative process is an ongoing one, with the emphasis in treatment varying in harmony with the changing needs and capacities of the client.

NOTES

1. Most of the references appropriate for this chapter have also been given in the chapters on treatment procedures. The following are of special pertinence:

On general relationships between diagnosis and treatment:

Lucille N. Austin, "Trends in Differential Treatment in Social Casework," *Journal of Social Casework*, 29 (June, 1948), 203–211.

Alex H. Kaplan, "Psychiatric Syndromes and the Practice of Social Work," *Social Casework*, 37 (March, 1956), 107–112.

Method and Process in Social Casework, Report of a Staff Committee, Community Service Society of New York, Family Service Association of America, New York, 1958.

Scope and Methods of the Family Service Agency, Report of the Committee on Methods and Scope, Family Service Association of America, New York, 1953.

Robert S. Wallerstein, Lewis L. Robbins, Helen D. Sargent, and Lester Luborsky, *The Psychotherapy Research Project of the Menninger Foundation*, Bulletin of the Menninger Clinic, 20 (September, 1956), 239–262.

On specific disturbances and treatment:

Lucille N. Austin, "Casework Treatment with Clients Whose Problems of Social Dysfunctioning Are Caused by the Neurosis of Anxiety Hysteria," in *Ego Psychology and Dynamic Casework*, Howard J. Parad, ed., Family Service Association of America, New York, 1958.

Casework Notebook, Family Centered Project, Greater St. Paul Community Chests and Councils, Inc., St. Paul, Minn., 1957.

Margaret Galston Grunebaum, "A Study of Learning Problems of Children: Casework Implications," *Social Casework*, 42 (November, 1961), 461–468.

Margaret M. Heyman, "Some Methods in Direct Casework Treatment of the Schizophrenic," *Journal of Psychiatric Social Work*, 19 (Summer, 1949), 18–24.

Sid Hirsohn, "Casework with the Compulsive Mother," *Social Casework*, 32 (June, 1951), 254–261.

Lillian Kaplan and Jean B. Livermore, "Treatment of Two Patients with Punishing Super-Egos," *Journal of Social Casework*, 29 (October, 1948), 310–316.

Beatrice Simcox Reiner and Irving Kaufman, *Character Disorders in Parents of Delinquents*, Family Service Association of America, New York, 1959.

Rosemary Reynolds and Else Siegle, "A Study of Casework with Sado-Masochistic Marriage Partners," *Social Casework*, 40 (December, 1959), 545–551.

Frances H. Scherz, "Treatment of Acting-out Character Disorders in a Marital Problem," *Casework Papers, 1956,* Family Service Association of America, New York, 1956, pp. 37–52.
Hank Walzer, "Casework Treatment of the Depressed Parent," *Social Casework, 42* (December, 1961), 505–512.

2. Anna Freud, *The Ego and the Mechanisms of Defense,* International Universities Press, New York, 1946, pp. 58–60.

3. Jerome Siller, "Socioeconomic Status and Conceptual Thinking," *Journal of Abnormal and Social Psychology, 55* (1957), 365–371.

4. See August B. Hollingshead and Frederick C. Redlich, *Social Class and Mental Illness,* John Wiley & Sons, New York, 1958; and Berta Fantl, "Casework in Lower Class Districts," *Mental Hygiene, 45* (July, 1961), 425–438. For important comments on Hollingshead and Redlich, see S. M. Miller and Elliott G. Mischler, "Social Class, Mental Illness, and American Psychiatry: An Expository Review," *The Milbank Memorial Fund Quarterly, 37* (April, 1959), 174–199.

5. Beatrice Simcox Reiner and Irving Kaufman, *Character Disorders in Parents of Delinquents,* Family Service Association of America, New York, 1959.

XIV

Three Variations

in

Treatment Emphasis

AS A CONCLUSION to this discussion of casework methods of psychosocial study, diagnosis, and treatment, we have selected three cases in which the relationship between diagnostic thinking and treatment methods and objectives can be demonstrated. These particular cases have been chosen because despite certain gross similarities among them there was for appropriate reasons considerable variation in treatment emphasis; in addition, almost all the major types of procedure discussed in earlier chapters were used at one point or another, in each of the cases. In the first, reflective discussion of current interactions, in combination with sustainment, was strongly emphasized; in the second, the emphasis was even more strongly on sustaining measures, with considerable environmental work, strong use of catharsis, and considerable reflective discussion of current interactions; in the third, greater emphasis was placed on consideration of dynamic and genetic factors, along with considerable reflective person-situation discussion and a good measure of sustainment.

] *A Character Disorder: Acting Out and Self-Devaluation*

Miss Milford, the first client, was a very attractive young woman recovering from tuberculosis, for which she had been hospitalized for several years. When she first came to the agency, she was living with a friend and was allowed to work several days a week. Her clinical diagnosis, arrived at after a period of study, was oral character disorder with some oedipal features, and a tendency toward depression. In spite of rigid defenses, Miss Milford had good capacity for inward perception. Because of the danger of further physical breakdown and of depression if the client felt too much emotional pressure, the caseworker refrained from anxiety-arousing treatment activities and rarely took the initiative in promoting dynamic or genetic understanding. Miss Milford's own need to understand herself was so great, however, that she herself sometimes found her way into beginning discussions of the dynamics of her reactions and of meaningful developmental experiences.

Miss Milford, whose mother had died when Miss Milford was born, spent her early childhood in an orphanage. During her latency and adolescence she had many different living arrangements, sometimes with relatives, sometimes in boarding homes, and sometimes with her father, who died when she was fifteen. Several subsequent living arrangements broke up because she could not get along with the women in the household and—according to her—because they were jealous of her good relationship with their husbands. She never felt that she could trust women.

Miss Milford's present problems arose from her illness and her personality rather than from external pressures. Her relatives were helping her financially, her living arrangements were adequate, and employment was available as her strength permitted her to undertake it. She was under good medical care. What difficulties there were with relatives and friends appeared to spring more from her own reactions than from unusual behavior on their part.

It was in personality patterns that Miss Milford most needed help. While her capacity for accurate perception, judgment, and reality testing was not impaired, she sometimes functioned poorly in these respects because of her low self-image and her tendency to project both this and her subsequent counter hostility onto other people, who then seemed to her to be hostile when they actually were not. Indeed, one of her most striking characteristics was the discrepancy between her attractive appearance, good intelligence, and interesting personality and her own deep-seated feeling that she was not lovable.

Both anxiety and guilt were high, though the guilt feelings were at first hidden even from Miss Milford herself. Her considerable sexual promiscuity at first seemed to indicate laxness in this area of the superego; it later developed, however, that a great deal of underlying guilt existed which she had handled by denial. There was a good deal of impulsive acting out, ambivalence, and hostility, and little ability to bear frustration. The client's chief defenses were denial, projection, and subtle forms of turning against the self.

Narcissism and dependence were also high, with very limited development of object relatedness. Miss Milford's sexual immaturity was evident in her need to have superficial relationships with many men rather than to develop a single stable relationship. It was apparent that she was still caught in a web of hostile feelings toward the mother who had "just died on her" and positive feelings toward her father. These ties seemed, however, to be on an oral dependent level rather than oedipal in nature. The client had no neurotic or psychotic symptoms, although there was a tendency toward mood swings and mild depressions in response to frustration.

Miss Milford's psychological difficulties, in other words, were many. The central problem was her devaluation of herself, combined with her strong dependency needs. The promiscuity with which she tried to solve this latter problem increased her guilt feelings—already intense on the unconscious level because of her feeling of responsibility for her mother's death—and deepened her distrust of her own worth. In addition, her mild depressive tendencies, impulsiveness, fear of criticism, distrust of women, defensive hostility and the defenses of denial and projection all became treatment themes.

Miss Milford's social problems were in three areas: employment, medical care, and relationships with other people, particularly men friends. The strong need for independence which she had developed in her effort to overcome her underlying dependence made it difficult for her to handle her medical and work situations realistically. She was constantly tempted to work harder than was medically advisable and to resist following restrictive medical advice. The worker was quite active in this area, whenever possible helping Miss Milford to think her medical and employment plans through realistically, but adding the weight of her direct advice when it was needed. At times, with her client's permission, the caseworker talked directly with the doctor and other medical personnel responsible for Miss Milford's care to make sure that the total health situation was accurately understood.

The early interviews gave the worker an opportunity to demonstrate her interest in Miss Milford and her concern for her welfare, her confidence in her ability and her wish for her to be well and to succeed in her work. She was also able to show her understanding of the client's feelings of frustration and resentment at her illness. Although she denied any discomfort about her sexual nonconformity, Miss Milford almost immediately brought out her fear that the worker would disapprove of her because of this. The caseworker's continued warm acceptance of Miss Milford began to overcome the barrier of her deep-seated distrust of any woman. Gradually she brought out her shame at having tuberculosis and her fear that no one would want to marry her because of her illness. After talking about these feelings with the worker, she lost the need to conceal her illness from friends and gradually learned from experience that her fears were not realistic.

Concurrently with these developments, Miss Milford began to bring out her conflicts about her relationships with men, her need to carry on several affairs at once and her desire to marry for security. Two different treatment dynamics became prominent at this point: rational discussion of the qualities of the men in whom she was interested and her ways of relating to them; and a strong sustaining element made possible by the client's constant testing of the worker's acceptance of her and willingness to let her choose her own way of life. Repeatedly Miss Milford brought up aspects of her promiscuity in ways that invited the caseworker to tell her to give it up. Each time, the worker made it clear that she was not interested in giving advice on this point or in talking in terms of right and wrong, but only in helping Miss Milford to think about what would be comfortable for her and how she could best achieve her own objectives. As the caseworker repeatedly refused to condemn her and as she more and more felt the worker's respect for her and interest in her, the client's own self-respect rose to the point where she could begin to face the guilt feelings she had always denied. She never talked about them per se, but she gradually began to curtail her promiscuity, at first offering the explanation that she was trying to live up to the worker's expectations. When the worker pointed out that she had never mentioned any such expectations, the client began to express her own opinion that her multiple relationships were self-defeating and that she felt better about herself when she exercised more control of her sexual impulses. Many times Miss Milford spontaneously referred to how much the worker's respect and interest meant to her and how in response to them her confidence in herself had increased. Toward the end of treatment she commented with satisfaction that now she had more regard for herself and therefore less need "to sleep around."

In exploring her feelings toward men and her fear that no man she respected would marry her, Miss Milford, without encouragement from the worker, brought out her great fear of abandonment and in association to this told of her strong feelings of anger when her brother said that she was responsible for her mother's death. It was apparent to the caseworker at this point that unconscious guilt about her mother's death and about her resentment of what she considered her mother's abandonment of her lay at the root of her low self-esteem and self-destructive tendencies. In subsequent interviews the possibility of psychoanalytic treatment was discussed. After careful consideration the client decided she did not want to go through the discomfort that analysis would involve. The consulting analyst advised against urging such treatment, partly because, in view of her medical history, it would be unwise to risk the degree of disturbance that might be involved, and partly because she was making such good progress with casework therapy that it might be best to be content with these gains in the face of the client's own resistance. The worker, therefore, accepted Miss Milford's decision as sound and continued to work in a strongly supportive way, constantly promoting the development of understanding of the client's current feelings and of ways of handling her situation. In addition, there was considerable ventilation of the strong emotions—anger and grief—that Miss Milford experienced in response to the frustrations of her life.

Dynamic understanding was sought in this case only in response to the client's own initiative, and in ways that would run a minimal risk of arousing anxiety. For the most part intrapsychic understanding was limited to the recognition of patterns of behavior and their effects rather than their dynamics. The worker did not initiate discussion of genetic material, but did help Miss Milford to understand life events which she spontaneously recalled.

Miss Milford was able to recognize her impulsiveness, her tendency toward depression and mood swings, her defensive hostility, and her projection. The impulsiveness was approached through reflective discussion of numerous specific instances of acting out in her current life. Miss Milford was able to recognize the trouble she made for herself and to see alternatives that would have been more helpful. Gradually she learned to stop and think before jumping into self-destructive actions. This capacity was reenforced by her growing identification with the caseworker. From time to time she would report: "I said to myself—'Mrs. W. would say . . .'" Later, shortly after her marriage, she came in for occasional interviews in which she would ventilate feelings of frustration. After one of these outbursts about current happenings, she quickly added, "But I didn't *do* anything silly."

Treatment of the depression and mood swings was limited to helping Miss Milford achieve awareness of these tendencies and of the ways in which they affected her judgment. This reduced her anxiety during periods of depression and enabled her to protect herself against misjudgments made under the influence of her moods. To have gone any further in this area of self-understanding might have involved Miss Milford in a greater amount of stress than she could have handled constructively.

The dynamics of the projection, and of the hostility based upon it, were never discussed as such, but individual instances in which they operated were taken up. Once when Miss Milford had misjudged an employer she was helped to see from details of actual events that there was no realistic basis for her feeling that the employer "rejected" her. The intent of this type of handling was to encourage Miss Milford to look more carefully at the realities of how other people acted toward her before jumping to the conclusion that they were hostile. Again, the emphasis was on current interactions.

Several very effective steps in treatment, involving consideration of the dynamics of her thought processes, were made possible by Miss Milford's reactions to the therapist. At one point, for instance, she thought that the worker, in conversations with the medical social worker, had divulged information she had given her in confidence, and she became very angry. Actually, there had been no breach of confidence, and it was possible for the caseworker to show Miss Milford that she had misjudged her. This incident was used dynamically to demonstrate Miss Milford's readiness to distrust even when a good relationship had existed for so long. She was able from this experience to recognize her general pattern of unjustified distrust of other people. Miss Milford herself put into words that this was one of her basic troubles, saying that she did not trust herself and therefore could not trust others. She subsequently commented that she had often broken up good relationships over trivial matters, or had expressed anger so strongly that other people had responded in the same coin and the relationship had ended. Some time later she commented that the caseworker's trust had enabled her to begin to trust other people. Here we see the combined effectiveness of dynamic understanding and a "corrective relationship" with the therapist.

In this example of treatment, then, the deep-seated source of the client's feeling that she could not be loved, combined with her serious physical disability, her tendency toward depression, her impulsiveness, and the extent of her libidinal immaturity dictated an emphasis on sustainment and the understanding of current feelings and interactions rather than on the goal of dynamic or genetic self-understanding.

] *A Character Disorder: Guilt and Impulsive Hostility*

It is interesting to compare the treatment of Mrs. Park, who was treated in a medical setting, with that of Miss Milford. In gross clinical diagnosis—oral character disorder—the two women were alike. Both suffered from a serious physical difficulty, in Mrs. Park's case, diabetes. There were many similarities, too, in the details of their personalities. Like Miss Milford, Mrs. Park had trouble with her superego because of promiscuity and because of deeply unconscious hostile feelings toward her mother, who had died when she still very much needed her. Mrs. Park too was impulsive and dependent; she too used hostility as a defense against her anxiety. Like Miss Milford, she had good capacity for accurate perception and judgment, although in current functioning it was impaired. She also suffered from periods of depression.

For Mrs. Park, too, it would have been unwise to press toward dynamic or genetic understanding because of the danger that anxiety aroused by this approach would result in increased physical illness, increased depression, or unwise acting out. The danger was even greater than with Miss Milford, for Mrs. Park had been in diabetic coma, close to death, on a number of occasions. Her diabetic condition was in general a serious problem, aggravated because she tended to disregard her diet and was obese; because of her neglect of her health she had had to have a leg amputated.

The personalities of the two women differed in that Mrs. Park's impulsiveness was greater than Miss Milford's. She would become violent in her rages, and even feared that she might do bodily harm to her husband or child. Her self-image was not so low as Miss Milford's, nor was she as afraid of abandonment. (This difference may be attributable to the fact that Mrs. Park's mother did not die until Mrs. Park was fifteen.) On the other hand, her guilt over her earlier promiscuity and her illegitimate child was so great that she was not able to express her feelings about it until after two years of treatment.

There were also sociocultural differences between these clients. Mrs. Park had somewhat less education than Miss Milford, she worked in a factory rather than an office, and she was harder pressed financially. Her husband was an unskilled laborer. Realities of periodic unemployment, inadequate housing, and episodic drinking on her husband's part added to her troubles.

Mrs. Park was referred to the caseworker because her general excitability and outbursts of hostility were detrimental both to her own health and to the welfare of her son. She had sought help for John who, she complained, was disobedient, did poorly in school, and had recently been truanting. Mrs. Park blamed his behavior on a head injury, sustained when he was hit by a car while going on an errand for her when he was five years old. His mother felt responsible for this injury, although it was in no way her fault. She also felt great guilt over the fact that John was an illegitimate child, and had not been able to tell him that Mr. Park was not his own father, even though during family quarrels remarks had been made which had aroused questions in John's mind on this point.

After her mother's death, Mrs. Park had gone through a period of rebellion, characterized by some drinking and a good deal of promiscuity. The only child born of her later marriage was feeble-minded. A few months before her application for help for John, this second child had been placed in an institution. Earlier, however, Mrs. Park had given her excellent care. After she had placed her daughter—a realistic step for both the child's welfare and her own—she experienced grave doubts about the care she was receiving. Her husband's relatives were also critical of her for having taken this step.

The objectives of treatment in this case included improvement in practical matters, such as employment, finances, housing and health, and the bettering of relationships between Mrs. Park and her husband and son. Psychological goals included reduction of her impulsiveness, defensive hostility, and guilt. Throughout treatment it was extremely important to guard against an increase in anxiety, for in all likelihood this would have led to further neglect of the diabetic condition and to withdrawal of John from psychiatric treatment. Thus no effort was made to develop dynamic understanding, and only once was genetic understanding promoted, in an instance in which such understanding led to reduction of guilt feelings. Rather, the emphasis was on sustaining procedures, relief of pressure by environmental means wherever possible, and reflective discussion of Mrs. Park's ways of dealing with the current realities of her life.

The caseworker's first task was to establish a therapeutic relationship. Here was a woman with intense hostility who immediately lashed out at the worker because more was not being done for her. Two things were immediately essential: first, obviously, that the worker not retaliate in kind but rather continue to extend good will and readiness to help, and second—a more subtle point—that she not be frightened or intimidated by the client's outbursts. The worker, as we have noted earlier, must be seen by the client not only as kindly disposed toward him but also as competent, or able to help. Clients like Mrs. Park are essentially children looking for strong and kind parents. They do not define competence in terms of professional education, but much more primitively; to them it is symbolized by someone who is not afraid of them and cannot be controlled or hurt by their outbursts. They are not aware of this, of course, but intuitively they know that they need someone who can help them to control themselves and who therefore must himself be strong.

During the early phases of the contact the worker, in addition to listening sympathetically to Mrs. Park's many troubles and accepting her during her periods of hostility, showed her concern and her wish to help in many practical ways. When Mrs. Park was worried about the care her daughter was getting in the institution and could not contact the doctors there, the worker took over and eventually worked out a special appointment with a doctor for her. She intervened with the housing authorities to hasten Mrs. Park's acceptance for public housing. She expedited plans for a new prosthesis for the amputated leg. She arranged for camp for John. In almost every interview some small practical service was either arranged for or reported on.

Throughout the worker's attitude was consistently one of sympathetic understanding, encouragement, and appreciation of the client's efforts. Gradually it became possible to encourage her, very tactfully, to see instance by instance some of her own provocations of other people by her hostile ways, with the result that Mrs. Park finally made a conscious effort to act differently and in time reported that people were nicer to her now that she was nicer to them. In this area of treatment and in discussions of her ways of dealing with John, the work was a combination of the development of understanding of current interactions and the use of direct influence to encourage wiser actions.

The core of treatment, however, was the reduction of Mrs.

Park's feelings of guilt, which lay at the root of her defensive hostility. She felt responsible for her son's bad behavior and his physical difficulties and for her daughter's institutionalization. On an unconscious level she no doubt thought all this was a punishment meted out to the children for the sins of the parent—her earlier promiscuity, unwed motherhood, and the hostility to her mother which underlay the latter. Close examination revealed that her anger arose not only in response to frustration but also burst forth with particular violence whenever she was criticized to the slightest degree or for any reason experienced feelings of guilt. Hence reduction of the trouble-making hostility depended upon lessening the guilt. In fact, if the worker had tried too soon to influence the impulsive hostility directly, she might have heightened the guilt, thereby increasing rather than decreasing the hostility.

The first and major approach to the problem was therefore a treatment relationship in which the worker, who no doubt represented the good mother, showed continuous liking and respect for the client. Opportunities were taken whenever it was justified to comment on ways in which Mrs. Park had handled her situation well or been helpful to members of her family. As the client acquired better control of herself, she experienced increasing satisfaction in her family relationships and was able to feel that she was making restitution to her son for the events about which she felt guilty. Among other things, she was able to tell him about his parentage in a way that relieved some of the anxiety he felt about it.

The one spot at which genetic or developmental understanding was gained was related to Mrs. Park's guilt about the acting out of her adolescent and young adult years and to some of her feelings concerning the loss of her mother. The opportunity arose in the third year of treatment, when Mrs. Park verbalized, with a great deal of feeling, her intense shame and guilt about her earlier promiscuity and illegitimate pregnancy. She related at the same time that a doctor some years ago had told her to forget all about it, and that she had tried but had been unable to do so. The worker encouraged her to talk about this period fully, so that in so far as possible the guilt would be brought into the open. She also agreed with Mrs. Park that it is not possible just to forget, and suggested that instead of forgetting she needed to forgive herself for what she had done.

Note that the caseworker did not try to deny that there was cause for guilt; rather she showed her own feeling that Mrs. Park was essentially a "good" person by advising her to forgive herself. Up to this point the handling was a combination of catharsis and sustainment. The worker went on, however, to talk with Mrs. Park about how what had happened was understandable in the light of the loss of her mother, the client having brought out her great dependence on her mother and the closeness of their relationship. The worker emphasized that the mother's death had occurred at a period in her life when a mother's love and guidance are especially important. The client then spoke of her difficulties with her stepmother after her father's remarriage, of her father's constant suspicions and accusations about her relationships with boys, and her own feeling that if he was going to accuse her anyway and insult her in front of her friends she might as well give him something to complain about. The worker's acceptance of the realities of the pressures Mrs. Park had been under helped her to re-evaluate her earlier life and fostered the process of self-forgiveness the worker had advised. Indication that this was occurring came at a later point, when Mrs. Park talked about her fears that she might still be promiscuous but at the same time decided this was no longer likely, because she now cared too much for her husband and son and would be concerned about the consequences for them. She felt she was very different from what she "used to be."

At no time did the worker attempt to uncover the hostility toward the diabetic mother Mrs. Park had had to spend her early adolescence nursing, although this undoubtedly was an underlying factor in her acting out and subsequent guilt. Genetic understanding, that is, could be sought in this case *only when it was primarily anxiety-relieving*. The hope was that with even partial alleviation of her guilt feelings, Mrs. Park would be less self-destructive and more able to handle her affairs in ways that would increase her satisfaction with herself and decrease her self-precipitated frustrations.

After this phase of treatment, Mrs. Park was greatly relieved and gradually terminated treatment. Her functioning was improved in terms of both her control of her diabetes and her relationship with John, who in turn showed improvement.

In this case the extent of the practical problems called for much more direct intervention in the environment on the client's behalf than was true with Miss Milford. Greater emphasis on sustainment, more catharsis, and more direct influence were also necessary. In consideration of the current person-situation interaction there was greater stress on actions and their results and less on drawing into the open feelings of which the client found it difficult to think or speak. The one instance of discussion of genetic content was extremely helpful, but could only be undertaken after three years of essentially supportive work and even then, despite its carefully guarded nature, Mrs. Park had a stormy time, lost her job, and had a recurrence of earlier symptoms. Close coordination with medical treatment was very important here.

It is difficult to judge the extent to which factors associated with social class influenced treatment in this case. The need for environmental work was, of course, a function of external presses, which are so much more commonly found in Mrs. Park's class. It is possible that had she had more education she would have pressed, as Miss Milford did, for more self-understanding. It is equally possible, however, that her personality pattern would have precluded this. In either case, in view of her emotional and physical condition, it would have been unwise to pursue any more anxiety-arousing treatment than was actually undertaken.

] *A Character Neurosis: Displacement and Inhibition of Aggression*

Like Mrs. Park, Mrs. Fillmore, our third client, was concerned about one of her children and felt very uncomfortable about her part in her daughter's adjustment difficulties. For her, however, the self-blame was associated not with a specific accident for which she felt responsible but with the way she handled the child. Like both other clients, Mrs. Fillmore suffered from a serious physical disability—recurring difficulty with a gastric ulcer. This condition did not assume serious proportions during treatment, and the client was under competent medical care; at times of stress, however, she did report gastric discomfort, and her physical condition had to be kept in mind. And like the other two women, Mrs. Fillmore had strong feelings of hostility toward her mother which were causing trouble in her current life; unlike Mrs. Park, she was well aware of them. The underlying cause of her hostility did not lie in the death of her mother at a period when she needed her, but rather in competitive feelings: her mother was socially at ease and outgoing, a cause of envy to Mrs. Fillmore, herself shy and lacking friends. She was very close to her father and critical of what she thought was her mother's insufficient affection for him.

Mrs. Fillmore was a well-educated woman, the family income was good, and her marriage satisfying. The only unusual external pressure she was experiencing—the situation that caused her to ask for help—was the difficult behavior of her daughter Joan, thirteen, who was not working up to capacity at school, indulged in temper tantrums, was nervous, uncommunicative, and responded negatively to almost anything her mother asked her to do. Mrs. Fillmore was at times over-protective of Joan and completely unable to control her, being afraid to discipline her even by such mild measures as sending her to her room. Although she felt great anger at Joan when she misbehaved, she was not impulsive and was able to control it. Early in treatment she admitted with much guilt that there were times when she hated Joan and felt sure that Joan hated her. Obviously, though this situation was actually a self-created environmental pressure, it was nevertheless a real one.

Assessment of Mrs. Fillmore's personality showed that perception, control and execution, and intelligence were on a high level. Her judgment in general was good, except as it was influenced by irrational elements in her reactions. Her chief defenses were inhibition and projection. Her self-image was somewhat distorted in that she undervalued herself as a socially attractive and likable person, and particularly lacked confidence in her ability to function as a mother. She found it difficult even to feel like a mother to her daughter and was guilty about her relationship to her. Behind this guilt was further guilt about her hostility to her mother, who in reality was a self-centered, unloving person. Her feelings toward her mother had been transferred in many respects to her daughter. Aside from this guilt, or superego anxiety, there was also an underlying anxiety about being neither loved nor lovable. This was not, however, so deep-seated a conviction as in Miss Milford. The possibility that the guilt feeling and other anxiety might create tension that would aggravate the gastric ulcer had to be kept in mind.

Mrs. Fillmore's superego seemed basically healthy. She felt realistic guilt over her poor relationship with her daughter, although she was somewhat too strict with herself about her hostility to her mother and hence about hostile feelings in general. As far as libidinal and aggressive characteristics were concerned, it could be said that Mrs. Fillmore's narcissism was not more than average. Her dependency needs were somewhat excessive, but her capacity for true object relationships was fairly well developed. Ambivalence was not unusually strong. Constructive aggressiveness, however, was definitely inhibited, and hostility toward her daughter was excessive. Details of her relationship with her husband were not explored but no sexual problem was known to exist. There were definitely unresolved feelings of hostility to her mother and indications of some excessive positive tie to her father. Finally, definite symptomatology lay in the physical area rather than in neurotic or psychotic manifestations.

In dynamic terms, Mrs. Fillmore's difficulty with Joan could be traced to her unresolved hostility to her own mother. This took two principal forms. First, in her effort to protect Joan from the hostility she displaced upon her, Mrs. Fillmore also inhibited her aggressiveness to the point where she could not exercise normal parental controls. Joan was therefore left at too early an age at the mercy of her own hostile aggressiveness because her mother did not help her to control it. And as so often happens in such instances, Joan's anxiety took the form of even greater aggression defensively, which in turn created more anxiety—a typical temper tantrum picture. Second, Mrs. Fillmore believed that there could not be a good relationship between herself and her daughter, that she could not be a good mother to a daughter and love her as she should be loved, and that her daughter in turn could not possibly love her—a combination of displacement and projection onto her daughter of her feelings toward her own mother.

From a clinical viewpoint, we first note the gastric ulcer, which is frequently due in part to anxiety caused by emotional stress, particularly hunger for love of an oral dependent or maternal type. We do not see specific psychoneurotic symptoms, but we do note character disturbances of the sort usually found in character neuroses of the oedipal type. Mrs. Fillmore's personality was more heavily accented with oedipal qualities than either Miss Milford's or Mrs. Park's. Her narcissism was much less than Miss Milford's. Although she did have unresolved dependency needs, they were not as great as those of the other two women. Her object relationships appeared to be considerably stronger, as was evidenced by her great concern about what she was doing to her daughter, a concern expressed not only in terms of fear of disapproval of herself but also of solicitude about what was happening to the child for the child's own sake.

The overall objective of treatment in this case was improvement in the parent-child relationship. Intermediate goals derived from Mrs. Fillmore's unresolved hostility to her mother, and included modification of several factors: her need to inhibit normal firmness in handling her daughter because she confused it with hostility; her displacement of feelings from her mother to her daughter; her fear of being a bad mother; her fear that her daughter could not love her; and her own feeling of being unlovable, or at least less lovable than she really was.

Earlier we noted Mrs. Fillmore's own awareness of her poor handling of her daughter and of her anger towards her. She did not realize, however, that her failure to exercise more control was a central problem. In the early interviews, her attention was called, as instances occurred, to incidents in which she seemed to feel helpless in the face of her daughter's rage. Such incidents, it was pointed up, constituted a problem that needed to be understood. Mrs. Fillmore was soon able to tie up her reaction of helplessness with her fear that she would be a "bad mother" if she allowed herself to become angry. She expressed the fear that her daughter would not love her, in fact did not love her, because of Mrs. Fillmore's own underlying anger. The worker was then able to point up instances in which Joan's love for her mother did show itself, and suggested that both Joan and Mrs. Fillmore were afraid to give expression to their love for each other because of the fear of each that she would be rejected.

In a subsequent interview, Mrs. Fillmore told of her anger at Joan for borrowing a piece of costume jewelry without permission. Since this had not created any actual difficulty for Mrs. Fillmore, the caseworker commented on her disproportionate reaction. Mrs. Fillmore immediately recognized the exaggeration and remarked that she never could have done anything like that with her own mother. She went on to tell of how ungiving her mother was both to her and to her father, and how angry this made her. She was then led to see that somehow she had equated Joan's taking something from her with her mother's depriving her and that she had reacted with the fury she had long harbored toward her mother.

An incident arose soon after in which Joan became so angry in a fight with her much younger brother that there was danger that the younger child would really be harmed. Mrs. Fillmore was unable to intervene and instead trusted to Joan's coming to her senses in time—which she fortunately did. The worker now made use of direct influence, pointing out the danger of the situation and definitely advocating that Mrs. Fillmore control Joan if such a situation arose again. She also pointed out Mrs. Fillmore's need to try to understand what was behind her inability to exercise normal parental authority. This technique brought into the open Mrs. Fillmore's confusion of firmness with hostile punishment and her belief that to be firm would mean that she did not love her daughter. Again she expressed her fear that her daughter would not love her if she exercised control of her. Further work on this theme enabled Mrs. Fillmore to see that her fear was excessive and was related to her feeling that her own mother had disliked her: again she was displacing her perception of her mother onto her daughter. It was actually impossible for her to believe that a good relationship could exist between a mother and daughter.

It is also true that part of Mrs. Fillmore's belief that her daughter did not love her was a projection of her own anger onto her daughter, but to have taken up this aspect of the problem would have created even greater anxiety for the client. As it happened, it was not necessary to go into it in any case, for her relationship with her daughter improved as she began to distinguish her from her mother.

It also proved possible for Mrs. Fillmore to begin to differentiate between disapproval of some of the things another person does and dislike or hostility toward him as a person. This developed in the context of the worker-client relationship. At one point Mrs. Fillmore said that she felt uncomfortable with the worker. Exploration of the remark brought out the client's feeling that the worker might be angry at her and was critical of her. A good opportunity was thus provided for the worker to explain that though she might think some of Mrs. Fillmore's ways of handling Joan were unwise, this did not at all mean that she was angry at Mrs. Fillmore or disliked her.

Shortly afterwards, further discussion of Mrs. Fillmore's relationship with her mother arose out of current difficulties between them in which Mrs. Fillmore's feelings had again been hurt, and she had concluded that her mother did not love her as much as she loved others in the family. Detailed discussion of how her mother reacted to other people brought out that she was in general an ungiving, hostile person. Mrs. Fillmore was then able to see that her mother's behavior was not directed particularly against her, nor was it evidence of Mrs. Fillmore's being less lovable than other people. Rather it was part of her mother's characteristic way of acting; she was just plain difficult with everyone!

These themes, involving both dynamic and genetic understanding, were reworked a number of times as different incidents brought them to the fore. At the same time there was constant discussion of the details of current happenings in an effort both to help Mrs. Fillmore understand Joan's feelings and reactions better and to think about wise ways of responding to her. As Mrs. Fillmore gradually became somewhat more free of the feelings toward her mother that she had displaced onto her relationship with her daughter, she became increasingly able to understand Joan's feelings, often equating them with her own adolescent reactions. She also became more comfortable about exercising necessary controls, and the child's problems became considerably less severe, partly in response to the improved mother-daughter relationship, partly as a result of treatment of Joan herself.

While Mrs. Fillmore's clinical diagnosis, like Mrs. Park's and Miss Milford's, fell in the general area of character disturbance, the fact that it was predominantly an oedipal rather than an oral type of character disturbance—that is, one of the character neuroses—made possible the strong emphasis on dynamic and genetic understanding, even though it was necessary to watch the anxiety level carefully lest tension should have a harmful effect because of the history of gastric ulcer. Mrs. Fillmore was less traumatized in childhood than either of the other two clients, her capacity for object relatedness was the greatest of the three, and her aggression, despite its central importance, was probably of less intensity. There was no problem of impulse control. Mrs. Fillmore was also far more aware of her own responsibility for the problem for which she sought help and therefore initially more motivated toward seeking understanding of her own involvement. All these qualities were consistent with her clinical diagnosis.

While there was a constant basis of sustainment underlying the work with Mrs. Fillmore, no unusual emphasis on sustaining procedures was needed. Direct influence was almost never used. Discussion of current interactions, as always in such work, was interwoven with the pursuit of self-understanding. As with Miss Milford, the client's strong motivation toward self-understanding was a clear factor in the direction treatment took, with the difference that in Mrs. Fillmore's case the worker was free to respond more fully to the client's desire for it since it was not diagnostically contraindicated. It should be noted, however, that treatment was centered around the theme of the parent-child relationships and that it was terminated at the end of one year without an effort to move further into Mrs. Fillmore's adjustment than was necessary to bring improvement in the parent-child functioning. No effort was made to reach the psychological factors in the physical illness.

These three cases are necessarily presented in very abbreviated form. Treatment lasted from one to five years, and with Miss Milford and Mrs. Fillmore was based on weekly interviews. These cases are certainly not offered as "proof" either of theories or results, but rather as demonstrations of the relationship among psychosocial study, diagnosis, and treatment presented in the previous chapters. They are among the cases from which the theories developed in this book derive.

XV

Perspectives

and

Current Issues

THIS BOOK HAS BEEN WRITTEN in the hope that it will add to the ability of caseworkers to help people who are experiencing trouble in their personal relationships. Casework is both an art and a science: an art in that it requires individual creativeness and skill; a science in that it is a body of systematized knowledge based upon observation, study, and experimentation.

No one can provide a caseworker with an exact formula for treatment of any individual. Rather, the worker must adapt general knowledge and principles to the needs of each person he treats. The best caseworkers are imaginative, inventive, and intuitive, molding their techniques to the nuances of the needs and personal qualities of their clients. They must be free to feel as well as to think. They must care deeply about helping their clients, and be warmly accepting of them as they are.

] *Perspectives*

But art is not enough. Casework began to grow into a scientific discipline a long time ago. Juan Vives experimented with rehabilitation in the sixteenth century. Charles Loring Brace began to place children in better environments in the 1850's. Octavia

Hill and other leaders of English charity organizations were thinking about how to motivate and enable people to improve their own lot in the 1870's. In this country Zilpha Smith, and afterwards Mary Richmond, studied methods of discovering the causes of individual maladjustment and of assisting people to overcome their difficulties and then taught "friendly visitors" what they had learned. Mary Richmond, as every social worker knows, was the first student and writer to systematize social casework and to emphasize the necessity of basing treatment upon social study and diagnosis. Her writings, dating from the turn of the century and including *Social Diagnosis* (1917) and *What is Social Casework?* (1922), set the framework for building a systematic theory of diagnosis and treatment.

The last forty years have seen a gradual accumulation of articles and books based on case studies and assimilating into casework whatever insights seemed potentially fruitful from the academically based social sciences and from other professions. Early in the century social, economic, and medical factors in causation began to be understood. During the first World War psychiatry and casework drew closer together, with the resulting emergence of psychiatric social work. The psychologies of Freud, Adler, and Meyer began to contribute to practice in the twenties; soon after, Rank's theories emerged; more recently the influence of Sullivan and Horney has been felt. Of all the dynamic psychologies, however, the main stream of Freudian thought has lent itself best to our needs. In the last few years the field has found the writings of sociologists and social psychologists of great interest. We are now in the process of testing concepts from these fields for their usefulness in individual therapeutic work, and of integrating them into the theory and practice of casework as their practical usefulness is demonstrated.

But casework is not merely the "practice" or "practical application" of any of these fields, any more than medicine is the "practice" of chemistry or physics or biology. Casework has its own entity, its own philosophy and its own methodology, related to but not identical with those of any of the other "healing professions."

Casework has certain distinctive characteristics. First, it is a psychosocial form of treatment: in diagnosis it gives weight to both the personality and the social situation; in treatment it works primarily with the individual, but also enters into the environment when such intervention is in the client's best interest. Second, it stresses a rational treatment approach that engages the client to think his way through his problem, rather than manipulating him psychologically. It is not, however, "intellectual" in the sense of relying on complicated psychological interpretations, but rather encourages the expression of down-to-earth emotions and the application of understanding to day-by-day experiences and activities. Third, it emphasizes the client's right to direct his own life. Fourth, it sets at the center of treatment true concern for the client's well-being and warm acceptance of him as he is. And fifth, it accepts responsibility for helping not only the actual applicant for treatment but also other members of his family or close associates whose problems are entwined with his own.

In common with other scientifically disciplined therapeutic methods, casework bases its treatment on a consistent, well-established body of theory, and with this as a frame of reference, studies each case individually, arriving at a working diagnosis and designing treatment according to the particular needs of the particular person.

In the building of theory, casework has drawn upon psychoanalysis for its understanding of the causation of psychological problems and of the means by which improvement can be brought about. It has not, however, turned itself into a watered-down imitation of psychoanalysis. The basic point of view of psychoanalysis toward people—its fundamental assumption that men can learn to guide their own lives better, that the role of the therapist is not to judge but to open men's eyes so that, seeing more clearly, they may be more free—is so in harmony with the aims and approach of casework that it provides a natural bridge between the two disciplines. Freudian theory provided reasonable explanations for the contradictions and inconsistencies in human beings which had so baffled and frustrated the practical-minded, activity-oriented social workers of thirty or forty years ago. In modern, reality-oriented casework the insights of psychoanalysis into human personality and the means by which it can be changed have been integrated with earlier understanding of the more overt personality, of family interactions, and of the nature of the social environment.

More recently the increasingly subtle and discerning theory emerging from the social sciences concerning social components in human behavior and human problems has attracted the attention of casework theorists and practitioners. How great the contribution of social science will be, or just what form it will take, is not yet clear, but it has already made valuable contributions and will no doubt continue to do so. Casework as a scientific art must continue to study new data and new theories as they are produced and articulated by any of the related behavioral sciences or humanistic professions. It must also increase and improve its own contributions to the knowledge of social behavior and methods of alleviating human distress.

In incorporating knowledge from other fields, however, as well as in evaluating new findings and theories from within its own ranks, casework must evaluate the evidence offered in support of new propositions and must weigh the new in the light of what is already reasonably well established. Though truth itself is absolute, the extent to which we can either understand or establish it is always relative. Theories concerning human and social behavior can rarely be established with as high a degree of certainty as biological or physical theories. They rest upon an accumulation of more or less well-recorded and well-controlled case studies, or on experiments which at best more or less simulate the conditions they seek to investigate, or on data subjected to statistical analysis which to a specified degree of probability indicate that this condition or that characteristic is associated to a specified degree with another condition or characteristic. Hence when incompatibilities emerge between new ideas and old assumptions we must look at the relative weight of evidence and the inherent reasonableness of each. Sometimes it is clear either that the old must be supplanted or that the new is not well founded. At other times both old and new appear to be well supported despite their incompatibility. Under such circumstances both old and new ideas will influence practice until better evidence emerges to settle the issue or seeming incompatibilities are erased in a broader theory that can embrace them all.

In a field such as ours, in which the attempt to validate knowledge is relatively new and the means of doing so are complicated and undeveloped, it must be kept firmly in mind that the fact that something has not yet been established as true by no means indicates that it is *untrue*. Gravity existed before Newton, and men used it and acted upon it long before they knew what they were using. After Newton they could use it more effectively. If "practice wisdom" indicates that certain assumptions are true, they should not be discarded merely because no one has yet found a way to prove them. If new evidence "disproves" them, however, or demonstrates a more effective technique or a more persuasive explanation, that is another matter.

] *Current Needs and Practical Problems*

Casework today has two great needs. One is for the development of greater skill among practitioners in using all that is already well established in casework theory. Any reading of a cross section of case records will show a serious gap between what is known in the profession and what is actually being used by the average practitioner. The other is for research into problems of casework practice, carried on by investigators who are skilled in research methodology, grounded in casework content, theory and practice, and thoroughly cognizant of the nature of the problems and treatment methods they seek to study. Both new ideas and old must be studied in an effort first to formulate them more clearly and then, if they seem worthy of it,* to establish their validity.

Progress in meeting either of these needs depends upon the quality of both schools of social work and casework agencies. Certain current developments in schools and agencies, sound in the main, nevertheless offer hazards to quality against which protection must be developed. Schools of social work are broad-

---

* "In our first contact with a set of propositions, *we commence by appreciating their importance*. . . . We do not attempt, in the strict sense, to prove or disprove anything, unless its importance *makes it worthy of that honour*." (my italics) Alfred North Whitehead, *The Aims of Education,* Mentor Books, New York, 1960, p. 15.

ening the content of their curricula. This in itself is a sound development, but breadth alone is not enough; it must be accompanied by greater depth and greater intellectual rigor, in the casework sequence as well as in other parts of the curriculum.

Much attention is given in casework to attitudes and general knowledge, but rigorous intellectual discipline in the breadth and depth of casework theory is often lacking. Classroom teachers have sometimes been away from casework practice too long, and field instructors are sometimes not well informed about theory or not articulate about it. Teachers of casework theory must be thoroughly grounded not only in the literature of casework but also in its practice. Until recently, most instructors in casework had practiced in agencies for many years before beginning to teach. It is undeniable that as content has expanded doctoral work has become more and more essential in the preparation of faculty members. Younger practitioners are undertaking doctoral work after only a few years of experience and going directly from their studies into teaching posts. These new instructors are often better prepared than their predecessors in their knowledge of the literature of casework, their sophistication about research, and the breadth of their familiarity with modern social and behavioral science. This in itself is good; but if the art of casework is to be passed on in schools of social work course content must be the product of seasoned, first-hand knowledge, and if new ideas are to be adequately screened for their usefulness, teachers must find ways to continue to engage in casework practice. In other disciplines the teacher does not give up the practice of his profession. Casework has here an administrative problem, one that can be solved, however, if faculty members and deans become convinced of its importance.

I cannot resist commenting on several other practical problems that confront the profession today. Recent economies in agency operations have made serious inroads into two most useful means by which caseworkers have improved their practice and protected their clients: record-keeping and supervision. To a certain extent, changes in the dictation and supervisory systems have been warranted. These systems had become routinized. In many agencies detailed dictation was kept automatically on every interview of every case, and all workers had two-hour supervisory conferences every week. It does not make sense, however, to jump from overroutinization to the extreme of requiring only dictation of the first interview and a closing summary, or to consider as adequate supervision group discussion for the worker who has had only one year of practice since acquiring his degree. It is true that some workers are happy with this arrangement. We all know it is more interesting to talk with a client than to a dictating machine, and easier not to have to expose one's work to examination. But is it good for the client?

It is not necessary to return to routine process recording on every case. But a substantial amount of dictation should be done on a selective basis. There should certainly be a definitive summary at the end of the exploratory period for every case. If workers prefer, such a summary can be drawn from longhand written notes of the interviews on which it is based. Tentative treatment plans should be formulated on the basis of this summary, and should also be recorded.

Beyond this, some cases do not need more than occasional brief summaries; for others, more detailed periodic recording is suitable. Where treatment becomes unusually complicated, there is no greater help to its guidance than detailed recording of each interview. Whether it is used by the worker alone or in supervision, the picture of client and worker that emerges in process recording reveals significant nuances that are otherwise completely lost. In such cases the reading of one interview in preparation for the next sensitizes the worker to common threads in context and can save both client and worker much time and effort in moving ahead.

Every worker should be dictating in detail at least two cases on which he is currently working in order to provide himself, and if he is in an agency his supervisor, with a sample of his work for study. Tendencies found in one case are apt to appear in another. Sometimes the worker is doing more suggesting than he realizes, sometimes falling back too much on reassurance, sometimes intellectualizing, sometimes drifting. Experienced as well as inexperienced workers can fail to recognize countertransferences, and can fall into ways that impede the client's progress. Detailed dictation will reveal such errors more quickly than any other device.

It matters very little what design is followed in choosing which cases to record. Nor must it be the same case from beginning to end. It is sometimes useful to follow through on a difficult period in one case and then switch to a difficult period in another. Sometimes such dictation can be combined with research, a group of workers recording in detail on cases that have certain features in common.

The amount of time such dictation will take varies. The most detailed form may require from forty minutes to an hour per interview; on the other hand, very useful procedural notes can be dictated in fifteen to twenty minutes. Clients make better progress in a well-directed forty-five-minute interview than in sixty minutes of drifting; the fifteen minutes saved for dictation may make the difference. This plan requires, of course, that agencies have machines at hand for dictation between interviews, and that transcriptions be ready in time for use. This costs money, but the cost is small in comparison to the widespread *hidden* costs of work that is less effective than it could be. Many hours of casework time are thrown away because movement is slowed down by lack of focus and because work is prolonged beyond its usefulness. For the worker just out of professional school the elimination of all dictation between opening interview and closing summary is nothing less than malpractice.

It has long been known that in supervisory conferences an occasional impromptu description of an interview rather than reporting from dictation has certain advantages. Tone of voice, gestures, and so on reveal things about the worker's methods and reactions to the client which do not come through in written material. Oral description should certainly be used from time to time, and will inevitably be employed with those cases that are not available in dictated form for the conference. It is not, however, an economical nor useful practice to follow routinely. It wastes the time of both supervisor and worker; it limits drastically the amount of ground that can be covered in a conference, and it reduces the consultation to off-the-cuff reactions. Spontaneous supervisory comments are interesting and useful, but they do not have the same value as well-considered opinions based on previous study of written material.

Supervision itself has also fallen victim to the cult of economy.

There is no question but that, ideally, workers should reach a point at which "consultation" can be substituted for supervision. In consultation the worker himself decides which cases he needs to discuss, how frequently, and so on. He is free to evaluate the worth of any suggestion the consultant makes, and to act accordingly. It is very important, however, that consultation be available in sufficient quantity. Skilled workers usually have very complicated case loads and may need several hours of consultation every alternate week; it is best to schedule these hours regularly.

It usually takes from four to six years of experience to reach self-dependent practice. During this time there should be a gradual transition from supervision to consultation. Initially, until the supervisor knows the new caseworker's abilities, he should be familiar with all the supervisee's work. Subsequently, all new cases should be followed up to the diagnostic summary, with a decision made at that point as to whether supervision or consultation is appropriate for the ongoing work. Occasional sampling of consultation cases provides an opportunity to check on the wisdom of these decisions, especially in the first year or two. Gradually the number of consultation cases should increase, until the shift to full consultation is made. Workers differ in their readiness for it, but the sooner this point can be reached, the better. Time is saved for everyone, and workers usually enjoy more independent practice. It is possible, too, that more innovations in practice emerge when workers are free to follow their own intuitions without the self-consciousness often engendered by supervision. It must always be kept firmly in mind, however, that the client's welfare is the first consideration in any administrative practice. The shift to consultation can be justified only when *his* interests will be served by it. He will not benefit from the worker's freedom to follow his intuitions and to innovate unless the worker's skills have matured to the point where his intuitions can be trusted.

In recent years there has been a tendency to move away from supervision, on the ground that it fosters an unnecessarily long period of dependence in the worker. Such a situation can arise if the supervisor does not give real allegiance to the goal of the worker's moving as rapidly as possible into consultation. It is also true that in this imperfect world some individuals in supervisory posts are incompetent. Workers quite naturally resent such a situation, and every effort should be made by agency executives to prevent it. To qualify as a supervisor a caseworker should himself have demonstrated treatment skill of a high order. To maintain this skill he should not only constantly enrich his knowledge by reading and participation in professional seminars but he should also engage in casework practice himself, ideally devoting about a third of his time to treatment. Under such a system there would be far fewer incompetent or half-competent supervisors.

It is a mistake, however, to confuse necessary dependence with neurotic dependence or domination. The treatment of problems of personal interrelationships is extremely complicated. The graduate of a two-year curriculum is at an early stage of competence in casework. The first two years of practice are in the nature of an internship, and the next two may be equated to a residency in medical training. What is really important is the sound maturation of the worker's skill. When that has been achieved, both client and caseworker will benefit from the worker's self-reliant practice. Such practice—whether carried on in an agency or privately—carries with it the responsibility to seek consultation whenever it is needed, to read professional publications regularly, and to find means of discussing professional matters with colleagues from time to time.

The ultimate responsibility of casework is to the client. In the end all theory must be measured against a single criterion: will it make it possible to help clients more effectively? Teaching, learning, and putting to proof require clarity of concepts, a sense of the logical relationships between concepts, and orderly organization of knowledge concerning the nature of the concepts. To practice skillfully, the worker must first have a firm intellectual grasp as well as an intuitive understanding of the principles of casework. To undertake research, the investigator must be thoroughly and appreciatively cognizant of what is already partially established or has been tried and found wanting. Otherwise he will waste his time in inconsequential efforts, in confusing spurious findings with real conclusions, and in tangential experiments that never quite test the real issue because the nature of the issue is not comprehended.

꙳ Casework is a demanding discipline. Like other humanistic professions it requires constant alertness and concentrated attention to the needs of others. It is impossible to know ahead of time the moment at which a client may be ready to talk about carefully guarded thoughts or, behind a passive or "it-couldn't-matter-less" facade, may be watching intently the worker's every reaction for indications of condemnation or acceptance. The right moment for helping a person to talk or the subtle lead to meaningful content is often imbedded in the most casual conversation.

Because so little is known with a high degree of certainty about people and how they can change, the caseworker is constantly confronted by uncertainty. Again and again decisions about treatment have to be made without knowing for sure what is best. *This* is *probably* better than *that,* and so we do *this.* The worker, therefore, must constantly be alert to the client's responses to his comments, ready to explain further, to reassure, or to be silent. He must be prepared to pursue the same line of thought further, to retract if a misinterpretation has been made, or to allow the subject to be changed. The client's facial expression, posture, and tone of voice, as well as his words, indicate how he is responding to treatment and whether or not the current approach should be continued. No blueprint of treatment can ever be given, any more than a skier can know the twists and turns he will have to take on a steep, unknown course toward a distant objective. Like the skier, the worker knows his general direction, but he can see only a little way ahead and must quickly adapt his technique to the terrain. To do this he must be a master of technique, know what to do to accomplish what, and when a given procedure is necessary.   ꭓ

Since new ideas are constantly coming to his attention, usually without much more to recommend them than the opinions of their proponents and their inherent persuasiveness, the worker must not only find ways of keeping in touch with the experience and opinions of his colleagues but also be both open-minded and hard-headed. This means he must read, and exchange ideas, and above all—think!

As a profession, all of us—practitioners, supervisors, consultants, teachers and executives—carry responsibility for thoroughly assimilating what is already known about casework treatment, for pushing the borders of knowledge ahead by research, for evaluating new findings as they become available, and for integrating those that prove sound into the main body of theory and practice.

BIBLIOGRAPHY

ABRAMS, RUTH D., and BESS S. DANA, "Social Work in the Process of Rehabilitation," *Social Work*, 2 (October, 1957), 10–15.

ACKERMAN, NATHAN W., "The Diagnosis of Neurotic Marital Interaction," *Social Casework*, 35 (April, 1954), 139–147.

———, *The Psychodynamics of Family Life: Diagnosis and Treatment of Family Relationships*, Basic Books, New York, 1958.

———, "The Training of Caseworkers in Psychotherapy," *American Journal of Orthopsychiatry*, 19 (January, 1949), 14–24.

———, and RAYMOND SOBEL, "Family Diagnosis," *American Journal of Orthopsychiatry*, 20 (1950), 744–753.

ADLAND, CHARLOTTE, "The Attitude of Eastern European Jews Toward Mental Disease: A Cultural Interpretation," *Smith College Studies in Social Work*, 8 (December, 1937), 85–116.

AINSWORTH, MARY D., "The Effects of Maternal Deprivation: A Review of Findings and Controversy in the Context of Research Strategy," in *Deprivation of Maternal Care: A Reassessment of Its Effects*, World Health Organization, Geneva, 1962.

ALEXANDER, FRANZ, "The Neurotic Character," *International Journal of Psychoanalysis*, 11 (1930), 292–311.

———, and HELEN ROSS, eds., *Dynamic Psychiatry*, University of Chicago Press, Chicago, 1952.

American Psychiatric Association, *Mental Disorders: A Diagnostic and Statistical Manual*, American Psychiatric Association, Washington, D.C., 1952.

AUSTIN, LUCILLE N., "Diagnosis and Treatment of the Client with Anxiety Hysteria," in *Ego Psychology and Dynamic Casework*, Howard J. Parad, ed., Family Service Association of America, New York, 1958.

———, "Qualifications for Psychotherapists, Social Caseworkers," *American Journal of Orthopsychiatry*, 26 (1956), 47–57.

———, "Trends in Differential Treatment in Social Casework," *Journal of Social Casework*, 29 (June, 1948), 203–211.

BEATMAN, FRANCES LEVINSON, "Family Interaction: Its Significance for Diagnosis and Treatment," *Social Casework*, 38 (March, 1957), 111–118.

BEHRENS, MARJORIE L., and NATHAN W. ACKERMAN, "The Home Visit as an Aid in Family Diagnosis and Therapy," *Social Casework*, 37 (January, 1956), 11–19.

BELLAK, LEOPOLD, "Psychiatric Aspects of Tuberculosis," *Social Casework*, 31 (May, 1950), 183–189.

BENNY, CELIA, "Casework and the Sheltered Workshop in Rehabilitation of the Mentally Ill," *Social Casework*, 41 (November, 1960), 465–472.

BERKOWITZ, SIDNEY, "Some Specific Techniques of Psychosocial Diagnosis and Treatment in Family Casework," *Social Casework*, 36 (November, 1955), 399–406.

BERLATSKY, MARJORIE, "Some Aspects of the Marital Problems of the Elderly," *Social Casework*, 43 (May, 1962), 233–237.

BETZ, JACQUELINE, PHYLLIS HARTMANN, ARLENE JAROSLAW, SHEILA LEVINE, DENA SCHEIN, GORDON SMITH, and BARBARA ZEISS, "A Study of the Usefulness and Reliability of the Hollis Treatment Classification Scheme: A Continuation of Previous Research in This Area," unpublished master's thesis, New York School of Social Work, Columbia University, New York, 1961.

BIBRING, GRETE L., "Psychiatric Principles in Casework," *Principles and Techniques in Social Casework*, Cora Kasius, ed., Family Service Association of America, New York, 1950, pp. 370–379.

———, "Psychiatry and Social Work," *Journal of Social Casework*, 28 (June, 1947), 203–211.

BISNO, HERBERT, *The Philosophy of Social Work*, Public Affairs Press, Washington, D.C., 1952.

BORGATTA, EDGAR F., "Role and Reference Group Theory in Social Science Theory and Social Work Research," in *Proceedings of an Institute Held by the Research Section of the National Association of Social Workers*, L. Kogan, ed., National Association of Social Workers, New York, 1960.

BOWLBY, JOHN, "Grief and Mourning in Infancy and Early Childhood," *The Psychoanalytic Study of the Child*, 15, The International University Press, New York, 1961.

———, *Maternal Care and Mental Health*, 2nd ed., World Health Organization: Monograph Series No. 2, Geneva, 1952.

BRENNER, CHARLES, *An Elementary Textbook of Psychoanalysis*, Doubleday Anchor Books, Garden City, New York, 1955.

BRIAR, SCOTT M., "Use of Theory in Studying Effects of Client Social Class on Students' Judgments," *Social Work*, 6 (July, 1961), 91–97.

BRITTON, CLARE, "Casework Techniques in Child Care Services," *Social Casework*, 36 (January, 1955), 3–13.

BRONFENBRENNER, URIE, "Socialization and Social Class Through Time and Space," in *Readings in Social Psychology*, E. Maccoby,

T. Newcomb, and E. Hartley, eds., Holt, Rinehart, and Winston, New York, 1958.

Casework Notebook, Family Centered Project, Greater St. Paul Community Chests and Councils, Inc., St. Paul, Minn., 1957.

CHANCE, ERIKA, *Families in Treatment*, Basic Books, Inc., New York, 1959.

Child Therapy—A Casework Symposium, Eleanor Clifton and Florence Hollis, eds., Family Service Association of America, New York, 1948.

COLLINS, ALICE H., and JAMES R. MACKAY, "Casework Treatment of Delinquents Who Use the Primary Defense of Denial," *Social Work* (January, 1959), 34–43.

COCKERILL, ELEANOR, and others, *A Conceptual Framework for Social Casework*, University of Pittsburgh School of Social Work, Pittsburgh, 1952.

DAVIS, ALLISON, *Social Class Influences Upon Learning*, Harvard University Press, Cambridge, Mass., 1962.

DEUTSCH, HELENE, *Psycho-analysis of the Neurosis*, Hogarth Press, London, 1951.

————, *Psychology of Women*, Grune & Stratton, New York, 1944.

DOLLARD, JOHN, and NEAL E. MILLER, *Personality and Psychotherapy*, McGraw-Hill, New York, 1950.

DOMANSKI, TERESA P., MARION M. JOHNS, and MARGARET A. G. MANLY, "An Investigation of a Scheme for the Classification of Casework Treatment Activities," unpublished master's thesis, Smith College School for Social Work, Northampton, Massachusetts, 1960.

EISENSTEIN, VICTOR W., ed., *Neurotic Interaction in Marriage*, Basic Books, Inc., New York, 1956.

EISSLER, KURT R., "The Chicago Institute of Psychoanalysis and the Sixth Period of Development of Psychoanalytic Technique," *Journal of General Psychology*, 42 (1950), 103–157.

ENGLISH, O. SPURGEON, "The Psychological Role of the Father in the Family," *Social Casework*, 35 (October, 1954), 323–329.

ERIKSON, ERIK H., *Childhood and Society*, Norton, New York, 1950.

————, "Identity and the Life Cycle," *Journal of the American Psychoanalytic Association*, 4 (1956), 68–

————, "The Problem of Ego Identity," *Journal of the American Psychoanalytic Association*, 4 (1956), 56–121.

FANTL, BERTA, "Casework in Lower Class Districts," *Mental Hygiene*, 45 (July, 1961), 425–438.

————, "Integrating Psychological, Social and Cultural Factors in Assertive Casework," *Social Work*, 4 (October, 1958), 30–37.

————, "Preventive Intervention," *Social Work*, 7 (July, 1962), 41–47.

FARBER, LAURA, "Casework Treatment of Ambulatory Schizophrenics," *Social Casework*, 39 (January, 1958), 9–17.

FAUCETT, EMILY C., "Multiple-Client Interviewing: A Means of Assessing Family Processes," *Social Casework*, 43 (March, 1962), 114–120.

FEDERN, PAUL, *Ego Psychology and the Psychoses*, Basic Books, New York, 1952.

———, "Principles of Psychotherapy in Latent Schizophrenia," *American Journal of Orthopsychiatry*, 1 (April, 1947), 129–144.

———, "Psychoanalysis of Psychoses," *Psychiatric Quarterly*, 17 (1943), 3–19; 246–257; 470–487.

FELDMAN, YONATA, "A Casework Approach Toward Understanding Parents of Emotionally Disturbed Children," *Social Work*, 3 (July, 1958), 23–29.

FENICHEL, OTTO, *The Psychoanalytic Theory of Neurosis*, W. W. Norton and Co., New York, 1945.

FINESTONE, SAMUEL, "Issues Involved in Developing Diagnostic Classifications for Casework," *Casework Papers*, Family Service Association of America, New York, 1960.

FRAIBERG, SELMA H., "Psychoanalytic Principles in Casework with Children," Family Service Association of America, New York, 1954.

———, "Some Aspects of Casework with Children," *Social Casework*, 33 (November and December, 1952), 374–81 and 429–435.

———, and JEANETTE REGENSBURG, *Direct Casework with Children*, Family Service Association of America, New York, 1957.

FRANZ, ALEXANDER, "The Neurotic Character," *International Journal of Psychoanalysis*, 11 (1930), 292–311.

FREUD, ANNA, *The Ego and the Mechanisms of Defense*, International Universities Press, New York, 1946.

FREUD, SIGMUND, *An Outline of Psychoanalysis*, authorized translation by James Strachey, W. W. Norton Co., New York, 1949.

———, *Lines of Advancement in Psychoanalytic Therapy*, v. 17 of *Standard Edition of the Complete Psychological Works of Sigmund Freud*, Hogarth Press and the Institute of Psychoanalysis, London, 1955.

———, "The Unconscious" (1915), in *Collected Papers*, vol. IV, The Hogarth Press, London, 1949, pp. 98–136.

GARRETT, ANNETTE, *Case Work Treatment of a Child*, Family Welfare Association of America, New York, 1942.

———, "Historical Survey of the Evolution of Casework," *Journal of Social Casework*, 30 (June, 1949), 219–229.

———, *Interviewing: Its Principles and Methods*, Family Service Association of America, New York, 1942.

———, "Modern Casework: The Contributions of Ego Psychology," in *Ego Psychology and Dynamic Casework*, Howard J. Parad, ed., Family Service Association of America, New York, 1958, pp. 38–52.

———, "The Worker-Client Relationship," in *Ego Psychology and Dynamic Casework*, Howard J. Parad, ed., Family Service Association of America, New York, 1958, pp. 53–72.

GEISMER, L. L., and BEVERLY AYRES, "A Method for Evaluating the Social Functioning of Families Under Treatment," *Social Work*, 4 (January, 1959), 102–108.

GEIST, JOANNE, and NORMAN M. GERBER, "Joint Interviewing: A Treatment Technique with Marital Partners," *Social Casework*, 41 (February, 1960), 76–83.

GILL, MERTON, and others, *The Initial Interview in Psychiatric Practice*, International Universities Press, New York, 1954.

GIOSEFFI, WILLIAM V., "Culture as an Aspect of the Total Personality," *Social Casework*, 40 (March, 1959), 115–119.

GOMBERG, ROBERT M., "Family Oriented Treatment of Marital Problems," *Social Casework*, 37 (January, 1956), 3–10.

GREEN, SIDNEY L., "Psychoanalytic Contributions to Casework Treatment of Marital Problems," *Social Casework*, 35 (December, 1954), 419–423.

GREENACRE, PHYLLIS, ed., *Affective Disorders: A Psychoanalytic Contribution to Their Study*, International Universities Press, New York, 1953.

GRINKER, ROY R., and others, *Psychiatric Social Work: A Transactional Casebook*, Basic Books, New York, 1961, pp. 11–14.

GROSS, NEAL, WARD S. MASON, and ALEXANDER MCEACHERN, *Explorations in Role Analysis: Studies of the School Supertendency Role*, John Wiley & Sons, New York, 1958.

GRUNEBAUM, MARGARET GALSTON, "A Study of Learning Problems of Children: Casework Implications," *Social Casework*, 42 (November, 1961), 461–468.

HAAS, WALTER, "Reaching Out—A Dynamic Concept in Casework," *Social Work*, 4 (July, 1959), 41–45.

HALL, BERNARD H., and WINIFRED WHEELER, "The Patient and His Relatives: Initial Joint Interview," *Social Work*, 2 (January, 1957), 75–80.

HAMILTON, GORDON, "Basic Concepts in Social Casework," *The Family*, 18 (July, 1937), 147–156.

———, "Psychoanalytically Oriented Casework and Its Relation to Psychotherapy," *American Journal of Orthopsychiatry*, 19 (April, 1949), 209–223.

———, *Psychotherapy in Child Guidance*, Columbia University Press, New York, 1947.

———, "A Theory of Personality: Freud's Contribution to Social Work," in *Ego Psychology and Dynamic Casework*, Howard J.

Parad, ed., Family Service Association of America, New York, 1958, pp. 11–37.

————, *Theory and Practice of Social Work*, 2nd ed., Columbia University Press, New York, 1951.

HAVIGHURST, ROBERT, and ALLISON DAVIS, "A Comparison of the Chicago and Harvard Studies of Social Class Differences in Child Rearing," *American Sociological Review*, 20 (1955), 438–442.

HELLENBRAND, SHIRLEY, "Client Value Orientations: Implications for Diagnosis and Treatment," *Social Casework*, 42 (April, 1961), 163–169.

HEMMY, MARY L., and MARCELLA FARRAR, "Protective Services for Older People," *Social Casework*, 42 (January, 1961), 16–20.

HENRY, CHARLOTTE, "Motivation in Non-voluntary Clients," *Social Casework*, 39 (February–March, 1958), 130–136.

HEYMAN, MARGARET M., "Some Methods in Direct Casework Treatment of the Schizophrenic," *Journal of Psychiatric Social Work*, 19 (Summer, 1949), 18–24.

HIRSOHN, SID, "Casework with the Compulsive Mother," *Social Casework*, 32 (June, 1951), 254–261.

HOLLINGSHEAD, AUGUST B., and FREDERICK C. REDLICH, *Social Class and Mental Illness*, John Wiley & Sons, New York, 1958.

HOLLIS, FLORENCE, *Casework in Marital Disharmony*, doctoral dissertation, Bryn Mawr College, 1947, microfilmed, University Microfilms, Ann Arbor, 1951.

————, "Personality Diagnosis in Casework," in *Ego Psychology and Dynamic Casework*, Howard J. Parad, ed., Family Service Association of America, 1958, pp. 83–96.

————, "Principles and Assumptions Underlying Casework Practice," *Social Work* (London), 12 (1955), 41–55.

————, "The Techniques of Casework," *Journal of Social Casework*, 30 (June, 1949), 235–244.

————, *Women in Marital Conflict*, Family Service Association of America, New York, 1949.

INKELES, ALEX, "Personality and Social Structure," in *Sociology Today*, Robert K. Merton, ed., Basic Books, Inc., New York, 1959, pp. 249–276.

————, "Some Sociological Observations on Culture and Personality Studies," in *Personality in Nature, Society, and Culture*, Clyde Kluckhohn, Henry A. Murray, and David M. Schneider, eds., Alfred A. Knopf, New York, 1959.

ISAACS, SUSAN, *Social Development in Young Children*, Harcourt, Brace & Co., New York, 1937.

JOLESCH, MIRIAM, "Casework Treatment of Young Married Couples," *Social Casework*, 43 (May, 1962), 245–251.

JOHNSON, ADELAIDE M., "Sanctions for Superego Lacunae of Adolescents," *Searchlight on Delinquency,* International Universities Press, New York, 1949, pp. 225–244.

JOSSELYN, IRENE M., *The Adolescent and His World,* Family Service Association of America, New York, 1952.

————, *Psychosocial Development of Children,* Family Service Association of America, New York, 1948.

KAPLAN, ALEX H., "Psychiatric Syndromes and the Practice of Social Work," *Social Casework, 37* (March, 1956), 107–112.

KAPLAN, DAVID M., "A Concept of Acute Situational Disorders," *Social Work, 7* (April, 1962), 15–23.

————, and EDWARD A. MASON, "Maternal Reactions to Premature Birth Viewed as an Acute Emotional Disorder," *American Journal of Orthopsychiatry, 30* (July, 1960), 539–547.

KAPLAN, LILLIAN, and JEAN B. LIVERMORE, "Treatment of Two Patients with Punishing Super-Egos," *Journal of Social Casework, 29* (October, 1948), 310–316.

KLEIN, EMMANUEL, "The Reluctance to Go to School," *Psychoanalytic Study of the Child, 1* (1945), 263–279.

KLUCKHOHN, FLORENCE, "Variations in the Basic Values of Family Systems," *Social Casework, 39* (February–March, 1958), 63–72.

————, and JOHN P. SPIEGEL, "Integration and Conflict in Family Behavior," Committee on the Family, Group for the Advancement of Psychiatry, Report No. 27, August, 1954.

KOEHLER, RUTH T., "The Use of Advice in Casework," *Smith College Studies in Social Work, 23* (February, 1953), 151–165.

KOUNIN, JACOB, NORMAN POLANSKY, and others, "Experimental Studies of Clients' Reactions to Initial Interviews," *Human Relations, 9* (1956), 265–293.

KOZIER, ADA, "Casework With Parents of Blind Children," *Social Casework, 43* (January, 1962), 15–22.

KRIS, ERNST, "On Preconscious Mental Processes," *Psychoanalytic Quarterly, 19,* 4 (1950), 542.

KRUG, OTILDA, "The Dynamic Use of the Ego Functions in Casework Practice," *Social Casework, 36* (December, 1955), 443–450.

KUBIE, LAWRENCE S., "The Fundamental Nature of the Distinction Between Normality and Neurosis," *Psychoanalytic Quarterly, 23* (April, 1954), 167–204.

————, "Problems and Techniques of Psychoanalytic Validation and Progress," in *Psychoanalysis as Science,* E. Pumpian-Mindlin, ed., Basic Books, 1952, p. 91.

LAING, L. P., "The Use of Reassurance in Psychotherapy," *Smith College Studies in Social Work, 22* (February, 1952), 75–90.

LANDES, RUTH, and MARK ZBOROWSKI, "Hypotheses Concerning the Eastern European Jewish Family," in *Social Perspectives on*

Behavior, edited by Herman D. Stein and Richard A. Cloward, The Free Press, Glencoe, Illinois, 1958, pp. 58–75.

LEHRMAN, LOUIS, "Science, Art, and Social Casework," unpublished paper, mimeographed, University of Pittsburgh Graduate School of Social Work, 1957.

LENNARD, HENRY L., and ARNOLD BERNSTEIN, *The Anatomy of Psychotherapy*, Columbia University Press, New York, 1960.

LITTNER, NER, "The Impact of the Client's Unconscious on the Caseworker's Reactions," in *Ego Psychology and Dynamic Casework*, Howard J. Parad, ed., Family Service Association of America, 1958, pp. 73–87.

LEWIN, KURT, *A Dynamic Theory of Personality: Selected Papers*, translated by Donald K. Adams and Karl E. Zener, McGraw-Hill, New York, 1935.

LINDEMANN, ERICH, "Symptomatology and Management of Acute Grief," *American Journal of Psychiatry*, 101 (1944), 141–148.

LOWRY, FERN, "Objectives in Social Case Work," *The Family*, 18 (December, 1937), 263–268.

MAAS, HENRY, "Building Social Work Theory with Social Science Tools," *A Report of the Annual Meeting of the Research Department*, Welfare Planning Council, Los Angeles Region, Special Report Series, No. 41, 1950.

——, "Social Casework," in *Concepts and Methods of Social Work*, Walter A. Friedlander, ed., Prentice-Hall, Englewood Cliffs, N.J., 1958, pp. 48–65.

MAEDER, LeRoy M. A., "Diagnostic Criteria—The Concept of Normal and Abnormal," *The Family*, 23 (October, 1941), 171–179.

MASSERMAN, JULES H., ed., *Psychoanalysis and Social Process*, Grune and Stratton, New York, 1961.

MAUK, FERN STEWART, "Helping the Unemployed Father," *Social Casework*, 43 (October, 1962), 422–427.

McCORMICK, ELIZABETH S., DOROTHY D. MUELLER, and PHOEBE RICH, "Management of the Transference," *Journal of Social Casework*, 27 (October, 1946), 207–216.

MEAD, MARGARET, *Male and Female: A Study of the Sexes in a Changing World*, W. Morrow, New York, 1949.

——, *Sex and Temperament in Three Primitive Societies*, W. Morrow, New York, 1935.

MEIER, ELIZABETH G., "Social and Cultural Factors in Casework Diagnosis," *Social Work*, 41 (July, 1959), 15–26.

Method and Process in Social Casework, Report of a Staff Committee, Community Service Society of New York, Family Service Association of America, New York, 1958.

MEYER, CAROL H., *Complementarity and Marital Conflict: The Development of a Concept and Its Application to the Casework*

Method, doctoral dissertation, New York School of Social Work, Columbia University, 1957.

MICHAELS, J., "Character Structure and Character Disorders," *American Handbook of Psychiatry,* Vol. I, S. Arieti, ed., Basic Books, Inc., New York, 1959.

MILLER, S. M., and ELLIOT G. MISHLER, "Social Class, Mental Illness, and American Psychiatry: An Expository Review," *The Milbank Memorial Fund Quarterly,* 37 (April, 1959), 174–199.

MITCHELL, CELIA, "Family Interviewing in Family Diagnosis," *Social Casework, 40* (July, 1959), 381–384.

MITTLEMANN, BELA M., "Analysis of Reciprocal Neurotic Patterns in Family Relationships," in *Neurotic Interaction in Marriage,* Victor W. Eisenstein, ed., Basic Books, New York, 1956, pp. 81–100.

MYERS, JEROME K., and BERTRAM H. ROBERTS, *Family and Class Dynamics in Mental Illness,* John Wiley & Sons, New York, 1959.

NEIMAN, L. J., and J. W. HUGHES, "The Problem of the Concept of Role—A Re-survey of the Literature," *Social Forces, 30* (1951), 141–149.

NESER, WILLIAM B., and EUGENE E. TILLOCK, "Special Problems Encountered in the Rehabilitation of Quadriplegic Patients," *Social Casework, 43* (March, 1962), 125–129.

NICHOLLS, GRACE, "Treatment of a Disturbed Mother-Child Relationship: A Case Presentation," in *Ego Psychology and Dynamic Casework,* Howard J. Parad, ed., Family Service Association of America, New York, 1958, pp. 117–125.

NOYES, ARTHUR PERCY, *Modern Clinical Psychiatry,* 5th ed., Saunders, Philadelphia, 1959.

NUNBERG, HERMAN, *Principles of Psychoanalysis: Their Application to the Neuroses,* translated by Madlyn and Sydney Kahr, International Universities Press, 1955.

OLDS, VICTORIA, "Role Theory and Casework: A Review of the Literature," *Social Casework, 43* (January, 1962), 3–8.

ORMSBY, RALPH, "Interpretations in Casework Therapy," *Journal of Social Casework, 29* (April, 1948), 135–141.

OVERTON, ALICE, "Serving Families Who Don't Want Help," *Social Casework, 34* (July, 1953), 304–309.

PARAD, HOWARD J., and GERALD CAPLAN, "A Framework for Studying Families in Crisis," *Social Work, 5* (July, 1960), 3–15.

PARSONS, TALCOTT, "Illness and the Role of the Physician," *American Journal of Orthopsychiatry, 21* (July, 1951), 452–460.

——, "Psychoanalysis and the Social Structure," in *Essays in Sociological Theory,* The Free Press, Glencoe, Illinois, 1954.

PERLMAN, HELEN, "Intake and Some Role Considerations," *Social Casework, 41* (December, 1960), 171–177.

————, "The Role Concept and Social Casework: Some Explorations. I. The 'Social' in Social Casework," *Social Service Review, 35* (December, 1961), 370–381. II. "What is Social Diagnosis," *ibid, 36* (March, 1962), 17–31.

————, *Social Casework: A Problem Solving Process,* University of Chicago Press, Chicago, 1957, pp. 77–81.

PIAGET, JEAN, *The Child's Conception of the World,* Harcourt, Brace & Co., New York, 1929.

POLANSKY, NORMAN, and JACOB KOUNIN, "Clients' Reactions to Initial Interviews: A Field Study," *Human Relations, 9* (1956), 237–264.

POLLAK, OTTO, "Design of a Model of Healthy Family Relationships as a Base for Evaluative Research," *Social Service Review, 31* (December, 1957), 369–376.

————, *Integrating Sociological and Psychoanalytic Concepts,* Russell Sage Foundation, New York, 1956.

————, *Social Science and Psychotherapy for Children,* Russell Sage Foundation, New York, 1952.

————, HAZEL M. YOUNG and HELEN LEACH, "Differential Diagnosis and Treatment of Character Disturbances," *Social Casework, 41* (December, 1960), 512–517.

PRAY, KENNETH, "A Restatement of the Generic Principles of Social Casework Practice," *Journal of Social Casework, 28* (October, 1947), 283–290.

PUMPIAN-MINDLIN, E., "The Position of Psychoanalysis in Relation to the Biological and Social Sciences" in *Psychoanalysis as Science,* E. Pumpian-Mindlin, ed., Basic Books, New York, 1952.

RAPAPORT, DAVID, *Organization and Pathology of Thought,* Columbia University Press, New York, 1951.

————, "The Theory of Ego Autonomy: A Generalization," *Menninger Clinic Bulletin, 22* (January, 1958), 13–35.

RAPOPORT, LYDIA, and KATE S. DORST, "Teamwork in a Rehabilitation Setting: A Case Illustration," *Social Casework, 41* (June, 1960), 291–297.

REDLICH, F. C., A. B. HOLLINGSHEAD, and ELIZABETH BELLIS, "Social Class Differences in Attitudes Toward Psychiatry," *American Journal of Orthopsychiatry, 25* (January, 1955), 60–70.

REGENSBURG, JEANETTE, "Application of Psychoanalytic Concepts to Casework Treatment of Marital Problems," *Social Casework, 35* (December, 1954), 424–432.

————, and SELMA FRAIBERG, *Direct Casework with Children,* Family Service Association of America, New York, 1957.

REINER, BEATRICE SIMCOX, and IRVING KAUFMAN, *Character Disorders in Parents of Delinquents,* Family Service Association of America, New York, 1959.

REYNOLDS, ROSEMARY, and ELSE SIEGLE, "A Study of Casework with Sado-Masochistic Marriage Partners," *Social Casework, 40* (December, 1959), 545–551.

RICHMOND, MARY E., *Social Diagnosis,* Russell Sage Foundation, New York, 1917. *What is Social Casework? An Introductory Description,* Russell Sage Foundation, New York, 1922.

RIPPLE, LILIAN, "Motivation, Capacity, and Opportunity as Related to the Use of Casework Service: Theoretical Base and Plan of Study," *Social Service Review, 29* (June, 1955), 172–193.

———, and ERNESTINA ALEXANDER, "Motivation, Capacity, and Opportunity as Related to the Use of Casework Service: Nature of Client's Problem," *Social Service Review, 30* (March, 1956), 38–59.

ROBINSON, VIRGINIA P., "An Analysis of Processes in the Records of Family Case Working Agencies," *The Family, 2* (July, 1921), 101–106.

ROHEIM, GEZA, *Psychoanalysis and Anthropology: Culture, Personality and the Unconscious,* International Universities Press, New York, 1950.

ROSENBLATT, AARON, "The Application of Role Concepts to the Intake Process," *Social Casework, 43* (January, 1962), 8–14.

RUE, ALICE W., "The Casework Approach to Protective Work," *The Family, 18* (December, 1937), 277–282.

RUESCH, JURGEN, *Disturbed Communication, The Clinical Assessment of Normal and Pathological Communicative Behavior,* Norton, New York, 1957.

SCHAFFER, LESLIE, and JEROME MYERS, "Psychotherapy and Social Stratification," *Psychiatry, 17* (February, 1954), 83–93.

SCHERZ, FRANCES H., "Multiple-Client Interviewing: Treatment Implications," *Social Casework, 43* (March, 1962), 120–125.

———, "Treatment of Acting-out Character Disorders in a Marital Problem," *Casework Papers, 1956,* Family Service Association of America, New York, 1956.

———, "What is Family-Centered Casework?" *Social Casework, 34* (1953), 343–349.

SCHMIDL, FRITZ, "A Study of Techniques Used in Supportive Treatment," *Social Casework, 32* (December, 1951), 413–419.

Scope and Methods of the Family Service Agency, Report of the Committee on Methods and Scope, Family Service Association of America, New York, 1953.

SELBY, LOLA G., "Supportive Treatment: The Development of a Concept and a Helping Method," *Social Service Review, 30* (1956), 400–414.

SHEA, MARGENE M., "Establishing Initial Relationships with Schizophrenic Patients," *Social Casework, 37* (January, 1956), 25–29.

SHERMAN, SANFORD N., "Joint Interviews in Casework Practice," *Social Work, 4* (April, 1959), 20–28.

SILLER, JEROME, "Socioeconomic Status and Conceptual Thinking," *Journal of Abnormal and Social Psychology, 55* (1957), 365–371.

SILVERBERG, WILLIAM V., "Concept of Transference," *Psychoanalytic Quarterly, 17* (October, 1948), 303–321.

SKINNER, JOHN, "Transference Interpretations in Psychotherapy," *Journal of Psychiatric Social Work, 22* (October, 1952), 5–13.

Social Casework, Generic and Specific: An Outline. A Report of the Milford Conference, American Association of Social Workers, New York, 1929.

SPIEGEL, JOHN, "Resolution of Role Conflict Within the Family," *Psychiatry, 20* (1957), 1–6.

———, "The Social Roles of Doctor and Patient in Psychoanalysis and Psychotherapy," *Psychiatry, 17* (November, 1954), 369–376.

———, "Some Cultural Aspects of Transference and Counter-Transference," in *Individual and Familial Dynamics,* Jules H. Masserman, ed., Grune & Stratton, New York, 1959, pp. 160–182.

SPITZ, RENE A., "Discussion of Dr. Bowlby's Paper," *The Psychoanalytic Study of the Child, 15,* The International University Press, New York, 1960.

STAMM, ISABEL L., "Ego Psychology in the Emerging Theoretical Base of Casework," in *Issues in American Social Work,* Alfred J. Kahn, ed., Columbia University Press, New York, 1959, pp. 80–109.

STANTON, ALFRED H., and MORRIS S. SCHWARTZ, *The Mental Hospital,* Basic Books, New York, 1954.

STARK, FRANCES B., "Barriers to Client-Worker Communication at Intake," *Social Casework, 40* (April, 1959), 177–183.

STEIN, HERMAN, "The Concept of the Social Environment in Social Work Practice," *Smith College Studies in Social Work, 30* (June, 1960), 187–210.

———, "Social Science in Social Work Practice and Education," *Social Casework, 36* (April, 1955), 147–155.

———, and RICHARD CLOWARD, *Social Perspectives on Behavior,* The Free Press, Glencoe, Ill., 1958.

STERN, ADOLPH, "Transference in Borderline Neuroses," *Psychoanalytic Quarterly, 17* (October, 1948), 527–528.

STUDT, ELLIOT, "An Outline for Study of Social Authority Factors in Casework," *Social Casework, 35* (June, 1954), 231–238.

TAUSSIG, HELEN P., "Treatment as an Aid to Diagnosis," *The Family, 19* (January, 1939), 289–294.

TOWLE, CHARLOTTE, "Factors in Treatment," *Proceedings of the National Conference of Social Work, 1936,* University of Chicago Press, Chicago, 1936, pp. 179–191.

TURNER, FRANCIS J., *Social Work Treatment and Value Differences*, unpublished doctoral dissertation, New York School of Social Work, Columbia University, New York, 1963.

VAN OPHUIJSEN, JOHN H. W., *Lectures at Neurological Institute*, unpublished, New York, August, 1949.

————, "The Psychiatric Consultation," *American Journal of Orthopsychiatry*, 29 (July, 1949), 397–403.

VESPER, SUE, "Casework Aimed at Supporting Marital Role Reversal," *Social Casework*, 43 (June, 1962), 303–307.

VOILAND, ALICE L., MARTHA LOU GUNDERLACH, and MILDRED CORNER, *Developing Insight in Initial Interviews*, Family Service Association of America, New York, 1947.

VOILAND, ALICE L., and associates, *Family Casework Diagnosis*, Columbia University Press, New York, 1962.

WALLERSTEIN, ROBERT S., LEWIS L. ROBBINS, HELEN D. SARGENT, and LESTER LUBORSKY, *The Psychotherapy Research Project of the Menninger Foundation*, Bulletin of the Menninger Clinic, 20 (September, 1956), 239–262.

WALZER, HANK, "Casework Treatment of the Depressed Parent," *Social Casework*, 42 (December, 1961), 505–512.

WEISS, VIOLA W., "Multiple-Client Interviewing: An Aid to Diagnosis," *Social Casework*, 43 (March, 1962), 111-114.

WERBLE, BEATRICE, "The Implications of Role Theory for Casework Research," *Social Science Theory and Social Work Research*, L. Kogan, ed., National Association of Social Workers, New York, 1960.

————, CHARLOTTE S. HENRY, and MARGARET W. MILLAR, "Motivation for Using Casework Services," *Social Casework*, 39 (February–March, 1958) 124–137.

WHITEHEAD, ALFRED NORTH, *The Aims of Education*, Mentor Books, New York, 1960, p. 15.

WILSNACK, WILLIAM H., "Handling Resistance in Social Casework," *American Journal of Orthopsychiatry*, 16 (April, 1946), 297–311.

WILTSE, KERMIT T., "The 'Hopeless' Family," *Social Work*, 3 (October, 1958), 12–22.

WORBY, MARSHA, "The Adolescents' Expectations of How the Potentially Helpful Person Will Act," *Smith College Studies in Social Work*, 26 (October, 1955), 19–59.

WYMAN, MARIAN, "What is Basic in Case Work Practice?" *Proceedings of the National Conference of Social Work 1938*, University of Chicago Press, Chicago, 1939, pp. 179–191.

ZBOROWSKI, MARK, "Cultural Components in Response to Pain," *Journal of Social Issues*, 8 (1952), 16–30.

Index

Acceptance: of client by worker, 12, 26, 37, 42, 47, 84–85, 109, 120, 127, 132, 153, 156–157, 234, 255
client's testing of, 249
Acting out, *see* Behavior
Adaptive patterns, change or modification in, 54–60
Adler, Alfred, 266
Adolescent traits, 35–36, 47, 102
Adult world: adjustment to, 34, 46–49
behavior unsuited to, 118, 121
Advice-giving: avoidance of, 103
use of, 68, 89, 91, 94
see also Direct influence
Advocating, as a technique, 92, 94, 111
Agency function: and choice of treatment, 214
in environmental change, 220
Aggression, 16, 37, 226, 258
see also Drives, libidinal and aggressive
American Psychiatric Association classification of disorders, 194
Anxiety: allaying or reducing, 50, 51, 59, 72–73, 83–88, 91, 94, 106, 129, 225, 229–236
as cause of maladjustment, 20, 36–38, 88, 97, 137–138
as component of motivation, 209
as realistic response, 149–150
seeking significance of, 182, 188
ways of expressing, 90, 235, 248
Anxiety and guilt as key factors in treatment, 229–236
Attitude: basic therapeutic, 156–162
discussion of client's, 74, 108–110
realistic and unrealistic, 149–154
and response in client-worker relationship, 148–155
of worker toward client, 12, 84–85, 157–158
Austin, Lucille, 53
Authority, professional, 90
Awareness: of inner feelings, 104–107, 117–127, 149

of nature of problem, 205, 251
need for, in worker, 129, 153
of situational problems, 101–104
see also Perception; Understanding

Behavior: acting out, 66, 111, 159, 246–252
client expectations of worker's, 108–109
compulsive, 56, 94
determinants of, 10–11, 25, 42, 73, 75, 124
ego-alien, 118
ego-syntonic, 118
exploring dynamics of, 75, 117–129
genetic or developmental aspects of, 75
impulsive, 56
irrational, 47, 107
and social environment, *see* Environment
ways of influencing, 28, 45
Beliefs: of individual, 10–11, 74
see also Values
Bibring, Greta L., 29, 52, 54
Brace, Charles Loring, 265

Cabot, Richard, 170
Caplan, Gerald, 206
Casework: basic values of, 12, 267
needs and problems, 269–275
perspectives, 265–269
psychiatry, and social sciences, 9–12, 268
and psychoanalysis, 11, 267
psychosocial approach of, 9, 266–267
relationship, *see* Relationship
and the unconscious, 131–146
Casework history, current needs and problems, 265–276
Casework treatment: examples of practice in, 33–49, 246–264
of internal factors, 23–24
reaction of client to, 107–110
through reducing environmental press, 22–23

Casework treatment (Cont.)
use of relationship in, 149–162
see also Treatment goals; Treatment procedures; and similar entries
Casework treatment classifications:
direct and indirect, 52, 53
environmental modification, psychological support, clarification, insight development, 53
executive and leadership, 52
social therapy: supportive therapy, experiential therapy, insight therapy, 53
suggestion, emotional relief, immediate influence, clarification, interpretation, 52
supportive, 53–54
treatment aimed at maintaining adaptive patterns, treatment aimed at modification of adaptive patterns, 54–55
Casework treatment, techniques and methods of, 50–54, 59–62, 65–68, 83–98
advice-giving, 68, 89, 91, 94
clarification, 52, 54, 57–60, 62, 66–68
classifications, 50–55
environmental measures, 22, 50, 51, 53–54, 63, 76–78, 110–114
insight development, 52–54, 101, 138
procedures of direct influence, 72, 89–96
reassurance, 51, 54, 63, 68, 71, 85–88
reflective consideration of the current person-situation configuration, 73–74, 76, 90, 97, 100–114, 249
reflective consideration of dynamics of response patterns, 74–75, 117–122
reflective discussion of the development of response patterns, 75, 123–127
supportive treatment, 43, 53–59, 67, 68
sustaining techniques, 71–72, 74–75
ventilation (catharsis), 26, 73, 86, 96–98, 111, 127, 132, 207

Caseworker: need for skill and sensitivity, 129, 151–154, 168, 215
relation to persons in environment, 111–112
relationship with client, 149–162, 222, 234
response to client, 152–153
responsibility for treatment, 169, 172, 221
role of, 95, 108, 152–154, 168–172
training of, 152–154
and the use of unconscious material, 139
Categories: of clinical entities, 193–197
of environmental factors, 193
of family interaction, 193
of personal interaction, 193
of physical problems, 193
of problems, 192
Categorization, a step in diagnosis, 192–199
Catharsis, *see* Ventilation
Cathexis and countercathexis, 134, 137–138
Causation: faulty ego and superego functioning, 20–22
infantile needs and drives, 20–21
life pressures, 20–21
in psychoanalytic theory, 267
and treatment goals, 210–212
Character disorders, 27, 58, 66, 159
acting out and self-devaluation in, 246–252
classification of, 196
guilt and impulsive hostility in, 252–258
and treatment procedures, 241, 246–258
Character neurosis: as clinical diagnosis, 196
displacement and inhibition of aggression, a case illustration, 258–264
Childhood: early drives of, 15, 17, 22
thought processes of, 17, 27, 34, 39, 161
understanding material from, 45–49, 121, 123, 125, 132–133, 191, 231–232

Children: family problems involving, 102–103
special techniques used with, 88
Clarification, 52, 55, 59, 62, 100
Class, social: factor in diagnosis, 186
factor in treatment, 85, 239, 253, 258
influence on behavior, 14, 19
sociological studies in, 11
see also Ethnic factors; Values
Classification: Aristotelian and Galilean methods, 194
of behavior disorders, 194
of casework treatment, 50–63
its place in diagnosis, 192
of procedures based on dynamic considerations, 65–78
Client-worker relationship: attitudes and responses in, 149–154, 157
in the dynamics of treatment, 156–162
problems of communication in, 155–156
in psychosocial study, 169–172
transference and countertransference, 154
Clinical diagnosis: and choice of treatment, 240–242
as genotypical or Galilean classification, 194
illustrations of, 247, 253, 261
value of, 197
Collaboration: caseworkers, psychiatrists, social scientists, 9
of community services, 114
with psychiatrists and physicians, 145
Collaterals: place of in psychosocial study, 175
use of treatment procedures with, 110–112
Communication: problems of, between client and worker, 155–156
significance in interaction, 190
Community resources, use by worker, 112–114
Complementarity, 33, 175, 189, 213
negative, in marriage, 33–40
Conscious material, 66, 140
and unconscious factors, 119, 129, 131, 135, 138

see also Preconscious; Unconscious
Consultation: with community experts, 114
psychiatric, 196
with psychoanalysts, 250
supervisory, 273
Countertransference: counter-therapeutic response, 155–156
nature of, 152–155
and realistic response, 152
and transference, 154
Crisis situations, 206
Culture: as a factor in diagnosis, 208–209
as a factor in treatment, 85, 239
norms of, 185–186, 225
study of, 11
see also Class; Ethnic factors; Values

Death wishes, 132–133, 141
Defense mechanisms: building of, 15, 18
client's understanding of, 119–120, 122, 224
and infantile thought processes, 18
listing of, 119
regression, 36, 62, 66
repression, 59, 126, 132, 141, 238
use of, 26, 29, 58–59, 228, 235, 248
Delinquency: patterns of, 20
and self-image, 20, 188
trend toward, 41, 111
Dependence, 20, 29, 56–57, 90–91, 96, 122, 128, 157, 225–226
see also Transference
Development of understanding, 75, 90, 93, 96
of intrapsychic forces, 117–129, 160–162
of person-situation configuration, 101–107
Developmental factors, reflective consideration of, 117–129
Diagnosis, 179–203
assessment of facts, 179–184
categorization, 192–194
clinical, 193–198, 240–242
consideration of norms, 184–187

Diagnosis (Cont.)
　as distinct from psychosocial study, 167, 169, 170
　dynamic and etiological factors, 187–192
　family, 193
　reality testing in, 107
　reflective discussion in, 101
　use of unconscious material in, 131, 140
Diagnosis, a threefold process, 178–199
Direct influence: and client-worker relationship, 157
　of others in environment, 113–114
　procedures of, 72–73, 89–96
　to supplement dynamic understanding, 123
　illustrations of use in treatment, 249, 258, 262
Direct treatment, classification of techniques of, 72–75, 78
　early use of, 52
Directive procedures: avoidance of, 13, 27
　use of, 29, 43, 91, 132, 157
　see also Direct influence
Displacement, 34, 36, 45–48, 126, 258, 262
Dream content, use of, 141
Drives: development of, 15
　fear of, 86
　libidinal and aggressive, 11, 15, 20, 25, 181, 226
Dynamic considerations in treatment, classification based on, 65–78
Dynamic and developmental factors: case illustrations of treatment, 246–263
　in diagnosis, 181–182, 187–192
　reflective consideration of, 117–129, 227–236
　relation to person-situation understanding, 128–129
　use of treatment relationship in, 160–162

Economic problems: appearing in social study, 172, 179–180

met by referrals, 112–113
poor housing, 21, 211
unemployment, 21
Eductive interviewing, *see* Interviewing
Ego: adult, 27–28, 40
　-alien behavior, 118–119
　as component of personality, 11, 15, 191
　controls, 28, 57, 60–62, 103, 159
　-dystonic feelings, 134, 161
　faulty functioning of, 20–21, 23, 25–26, 28, 35–36, 57, 224
　-ideal, *see* Superego
　qualities of significance, 182
　-syntonic feelings, 118, 137
　see also Defense mechanisms
Eissler, Kurt R., 28
Emerson case, 41–45, 159
Employment, problems related to, 45, 118
Environment, social: conflicting forces in, 14–20
　demands of, 41, 73, 103
　evaluating pressures in, 180
　interpretation to persons in, 111–114
　reducing pressure in, 22, 76
　study of, in diagnosis, 188
　see also Person-situation configuration
Environmental casework, 22, 50–51, 53–54, 63
　treatment procedures in, 76–78, 110–114, 220–223
　see also Casework treatment
Ethnic factors: categorizing, 193
　and choice of treatment, 239
　and diagnosis, 186
　and ego-ideal, 185
　in establishing norms, 185
　and perception, 19
　relation to behavior, 16
　and values, 11, 85
　see also Class; Culture
Etiological and dynamic factors: in diagnosis, 187–192
　and goals of treatment, 210
Experiential therapy, 53–54
Exploratory period of treatment, *see* Psychosocial study

Family: conflicting needs of members, 17, 19, 34, 37, 254, 260
diagnosis, 174, 193, 213
in Freudian theory, 11, 15–16
see also Relationship
Family Service Association of America, treatment classification, 54–55, 59, 138
Father-figure, *see* Parent-figure
Father-son relationship, *see* Relationship
Fillmore case, 258–264
Free association: nature of, 142
not used in casework, 137
and unconscious material, 135–137
Freud, Anna, 225
Freud, Sigmund, 11, 15, 59, 134, 266
Freudian theory: analysts trained in, 143
contribution to casework, 15–17, 266–267
on derivatives from the unconscious, 47, 134–138
on ego-adaptive patterns, 59
oedipal factors, 47, 191, 247, 261
and terminology, 194
Fuller case, 45–49

Garrett, Annette, 67, 161
Genetic aspects of development, *see* Development of Understanding
Goals, *see* Treatment goals
Graham case, 56
Guilt: allaying or reducing, 73, 106, 225, 229, 231
in character-disorder case, 252–258
as key factor in choice of treatment, 229–236
sense of, 84–86, 259
about sex, 36, 84
unconscious feeling of, 48, 73, 132
see also Anxiety

Hamilton, Gordon, 52
Hard-to-reach clients, 20, 88, 109–110, 174, 221
Hartmann, Heinz, 136
Hidden material, 105, 126, 134, 137

Hill, Octavia, 266
Hollis, Florence, 53
Home visit: its importance in diagnosis, 174, 175, 183
as sustaining technique, 88
Horney, Karen, 11, 143, 266
Hostility: development of, 16, 18, 20, 111
dynamic understanding of, 102, 121, 127, 226
impulsive, illustration of, 252–258
infantile, 34, 132–133
as a realistic response, 85, 151–152
reducing, 24, 26, 29, 39, 127

Identification, 11, 43, 160, 251
Impulsive personality: case illustration of, 252–258
developing understanding in, 121, 238, 256
Indirect treatment, *see* Environmental casework
Infantile thought processes, distortions of, 17–18, 25, 27–28, 124, 132, 138
see also Primary thought process; Preconscious; Unconscious
Influence, direct, *see* Direct influence
Ingersoll case, 56–57, 60–61
Insight development, 52, 54, 100, 138–139
Instincts, in Freudian theory, 16
see also Drives
Interaction: in casework theory, 16
between client and worker, 105–110, 149–162
between environment and individual, 10, 15, 17–20, 75, 103, 188–190
between family members, 16, 17, 37–39, 101–102, 174, 213
in Freudian theory, 15–17
see also Relationship
Interpersonal adjustment: and casework treatment, 9–11
cause of breakdown in, 20–22, 211
complementarity in, 189, 213

Interpersonal adjustment (Cont.)
  conscious and unconscious fac-
    tors in, 131–146
  gathering facts on, 170–173, 180,
    187
  reflective discussion of, 101–103,
    113–114
  and sustaining techniques, 84–88
Interpersonal relationship, *see* Re-
    lationship
Interpretation: of behavior to client,
    106–107, 118, 121
  to environmental persons, 111
  limitations of, 169
  as a technique, 52, 54
  transference, 128
Intervention, in environmental prob-
    lems, 111, 113
  as a sustaining technique, 93–95,
    225
Interviewing: classifying content,
    76
  client's feeling toward, 83, 97
  collaterals, 111
  diagnostic, 43, 179
  duration and frequency, 141, 215
  eductive 26, 137, 142
  electrically recorded, 69
  at home, 174, 183
  joint and separate, 36, 72, 174,
    214
  and preconscious material, 59,
    140
  in social study, 170–175
  worker's technique in, 59, 84, 88,
    96, 171, 215
Intrapsychic factors: and diagnosis,
    181–182, 187–192, 240
  influence of, 11
  modification of, 24, 70, 75
  reflective discussion of, 75, 105–
    107, 224, 227
  see also Dynamic and develop-
    mental factors; Personality

Joint interview, *see* Interviewing

Kaplan, David, 206
Kaufman, Irving, 241
Knight case, 57
Kris, Ernst, formulations concern-
    ing the preconscious, 136–137
Kubie, Lawrence S., 135

Landers case, 57–58, 62
Lee, Porter, 52
Lewin, Kurt, 194
Libidinal and aggressive charac-
    teristics, *see* Drives
Life pressures, *see* Environment
Lindemann, Erich, 206
Lowenstein, Rudolph, 136

Manipulation: of the environment,
    17, 23
  as a type of treatment, 28, 52, 77,
    110
Marital adjustment: basis of diffi-
    culty in, 172, 189, 210
  cases involving, 24, 33–40, 56–57
  negative complementarity, 33–40
  of woman working outside the
    home, 24
Masters case, 58, 61
Maturation, stages in, 11, 29, 237
Medical problems: and choice of
    treatment, 145
  evaluation of, 173, 196
  help in understanding, 103
  as source of anxiety, 86, 249, 253
Methodology, *see* Casework treat-
    ment
Meyer, Adolf, 266
Milford case, 246–252
Modifiability of causative factors,
    211–212
Mother-daughter relationship, *see*
    Relationship
Mother-figure, *see* Parent-figure
Motivation: in exploratory period,
    169
  and goals, 207–210, 216
  punitive, avoidance of, 93
  toward self-understanding, 234

Narcissism, 15, 20, 122, 129, 237–
    238
Needs: in Freudian theory, 16–17
  infantile, 20, 23, 34, 91
  see also Drives
Neurosis: as casework diagnosis,
    196–198
  character, case illustration, 258–
    264
  compulsive, 197
  evidence of, 66, 229

Neurosis (Cont.)
Freudian theory on, 16
and treatment procedures, 241
types of, 196
Norms: in assessing client behavior, 184–187
as factor in treatment, 208
and frame of reference, 184
nature of, 184–185
sociocultural factors in, 185–186
worker's professional, 208
see also Class; Role

Object relationships, capacity for, 15, 236–237, 261
Oedipal conflict, 26, 47, 191, 261
Overprotection, 48, 212

Parad, Howard, 206
Parent-figure, worker as, 26, 42, 56–57, 61–62, 88, 128, 155, 157–158, 160, 255
Park case, 252–258
Perception: of client by worker, 152
in decisions and consequences, 103–104
of dynamic factors, 118, 123, 227–229
and the environment, 10, 14, 17–19, 21
improvement in, 29, 38, 101–103, 127
of role performance, 19
see also Awareness; Understanding
Person-situation configuration: and diagnosis, 182
genetic factors in, 128, 140
observance of interaction in, 188, 228
and personality dynamics, 122–123
reactions of client in, 10, 29–30, 106–110
reflective discussion of, 73, 77, 97, 100–114, 132, 158
Personality: as a balance of forces, 25, 38, 124
changes and adaptive patterns, 54–59
change vs. change in functioning, 55–59

changes and methodology, 55–59
change through treatment, 23, 24, 27, 29, 38, 44, 54
development, 11, 15–16, 34
diagnostic evaluation of, 182–187, 247
dynamic factors involved in, 117–129
factors and treatment objectives, 212
neurotic, *see* Neurosis
and social functioning, 13–20, 35, 41, 207
structure, 41
Personality, social adjustment, and the casework method, 9–32
Pollak, Otto, 180
Preconscious, the: ego-dystonic elements, 134, 161
ego-syntonic elements, 118, 137
Freudian theory, 134–135
material from, 47, 52, 59, 66–67, 137
processes of, 136–138
theories of Kris, 136
and the unconscious, 133–138
see also Ego; Unconscious
Press, *see* Pressure
Pressure, also known as press, 10
assessed in diagnosis, 179–180
environmental, 17, 20–22, 34, 36, 54, 76, 113, 122
internal and external, 10, 179–180
relieving, 254
Primary thought process: Freudian theory, 15, 17, 134–135
in preconscious processes, 136
see also Infantile thought processes; Preconscious; Unconscious
Problem: assessment of, 179–192
categorizing, 193
classification, 192, 196, 242
as a concept, 242
of psychiatric nature, 195
see also Psychosocial study
Procedures: and choice of treatment, 219–243
of direct influence, 72–73, 89–96, 111
psychological, 77, 144

Procedures (Cont.)
  relationship to diagnosis, 66
  sustaining, 71–75, 83–89, 94–96
  see also Casework treatment
Protective casework, 93, 95
Psychiatric consultation, 139, 196, 250
Psychiatrist: as consultant or supervisor, 139, 196
  therapy conducted by, 144
Psychiatry: nature of, 10–11
  relation to casework, 11, 139, 195
  training in, 145
Psychoanalysis: contribution to casework, 11, 15–16, 52, 267
  differentiation of casework from, 28–29, 142–143, 160–161, 250
  formulations about the unconscious in, 59, 134–138
  personal use by caseworkers, 139–140
  and personality change, 29, 59
Psychoanalytic therapies, 11, 15, 28, 143, 266
Psychological factors in treatment, 11, 52
  casework's orientation to, 145, 267
  considering dynamics of, 117–123, 267
  see also Personality
Psychosis, 27, 93, 97
  avoidance of hidden material in, 140
  diagnosis of, 195–196
Psychosocial orientation of casework, 9, 16, 20–27, 266–268
Psychosocial study: as aid in treatment plans, 167–170, 204
  differentiated from diagnosis, 170
  interviews during, 170–175
  period required for, 170
  as preliminary to diagnosis, 167–169
  problems covered in, 171–173
  supplementary reports needed in, 175
Psychosocial therapy, casework as, 16, 20–27, 29, 143, 266–268
Psychotherapy: types of, 53
  as used in different professions, 143–146
  see also Casework treatment

Pumpian-Mindlin, E., 135

Rapaport, David, 136–137
Rational therapies: vs. directive, 27–30
  illustration of, 249
  in the sustaining process, 85–87
Reality testing, 29, 107, 224
Reassurance, use of, 51, 54, 63, 68, 85–88, 106, 109, 157
Recording, 270–272
Referral: of cases needing analytic psychotherapy, 145
  involving basic needs, 112
Reflective discussion: with collaterals, 111
  of development of response patterns, 75, 123–127
  of dynamics of response patterns, 74–75, 117–122
  of person-situation configuration, 73–74, 76, 90, 97, 100–114, 249
Reid, William, 76
Reiner, Beatrice Simcox, 241
Relationship: adult-object, 15, 236–237, 261
  basic therapeutic, 156, 221
  child-parent, 17, 34, 41–42, 45–49, 85–86, 104, 254
  corrective, 26, 40, 42, 158–159, 251
  in family, 11, 14, 33, 37, 42–43, 57, 173, 213
  father-son, 45, 47, 101
  influence of unconscious material on, 131–132
  interpersonal, 13–20, 103–104, 148–162
  in marriage, 14, 17, 33, 39, 172, 210
  mother-daughter, 34, 41–42, 126, 132–133, 258–263
  oral dependent, 15
  sexual, 34–38
  use in treatment, 19, 28, 37, 40, 42, 51, 57, 60–61, 72–74, 84–98, 108–110, 118, 127, 149–162, 222, 251
  see also Client-worker relationship; Transference
Relationship, the client-worker, 148–162

Religion: and norms, 185, 187
and treatment, 120–121
Richmond, Mary E., 52, 72, 170, 266
Ripple, Lillian, 242
Rogers, Carl, 144
Role: of caseworker in treatment, 95, 108, 152–154, 168–172
of client in treatment, 108–109, 149–162
concepts, 185–186
and diagnosis, 186–187
expectation, 10, 11, 19, 186, 209
expectation of worker's by client, 94–95
network, 108
and norms, 186–187
and perceptions, 11, 14
and values, 10, 14
Ryman case, 33–40, 205

Schools of social work, needs for practice by methods instructors, 270
Self-determination: as basic concern, 12
limitations of, 13, 28
and self-direction, 13, 95
and treatment planning, 168
Self-direction: capacity for, 95–96
value of, 13, 91, 95
Self-image: as factor in treatment, 159–160, 183
of potential delinquent, 20, 188
treatment of low, 44, 224, 247, 259
Sexual problems: as basis of anxiety, 36, 84
deviation, 182, 226
and diagnosis, 182
and guilt, 232
immaturity, 182, 227
and marital adjustment, 34–40, 118
promiscuity, 248, 256
treatment through healthy identification, 133
Situation-response, 10, 29, 75–77, 100–104, 182
see also Person-situation configuration
Smith, Zilpha, 266

Social adjustment, personality, and casework method, 9–32
Social casework, *see* Casework
Social class, *see* Class
Social environment, *see* Environment
Social functioning, improvement of: as aim of casework, 11, 13, 25, 29
as treatment goal, 205
see also Environmental casework
Social sciences: contribution to casework, 268
and psychoanalytic theory, 10–11
related to casework and psychiatry, 9–12
Social work education, *see* Schools of social work; Supervision
Social study, *see* Psychosocial study
Sociocultural factors, *see* Culture
Sociology, *see* Social science
Stereotype: of caseworker, 20
race, 19
and use of categories, 199
Stress, *see* Pressure
Study, Family Service Association of America treatment classifications, 54–55, 59, 138
of twenty-five cases to identify treatment techniques, 66–69, 71, 132
Suggestion, as technique, *see* Procedures of direct influence
Sullivan, Harry Stack, 11, 200
Superego: change in patterns, 61–62
as component of personality, 11, 15, 59, 84
and ego-ideal, 42, 160
faulty functioning of, 20–21, 23, 28, 40–45, 58
modification of, 120, 225
Superego disturbance, case illustration, 40–45
Supervision, or consultation, 273
need for, 272–274
trends in, 270–272
Supportive treatment, cases of, 40–45, 56–59, 60–63
see also Casework treatment
Suppressed material, 66–68, 119, 126
see also Preconscious

Sustaining procedures, 71–75, 83–
89, 94–96, 100, 105–106, 111,
113, 123, 222
   and anxiety, 234
   and client-worker relationship,
157
   and client's unconscious self,
131–132
   illustrations of use in treatment,
246–249, 252–254, 256–257,
264
Symbols, as cause of distortion in
communication, 155
Symptomatology: in diagnosis, 182,
192
   as part of genotypical diagnostic
system, 194
   and psychoneurosis, 198

Techniques and methods, see Casework treatment
Therapies, directive vs. rational,
27–30
   range of, 143–146
Therapy: experiential, 53–54
   insight, 53–54
   in psychiatry, 143
   in psychoanalysis, 143–144
   in psychology, 144
   supportive, 53–54
Towle, Charlotte, v–xii
Transaction, between individuals,
188–190, 213
   see also Interaction
Transference: and countertransference in treatment dynamics,
154, 156–162
   cures, 28, 44–45
   and infantile thought, 18
   neurosis, 161
   problems in joint interview, 175
   in psychoanalysis, 28, 143
   and realistic relationship, 149–
151
   regressive, 143, 161
   situation, 54, 57, 128, 149, 160
   see also Client-worker relationship
Trauma: of early experience, 44,
127, 132, 232
   situational, 24, 36

Treatment emphasis, three variations in, 246–264
Treatment goals: and causation,
210–213
   intermediate and long-range,
205–207
   and motivation, 207–210
   from viewpoint of client, 95
Treatment objectives, choice of,
204–216
Treatment procedures, choice of,
219–243
   see also Casework treatment
Treatment process: client relation
to, 107–110, 156–162
   psychosocial study in, 167–176
   relation to problems, 242
   see also Casework treatment;
Psychotherapy

Unconscious, the: and casework,
131–146
   differentiated from the preconscious, 133–138
   directing comments to, 132–133
   in Freudian theory, 11, 47, 134–
138
   material from, 47, 52, 119, 132,
143, 161
Understanding early life experiences, 45–49
   see also Development of understanding

Values: of casework, basic, 12,
265–268
   and ethnic factors, 11, 14, 208
   effect on choice of treatment procedures, 85, 208, 221, 223
   of individuals, 10–11, 74, 85, 208
   worker's, 208
   see also Class; Norms; Role
Ventilation (catharsis): as a treatment technique, 26, 73, 86,
96–98, 111, 127, 132, 231–232,
237
   feelings brought out by, 106, 124,
127
   and treatment goals, 207
Vives, Juan, 265